18.95

M000286564

* summary

What do people think when they imagine themselves as
part of a nation? *Nation and commemoration* answers this
question in an exploration of the creation and recreation
of national identities through commemorative activities.
Extending recent work in cultural sociology and history,
Lyn Spillman compares centennial and bicentennial celebrations in the United States and Australia to show how
national identities can emerge from processes of "cultural
production." She systematically analyzes the symbols
and meanings of national identity in these two "new
nations," identifying changes and continuities, similarities and differences in how visions of history, place in the
world, politics, land, and diversity have been used to
express nationhood. The result is a deeper understanding,
not only of American and Australian national identities,
but also of the global process of nation-formation.

Nation and commemoration

Cambridge Cultural Social Studies

General editors: JEFFREY C. ALEXANDER, *Department of Sociology, University of California, Los Angeles, and* STEVEN SEIDMAN, *Department of Sociology, University at Albany, State University of New York.*

Editorial Board
JEAN COMOROFF, *Department of Anthropology, University of Chicago*
DONNA HARAWAY, *Department of the History of Consciousness, University of California, Santa Cruz*
MICHELE LAMONT, *Department of Sociology, Princeton University*
THOMAS LAQUEUR, *Department of History, University of California, Berkeley*

Titles in the series
ILANA FRIEDRICH SILBER, *Virtuosity, charisma, and social order*
LINDA NICHOLSON AND STEVEN SEIDMAN *(eds.)*, *Social postmodernism*
WILLIAM BOGARD, *The simulation of surveillance*
SUZANNE R. KIRSCHNER, *The religious and Romantic origins of psychoanalysis*
PAUL LICHTERMAN, *The search for political community*
ROGER FRIEDLAND AND RICHARD HECHT, *To rule Jerusalem*
KENNETH H. TUCKER, JR., *French revolutionary syndicalism and the public sphere*
ERICK RINGMARR, *Identity, interest, and action*
ALBERTO MELUCCI, *The playing self*
ALBERTO MELUCCI, *Challenging codes*
SARAH M. CORSE, *Nationalism and literature*
DARNELL M. HUNT, *Screening the Los Angeles "riots"*

Nation and commemoration

Creating national identities in the United States and Australia

Lyn Spillman
University of Notre Dame

CAMBRIDGE
UNIVERSITY PRESS

Published by the Press Syndicate of the University of Cambridge
The Pitt Building, Trumpington Street, Cambridge CB2 1RP
40 West 20th Street, New York, NY 10011-4211, USA
10 Stamford Road, Oakleigh, Victoria 3166, Australia

First published 1997

Printed in Great Britain at the University Press, Cambridge

A catalogue record for this book is available from the British Library

Library of Congress cataloguing in publication data

Spillman, Lynette P.
  Nation and commemoration: creating national identities in the
United States and Australia / Lyn Spillman.
    p.   cm. – (Cambridge cultural social studies)
  Includes bibliographical references and index.
  ISBN 0 521 57404 8 (hc) – ISBN 0 521 57432 3 (pbk)
  1. Nationalism – United States – History.   2. Nationalism –
Australia – History.   3. United States – Centennial celebrations,
etc.   4. Australia – Centennial celebrations, etc.   5. American
Revolution Bicentennial, 1776–1976.   6. Australian Bicentenary,
1988.   I. Title.   II. Series.
E188.S73   1997
320.5′4′0973 – dc20   96–3024 CIP

ISBN 0 521 57404 8 hardback
ISBN 0 521 57432 3 paperback

For Pat and John Spillman

Contents

Acknowledgments

My warm thanks go to many people whose support contributed to this work.

Librarians at the Library of Congress in Washington, DC, the National Library of Australia in Canberra, the Mitchell and Dixson Libraries in Sydney, and the libraries of the University of California at Berkeley, the University of Queensland, and the University of Notre Dame made this research possible. They preserve rich records of human action, and the importance of this work – and even the excitement it sometimes generates – deserves wide and public appreciation.

The Graduate Division of the University of California at Berkeley provided early support for the research. The Institute for Scholarship in the Liberal Arts, College of Arts and Letters, University of Notre Dame, was helpful at two crucial junctures in the project. The University of Notre Dame Faculty Research Program and a University of Queensland travel grant also helped make some of the research possible. And acknowledgments are due to the Human Sciences Press for permission to reprint parts of chapter 4 which have appeared previously in *Qualitative Sociology*.

Members of the Department of Anthropology and Sociology at the University of Queensland made a welcoming scholarly environment for some of the work. My colleagues in sociology at the University of Notre Dame deserve recognition for their appreciation of the time demanded by research of this sort. Thanks go too to Sung-Chang Chun, Dave Brunsma, and Beth Schaefer Caniglia: their hard work developing parts of the book has been much appreciated. Neil Smelser, Ann Swidler, Michael Rogin, and Kim Voss all read early versions and made the ultimate product better. Beyond their comments and support, I have been sustained by Neil Smelser's consistent responsiveness, and Ann Swidler's talent for encouraging accessible presentation. Toward the end of the project, I have appreciated very much Catherine Max's work at Cambridge University Press, and the fine copy-editing of Karen Anderson Howes.

Among the many other people who have commented on parts of this work, or contributed in other important ways, are Jorge Arditi, Alasdair Bowie, Doris Bermingham, Sam Blazer, Dorothy Capoletto, Mark Chaves, Nina Eliasoph, Rosemary Frederick, Anita Garey, David Glassberg, Ted Goode, David Greenberg, Karen Hansen, Jean and Marge Harrison, Kim Hays, Peter Hoffenberg, Rich Kaplan, Desmond Kennard, Clive Kessler, Paul Lichterman, Wendy McCarthy, Patrick Miller, Denis O'Brien, Timothy Phillips, Jennifer Pierce, Arvind Rajogopal, Ron Ramsay, Marc Rothenberg, Eli Sagan, April Schultz, Phil Smith, Ken Spillman, Chuck Stephan, Terry Strathman, Kathleen Taperell, Marge Terrafranca, Samuel Valenzuela, and Pam Wright. I've appreciated what they've done. I'd especially like to record the value of the intellectual communities provided in Berkeley in the late Leo Lowenthal's seminar and in the Culture Club.

Three people may justifiably consider the book theirs as well as mine. Pat and John Spillman have always valued scholarly inquiry and supported mine, and I thank them for that and immeasurably more. It's also difficult to truly acknowledge the contributions of Russell Faeges without sounding unduly effusive: but as a scholar and a companion, he has done more than I can say toward this book. I'm often stimulated by his theoretical wisdom, impressed by his wide knowledge, startled by his unusual intuition, and thankful for his constant encouragement.

1

Comparing national identities

Long before most people took their nationalities for granted, Elbridge Gerry, a delegate to the American constitutional convention in Philadelphia, was puzzled about what it could mean to be American. "We were neither the same Nation nor different Nations," he said of Virginia, Pennsylvania, Massachusetts, and the other former colonies. What could it mean to be "American," he seemed to be asking, when all the states appeared quite different? A century later, at their own convention, Australians had a nationality problem too: trying to work out their links to Britain, some wondered whether they might be "a nation within a nation," or "part of a nation." Americans and Australians faced questions about their national identities which have been encountered, in one way or another, by people around the globe. They wondered what they all shared; and they wondered how to draw the boundaries between themselves and others. There were many possible responses to these questions; what answers did they find, and why did they choose them?[1]

This book addresses the question of how two similar sets of people with many similar experiences formed and reformed their different national identities. Comparing major celebrations of national identity in the United States and Australia – the centennial of the American Revolution in 1876 with the Australian centennial of settlement in 1888, and the American bicentennial commemoration in 1976 with the Australian bicentenary in 1988 – I ask how different national identities developed and why each nation came to mean what it did. I compare the national identities which people created and recreated in big national rituals in these two "settler nations," and explain how similarities and differences in American and Australian national identities emerged.

We often take our nationalities for granted now. The nation-state has become a norm of social organization, and nationality a commonsense

1

frame of reference. According to the Universal Declaration of Human Rights, "everyone has the right to a nationality," and most people say they are proud of their nations. Indeed, our nationality is one of those assumptions – like our gender – which lie unacknowledged behind many of our everyday actions, which, as cultural sociologist Pierre Bourdieu puts it, "structure what is thought." In the United States and Australia, as elsewhere, national identity flavors everyday life in familiar ways, and a commonsense rhetoric of nationality makes an unnoticed backdrop to public life. We hardly question the grounding of common appeals to national identity, like that of the yachting commodore who thought it was "traitorous to commit our club in litigation against another American yacht club," or the "patriotic Australians objecting to the sell-out of the nation's independence." These particular claims happened to be obscure, fleeting, and debatable; but they were also archetypical.[2]

These days, Americans and Australians may often differ among themselves about what exactly characterizes their nations, and some are disillusioned. But rarely do they wonder whether they are somehow composed of other nations, or part of some larger nation. Few people now doubt that they are, or should be, part of a nation, although this identity may sometimes be less salient than other identities. Like our gender, a sense of nationality is deeply part of our common sense. Perhaps, as philosopher George Santayana once wrote, "nationality . . . [is] like our love and loyalty toward women . . . too radically intertwined with our moral essence to be changed honourably, and too accidental to the free mind to be worth changing."[3] But many of our assumptions about gender have indeed been altered in the course of a wide-ranging critical analysis (like the apparent presumption in the passage that readers were heterosexual men). We are now well aware of many different ways that gender attachments may be expressed and interpreted. Our commonsense interpretations of national identity also deserve such attention.

What, then, does it mean to be part of a nation, and how do ideas about nationality change? In what terms is the nation seen as a natural unit of society, in contrast to more local or more cosmopolitan groups? When people talk about their national identities, they are making special sorts of claims about what they share; in Benedict Anderson's useful formulation, they are appealing to "imagined political community – imagined as both inherently limited and sovereign." Cultures of national identity are those sets of meanings and values with which we talk of our actual or prospective political communities. People in the United States and Australia formed their ideas about their nationalities on the basis of a shared cultural frame of what it meant to be a nation-state – collectively, to have things in common and to be different from others. National identity is the symbolic elaboration of this imagined community.[4]

Claims about shared experience of language, ethnicity, land, religion, or history sometimes seem to make a self-evident symbolic grounding for national communities. But themes expressing national identities are volatile and various: national identity may be based on many different sorts of meanings and values, and the many symbolic associations used to characterize nations have defeated easy understanding. Further, Max Weber early concluded that "the concept of 'nation' . . . cannot be stated in terms of empirical qualities common to those who count as members of the nation."[5] Not only are there many variations and possibilities in how nations are symbolized; the acute listener in a new land will also be struck by the fact that the same symbols may have a very different meaning and importance in different contexts. The process of endowing the commonalities and boundaries of imagined national community with meaning is complex and intriguing, but the very contingency and creativity of such symbolizing often makes it hard to grasp. A sense of nationality, something like an emotional attachment to a particular symbol such as a flag, often seems both too trivial and too messy to fit into any general categories, to be accessible to the sometimes blunt tools of general social explanation. How can we explain such fluid and subtle cultural differences as differences in national identity?

The general question of how and why nations come to be characterized in particular ways becomes even more puzzling as we consider the United States and Australia. These days, when they mention "the nation," Americans might often talk of their political values or their founding; Australians might commonly talk of their land or their place in the world. Comparing two similar nations shows vividly that it is not merely natural that they associate these symbols with their nations; some few Americans would talk of the land, some few Australians would talk of their political values, and a century ago Americans emphasized their place in the world much more, and Australians their founding moment. What is more, many people from other places would see the United States and Australia as more similar than different. Visitors to both countries will now find functioning democracies, predominantly English-speaking peoples, extensive and varied lands, big cities, and developed economies. The two countries also share many important historical experiences: European conquest, British settlement, long-established liberal political culture, extensive exploration, immigration and settlement, the joining of smaller polities to form the nation-state, and economic growth. In both countries, those who wanted to find shared qualities, and to draw boundaries between themselves and others, faced circumstances which were analogous in many respects, and could draw on many similar experiences to talk about their nations. In such circumstances, one might expect that American and Australian national identities would be very similar. On the other hand, uniqueness can be an important claim in a national identity. So do Americans and Australians think of themselves in the same ways? Or have their national identities developed very differently?

Australia and the United States are rarely compared, but answering these questions is important for two reasons. First, neglected mid-range comparisons like this one between two settler countries provide national historians with a deeper and more systematic understanding of what is really different about their country, and why. Most investigations of national identity focus on one country alone: most of what we know of nation-formation in the United States and Australia we know from the work of national historians. In the fine grain of national historiography, other nations are often thought to be irrelevant. But for those who are interested in understanding the United States or Australia, this study highlights some curious absences by placing talk of national identity in each country in a new comparative light. For instance, while the highly urbanized Australians now think first of their distinctive continent when they think of what they share as a nation, the equally impressive and much richer American land is not now a central symbol of the nation, and its exploration and development is more the subject of local than national myth and legend. How can we explain this difference? Political values are another example of the apparent unaccountability of claims about national identity. While we know that democratic political values in the United States have been seen as crucial to American national identity, by scholars as well as nationalists, it seems strange to find Australians in the late nineteenth century viewing themselves, and not Americans, as the most politically advanced nation on earth. On the other hand, the American experience has sometimes led us to assume that all new nations will use ideas about shared political values to express their national identities – but for contemporary Australians, such ideas are not the first things they think of when they celebrate their national identity. National historians more often look at what is said than what is not, but might have been; the comparative analysis of two cultures of national identity allows us to understand more systematically the themes of national identity which do emerge by contrasting them with those which do not.[6]

Secondly, examining the development of national identity in these two similar countries is important for the comparative study of nation-formation. Until recently, the historical record most important for generating accounts of nation-formation has emphasized places where it has been most politically consequential, where strong states or critical national movements promoted national ideas. We know very little about how the process by which the United States and Australia became nations fits into this bigger story, because the settler countries show a pattern of nation-formation which is both more subtle and less contested than elsewhere. In these cases, cultures of national identity did not emerge fully formed from prior historical experience; nor can they be attributed simply to the powerful visions of nationalist political actors.[7]

Yet these countries show a neglected side of the process by which nations came to seem natural. They suggest that national identity need not be a simple function of strong states or critical social movements, often the most obvious causes in other countries. They allow us to examine the development and meaning of national identity in the relative absence of such proximate causes. Rather, the process by which Australians and Americans came to think of themselves as naturally grouped, as natural social units, suggests the importance of what some sociologists have called a "world cultural frame" – especially of nations in a world of nation-states – as a model for the interpretation of emerging global realities. We see both Australians and Americans using this model as they try to think about what they have in common and how they are different from people elsewhere. For Australia and the United States, the availability of the idea that nations were natural social units was enough, with comparatively little in the way of nationalist movements or officially promoted nationalisms, to form their identities as nations. While the detailed comparison of these two similar countries does not show conclusively the more widespread influence of "world cultural frames," it does suggest that the global availability of cultural models of the nation has been important and sometimes crucial as the world became a world of nation-states, and tells a neglected part of the story of how nation-formation occurred. These cases show in purer form the process by which elements of local cultural repertoires were reconceptualized as national, as nation-states became plausible and later necessary forms for political action in the larger geopolitical context.[8]

Comparing national identities in the United States and Australia provides a deeper and more systematic understanding of each country, and it broadens our understanding of the global process of nation-formation. My purpose here is to account for previously unexamined differences and similarities in national identity in these two settler nations, and, taking them together, to extend our understanding of how national identity has come to "structure what is thought."

National identities and cultural explanation

Comparing and explaining cultures often seems an unwieldy task. But "culture shock" is such a common experience that it is strange that cultural sociologists have so far devoted little systematic attention to understanding it. Here, I draw from recent cultural sociology to specify the terms of this cultural comparison and the analytic tools I use to build a comparative account of what American and Australian national identities have come to mean and why.[9]

It is important to be precise about what we are comparing. Any visitor to another country is struck by a variety of differences, and learns to be conscious of his or her own assumptions about society in many new ways. Some of the differences are interactional: the easy way of dealing with shop assistants may suddenly be a puzzle, for example, or the proper tone of debate among friends. Some of the differences are larger: patterns of institutionally available resources and dependencies run counter to what seems natural. What children learn in school may be decided nationally rather than locally, for example, or there may be more poverty, or fewer banks. But what are most obvious to the visitor are symbolic differences: even if we speak the same language, we see more flags, or hear more talk about the working class or ethnic groups, or observe more obvious pride in the land or sports. When we talk loosely of "another culture," we sometimes mean interactional or institutional differences. But a term which can mean anything means little; to understand cultures we first need to think about culture more precisely. Cultures are symbolic repertoires of meanings and values, some of which are heard widely, some of which are less commonly heard. Here I analyze the persistent and influential sets of meanings and values which have been used in making claims about American and Australian national identity.[10]

One of the best ways to see what nations mean to us is by comparison, and one of the best ways to compare systematically the ways we formulate our national identities is to compare what people say about their nations in very similar circumstances. Both the United States and Australia celebrated what they labeled as centennials in the late nineteenth century with huge international exhibitions, parades, and other ceremonies. Each country also held a national bicentennial commemoration in the late twentieth century, and these too were organized in very similar ways. Such organized public festivals have long been seen as important representations and affirmations of collective identity, and they became important instruments for the constitution of national identities during the nineteenth century.[11]

I draw the analytic tools for understanding national identity in centennials and bicentennials from the recent work of cultural sociologists. I use these tools to avoid as far as possible the long-recognized tension between idiographic and nomothetic, particular understanding and general explanation. If national identity is a form of imagined community which is understood in many different ways, we need the conceptual tools to understand cultural variety and contingency, while placing this understanding in the context of more general explanation. We need an approach which allows us to see the forest through the trees, without clearfelling the woods in the process.[12]

To this end, I ask questions drawn from three types of cultural analysis as I examine and explain what people said about their nations in the centennials and bicentennials. These different approaches to cultural analysis can be seen as different sorts of lenses on the celebrations; I combine these lenses, as an optician might, for greater depth and focus.[13] To understand and account for national identity in these cases, we first need "thick description" of that symbolic repertoire as people used it in contingent and complex figural action. Second, we need to understand the context in which it was produced. Third, we need to understand the broader discursive field within which the symbols were organized and became meaningful as *national* symbols. Different cultural analysts have stressed these different aspects of cultural explanation to different degrees, but this book combines these different insights. Taken together, these lenses, illuminating different aspects of the social process of making meaning, provide both interpretive context and general explanation as I account for similarities and differences in the ways national identity developed in Australia and the United States.

The central part of the story of national identity in the centennial and bicentennial celebrations is the story of the many symbols with which people have expressed American and Australian national identity in national celebrations – symbols appealing, for instance, to national freedom or progress. For each celebration, I look at the particular meanings and values people associated with their nation, at what people said as they spoke about what they were celebrating and why. What was the range of meanings and values they attributed to the nation, the range of possible claims about national identity? By answering these questions about public culture for each event, I show the symbolic repertoires expressing national identity available to cultural actors in Australia in 1888 and 1988, and in the United States in 1876 and 1976. We will see reflection on such themes as place in the world, collective memory, political values, the land, diversity, and spectacle itself to different degrees in each event.

This examination of what their nations have meant to Americans and Australians in their big national celebrations provides a new perspective on important symbols of national identity, allowing us to see what has persisted and what has changed about how national identity has been understood.

Cultural sociologists have sometimes viewed culture as the result of a production process, and this is the second lens I use to view national identity in the centennials and bicentennials. Symbolic repertoires are frequently produced and reproduced in specific organizational contexts: available meanings and values are often influenced by the goals, constraints, resources, conventions, and technologies of particular culture-producing groups, and their audiences. Particular sets of meanings and values are often effective or ineffective depending on the resources and conditions which accompany their production, selection, and institutionalization.[14] Symbolic repertoires available to express national identity may be produced by state organizations or nationalist movements, for instance, or by those who write national textbooks or arrange local Fourth of July parades; and the chosen themes of national identity may vary accordingly.

In the centennials and bicentennials, specific sets of organizations produced and elicited claims about national identity as they tried to make plausible celebrations in their broader public spheres. By looking at these patriotic commemorations as cultural productions, we can also see in each case organizational constraints which influenced the cultures of national identity produced. The sorts of themes which could be claimed to express national identity depended especially on the relationship between planning organizations (themselves often composed of quarreling elites) and other groups – groups which were sometimes enthusiastic but just as often dissenting or apathetic. I note, for instance, that organizers of the American centennial made a deliberate appeal to the revolutionary founding moment across contemporary North/South divisions, and that organizers of the Australian bicentenary deliberately muted references to the Australian "founding moment" of British invasion in the face of contemporary Aboriginal protest. For each event, I examine the constraints and possibilities of production context, asking who produced the national rituals, for whom, why, how they saw the problems they faced, and how they addressed them.

Each of these events deserves more specific historical attention in its own right. Much that is interesting in the history of each event – like more detailed pictures of each social group involved, or the stories of intra-organizational politics – is neglected here in favor of the larger comparative picture. Thus, for instance, I do not examine the changing social composition of organizing elites so much as the similarities and differences in the challenges they faced in expressing national identity. But keeping such constraints and the possibilities of the context of cultural production in mind, I do ask whether dominant cultural repertoires seem to have been widely shared in each event, and how what was said was influenced by prospective audiences and available organizational technologies. Each set of events I examine shows variations in the salience and meaning of national identity claims among different groups. So as I account for the emergence, persistence, and disappearance of aspects of what it has meant to be Australian or American, I will be situating those themes in the context of their cultural production.

It is worth noting here that the "cultural production" lens shows the value of these national patriotic events as evidence of repertoires of national identity claims. In these events, there were many claims about the nation made by a number of different elite groups to whom national identity was most important, but at the same time the plausibility of their claims depended on many more peripheral social groups, and organizers often spoke to elicit a wide response. The centennials and bicentennials were both culturally dense and relatively inclusive. Of course, focusing on these events also has limitations. First, we would expect to find some difference in emphasis in themes of national identity if we looked at other sorts of cultural productions, because some symbols may be more meaningful or useful in some contexts than others, and there are likely to be some differences between the versions of national identity produced by different groups and for different audiences. Nevertheless, the centennials and bicentennials are more likely than most other indicators to give a broad overview of what Australians and Americans have associated with their nations. Second, of course, we would expect to learn more of each national identity with more detailed attention to familiar historical developments in the century intervening between the centennials and bicentennials. The comparative overview of events largely similar in their cultural production is not a substitute for more particular historical understandings; rather, it shows those histories in a new light.

Organizers of centennials and bicentennials in each country faced very similar tasks. The cultural production of centennial celebrations was largely comparable in the United States and Australia, as was that of the production of the respective bicentennials. Centennial talk differs much more from bicentennial talk in its general themes and style than the two countries differ in their respective centennials or bicentennials. Methods of organizing national celebrations, and the problems organizers faced, changed significantly between the late nineteenth and the late twentieth centuries, and thus help to account for the ways the national identities produced in such celebrations changed over time. Languages of popular inclusion – appealing to "progress" or "diversity," for example – were very different in centennials and bicentennials. Production organization and constraints account for many differences between centennials and bicentennials; viewing the events through the lens of "cultural production" helps to show what we can expect to be similar in national celebrations in each country, and also what will change over time.

The third analytic lens I bring to these celebrations reveals a common discursive structure underlying the contingent and various sets of meanings and values in each of the four events. I draw here on the work of those cultural analysts who suggest that particular symbols become meaningful within discursive fields. Discursive fields establish "limits of discussion" and define "the range of problems which can be addressed." They delineate the meaningful and valuable from a large range of potential meanings and values available. All talk of national identity, whatever its themes, is framed by a discursive field which is defined by concerns about international position and internal integration. Particular themes and symbols gain their meaning as elements of national identity to the extent that, in specific historical contexts, they can be seen to be answering one of two questions: "What can we agree that we share?" and "What is our position in the world?" As I analyze symbolic repertoires in each set of events, I compare and contrast the ways Americans and Australians spoke of what they shared and how they were placed in the world.[15]

Seeing national identity as a discursive field is useful for several reasons. First, it furthers the comparative analysis of national identities without denying their variety or the indeterminacy in their production. We can generalize across the many particular ways in which national identity has been characterized, seeing the cultural forest through the trees. The discursive field provides a systematic basis for identifying similarities and differences in national identities both cross-nationally and over time.

Second, identifying the common discursive structure behind different symbolic repertoires can help to explain important cross-national differences. With this general framework, we can see that "what may appear to be cross-national differences may really be instances of lawful regularities, if thought of in terms of some larger, more encompassing, interpretation." Specifically, I ask here, as I develop the comparison of the centennials and bicentennials, whether integration concerns or geopolitical concerns were more important for plausible national identity in each event.[16]

So in the chapters which follow I compare the Australian and American national identities which were formulated in centennial and bicentennial

Summary

celebrations by comparing the symbolic repertoires which were created and recreated by cultural producers, examining the organization of this cultural production, and showing the shared but differentially salient discursive field which structured the production of meaning in these symbolic repertoires. I view each event through the three lenses of symbolic repertoire, cultural production, and discursive field. Together, these three lenses provide an account of the similarities and differences which emerged as American and Australian national identities were created.

Centennials, bicentennials, and inference about national identity

These centennials and bicentennials were public events which were meant to be remembered. Many documents recorded their organization and their themes. My analysis of Australian and American national identities is based on these primary documents. They included commemorative volumes, official reports, promotional materials, minutes, pamphlets, debates, sermons, speeches, poems, records of ceremonies and parades, newsletters, magazines, histories, souvenirs, and programs. For each event, I examined in detail most of the available records of the organizers and producers. For centennials and again for bicentennials, very similar sorts of records were available in each country. I also examined available information and talk of national identity in some groups only remotely connected with organizers, and in oppositional claims surrounding the events.[17]

Sources

I treated these documents as evidence of public languages of national identity, as if they were rather elaborate sets of responses to a sentence completion test: "What characterizes my nation is . . ." The range of documents available shows dominant themes of national identity, but also themes in the symbolic repertoire which were used less widely. I also used more indirect inference, as I examined assumptions about who was included in the claims, about what was omitted, and about how various claims were related. An important sort of indirect inference came in answer to questions about why writers or speakers considered their topics relevant to a national celebration.[18]

Records from more remote and oppositional groups are much less complete than those from organizers, and more importantly, there is little basis to judge just how representative are the records which do exist. Where peripheral or oppositional records seemed to show similar themes to those evident in records of organizers, I took this as further support for the importance of themes in dominant repertoires of national identity. I also show, where possible, how the meanings of the nation to central organizers differed from those of other groups, noting some intriguing

Contradictions?

variations in what the nation has meant to members in different social locations.

Records available from centennials and bicentennials, though extensive for both sorts of events, are quite dissimilar. Central events of 1876 and 1888 were grand international exhibitions; in both Australia and the United States, the exhibitions provided much, though not all, of the occasion for talk about the nation. Typical forms of celebration were different by the end of the twentieth century. In the bicentennials, the emphasis was on more syncretic, vague, but systematically mobilized, ways of marking the year. In both centennials and bicentennials, organizers were conscious of apathy about their projects and potential disagreement with their actions and claims; but the relevant public sphere which formed their broader reference group excluded more groups in the centennials than the bicentennials. By the time of the bicentennials, the techniques for mobilizing the celebration of national identity were more penetrating, and under state guidance most elite groups and many peripheral communities participated directly in the construction of national identity in the celebrations. At the same time, oppositional opinion from a greater variety of groups influenced the themes adopted and the way the events were marked; elites were concerned to pre-empt criticism from a wider range of groups. The ways national celebrations changed – in rhetoric, ritual forms, and in the relevant public sphere – influences the evidence of national identity available. This does not, on the whole, affect the comparisons between Australian and American centennials, and even less does it affect the bicentennial comparison, but I take this into account in assessing the ways national identities changed between the two sets of celebrations.

There are two steps in explaining differences between American and Australian national identities on the basis of this comparison of centennials and bicentennials. First, I use the logic of "similar-case comparison" to suggest important factors accounting for different meanings and values which have become associated with each nation. Second, I also suggest that we should embed this account of relevant differences in a more historically sensitive account recognizing the influence of "global time" – the fact that these events are "differentiated *outcomes* or *moments* of an historically integrated process" of nation-formation. Changing international organization, both geopolitical and economic, influenced the presuppositions of cultural producers about national identity.[19]

In the similar-case comparison, controlling many sources of variation in national identity by choosing similar countries and similar ritual events highlights those variations which do occur by eliminating many competing explanations of the differences:

if two societies share some important conditions in common, it is relatively more permissible to treat these common conditions as parameters, and proceed to examine the operation of other variables as if these common conditions were not operative, because their operation is presumably similar in both cases.[20]

Of course, similarities and differences lie in the eye of the beholder. As I have noted, this particular comparison has escaped most scholarly vision, whether the particularist gaze of the national historian or the typologizing overview of nationalism scholars. Some of the distinctive qualities of each national experience will indeed gain new significance in this comparative explanation of national identities; but equally, the comparative explanation will draw attention to many similarities shared by these countries as settler nations in contrast to older or younger polities.

Because Australia and the United States share some historical similarities, the comparison helps to eliminate some explanations for differences in national identity. National differences here are not easily explained by referring to space, economic opportunity, or democratic politics, for example, at least not without much more precise specification. For instance, some suggest that Americans do not now stress the land in the dominant construction of national identity because it draws attention to the conquest of native peoples; but this explanation seems doubtful because in Australia there was also conquest, but the land is a dominant theme, and sometimes used as a theme to underline the imagined integration of Aborigines in the nation. Similar-case comparison is also "fruitful analytically" because it "enables theoretical results to be gone into more deeply in order to break up categories that have become insufficiently discriminating." So, for instance, while both Americans and Australians talked about international recognition in their centennials, they did this in somewhat different ways – Australians stressing more their identification with powerful others, Americans stressing more national display to powerful others. There are different nuances to their consciousness of others which become clearer in the process of comparison.[21]

On the basis of this "similar-case comparison," I conclude that, overall, producers of Australian national identity have been more deeply and persistently influenced by concerns about the position of their forming nation in the world, and producers of American national identity by problems associated with the internal integration of their populations. While, in all events, concerns about internal integration and world position both help define national identity, the different salience of internal integration and world position explains some important emergent differences in American and Australian national identities.

Similar-case comparison suggests important determinants of national identity in these events; because the countries share many features, the differences they display in integration and geopolitical position gain more weight as the crucial differences influencing different forms of national identity in American and Australian centennials and bicentennials. But such causal argument, taken alone, assumes that social conditions can be so controlled that variations of time and place could become irrelevant; historical differences then become simply parameters of the causal claim. To the extent that this is possible, comparing these centennials and bicentennials does control for many background variations. But ultimately, to hold historical developments "constant" would be to neglect important temporal changes in national institutions, cultural repertoires, and geopolitical relations. Rather, the "causes" of different national identities, identified in the similar-case comparison, themselves emerge from and are embedded in a larger political and economic history of nation-formation. In this larger history, the two countries differed in the timing of their founding and their integration in the system of nation-states. If Australian cultural producers in these national events display greater consciousness of issues of geopolitical position and their relations with others, and American cultural producers greater concern with symbolizing internal integration, these differing presuppositions are largely attributable to historical changes in conditions of nation-formation. These changing conditions meant that, from their foundings, Australians and Americans faced cumulatively different worlds as they imagined links among themselves and relations with others.

In the following chapter I begin to build this argument by examining the different trajectories which brought people in the United States and Australia to celebrate "centennials" in the late nineteenth century. I go on to discuss how centennial celebrations were organized. Using the work of Edward Shils, I argue that these big, dense, inclusive, but transient, rituals were mobilized by "cultural centers" to invite the participation of "cultural peripheries." Understanding this distinctive form of cultural production helps to understand who spoke about nations, what was important to them, what problems and opportunities they faced, and how they understood their audiences. Viewing the centennials through this lens, I tell the long-forgotten stories of the "collective effervescence" which sparkled in many corners of each country in 1876 and 1888.

Against this background, chapter 3 focuses on what national identity actually meant in American and Australian centennials. I ask how members of each nation spoke of what they shared, and how they spoke of their place in the world. What did they think was worth celebrating? Did they talk about history, language, agriculture, art, industry, land, ethnicity, wars, freedom, language? What were the patterns of emphasis and association among the different themes by which the nations were characterized? How similar or different were the themes they chose? I compare the ways each nation was imagined in each centennial by analyzing the symbolic repertoires available for characterizing national identity, and the discursive fields which gave significance to commonly used themes.

Chapter 4 shifts the focus to national identity in the bicentennials a hundred years later. The world facing organizers and participants in these events is more familiar to us than the world of the centennials: nevertheless, the intensive organization and widespread talk of the nation in these big national rituals has quickly been forgotten. I analyze the elaborate cultural production of bicentennials as I tell the story of how the events were planned and created, what happened, who spoke of the nation, and the problems and opportunities they faced. Once again, cultural centers produced and encouraged ritual commemoration for and with cultural peripheries which were sometimes enthusiastic and sometimes critical and resistant. I then turn to the question of the meaning of each nation in the bicentennials, asking again how members of each country spoke of what they shared and their place in the world. What symbols and claims made best sense as representations of American and Australian national identity in the late twentieth century? What was persistent and what had changed since the centennials a hundred years earlier?

The stories of the two celebrations will suggest many intriguing directions for comparison and cultural explanation as we see persistence and variation in forms of collective memory and such points of national pride as political values or the land. In the course of the centennial and bicentennial analyses I sometimes refer forward or backward to note important points of comparison; but I reserve the larger comparative picture for the final chapter. In chapter 5, on the basis of the more detailed analyses, I draw the threads of the extended cultural comparison together. Summarizing the symbolic repertoires available to express national identity in each of the four events, I outline how national identities changed in each country in the course of a century, how American and Australian national identities compared, and how the similarities and differences between these two settler nations changed between centennials and bicentennials. I explain why meanings associated with the two nations have changed, and what accounts for emergent differences between them.

The two countries shared many ways of expressing their national identities. Many of these similarities are attributable to the analogous cultural production processes available to nationalizing cultural elites at the end of the nineteenth century, and at the end of the twentieth century.

But the comparison also shows important differences. These differences suggest that for Australians, themes and symbols of national identity are more charged with meaning as they are useful in expressing position in the world, and that for Americans, particular themes and symbols of national identity are more meaningful to the extent they can represent integration across salient social boundaries. Already evident in the late nineteenth century, this fundamental difference in cultures of national identity was very strong by the time of the bicentennials. Variation in the importance of issues of integration and world position emerged because of the different timing, for the United States and Australia, of their formation and integration into a world of nation-states which was itself forming.

Although there were differences in emergent national identities, though, there was a more encompassing similarity shared by these two new nations as many others; by the end of the twentieth century, national identities, though fluid and contested, were no longer overshadowed by narrower or broader imagined communities. By the end of the twentieth century, the early American concern that "we were neither the same Nation nor different Nations" and the early Australian suggestion that Australians might be "a nation within a nation" no longer meant much to most Australians or Americans. Links between citizens and imagined geopolitical boundaries had been constructed. The following chapter begins the story of one of the more vivid episodes in that process.

2

"Every one admits that commemorations have their uses": producing national identities in celebration

By the late nineteenth century, ideas of "American" and "Australian" nationality were "acquir[ing] their taken-for-granted status" for important groups in each country. The centennials they celebrated in 1876 and 1888 were often treated as significant and exciting crystallizations of existing national identity and experience. As an Australian journalist reflected about the ceremonial opening of "Centennial Hall" in Sydney, "the outward and visible sign arouses thought and ofttimes something more ... it shows the place we have come in the march of our progress; it recalls the past; it suggests the future." Many people in both countries took part in exhibitions, parades, ceremonies, and banquets for the centennials; they made speeches, wrote poems, gave sermons, built halls, published magazines, sent letters, and counted products to the greater glory of their nations. In some groups, people worked so intensively on making the celebrations that they may well have been as burnt out as the Connecticut woman who wrote to fellow organizers in 1875: "every one admits that commemorations have their uses; this will, it is hoped, be true of us, though we be done to death by over-commemorating." She was unusual, though, in publicly admitting limit to the excitement of the celebration. How had people in these new nations come to this point? And how are we to interpret the beliefs about nationality they expressed?[1]

Many people in each country were claiming shared identities which had hardly existed a century earlier. And in these settler countries, the changes which transformed new mixes of land, peoples, and political arrangements into "new nations" had been slow, subtle, and diffuse in their origins. Even though characterizations of national identity had been available for some time, for most of that time they had been subordinated to stronger local or transnational loyalties. National cultures were frequently overshadowed by local and regional identifications in the United States and dominated by imperial loyalties in Australia. Even more puzzling, Australians and Americans were making similar sorts of claims about their nationalities in the centennials, even though they were celebrating very different centuries. In both cases, the future of national identity was perhaps even more important than its past; many important symbols, rituals, and patriotic organizations were yet to be established.[2]

Two shared cultural developments made the similarly energetic celebration of centennials possible, despite brief histories, competing loyalties, and, in Australia's case, the absence of any unified, independent sovereignty. First, nationality was gradually becoming a "world cultural frame" for the interpretation of the human experience of sharing and difference in political community. Second, the exposition as a genre of large-scale national celebration was adopted and adapted in both the United States and Australia; exhibitions helped mobilize national celebration, provided a focus for many other ritual events, and made the way cultural claims about nationality were produced in each centennial very much the same. A global belief in nationality was being institutionalized, and elites in each country adopted similar organizational frameworks and strategies to promote that belief. These two global influences were shared by Australia and the United States, and they made the centennials comparable celebrations of national identity.

Before examining exactly what people thought about their new nations, it is important to understand the context in which they came to think of themselves as nations at all, and to devote their energies to celebrating centennials. Here, I will first trace the different paths by which Americans and Australians came to the point of celebrating centennials, noting that these paths bear little resemblance to those of cases more typically explained by theories of nationalism. I argue that the organized celebration of national identity in these centennials is best understood as a distinctively intense yet transient cultural production process, characterized by the mobilization by self-constituted "cultural centers" of their peripheries. This framework helps illuminate the background to talk of the nation in these ritual events, and provides a basis for comparing centennials, and bicentennials, in both countries. In the final part of this chapter, I will show how the centennials were celebrated, and how claims about national identity were produced by organizing elites who attempted to affirm shared identity in the face of significant political difference and social distance.

Becoming nations: American and Australian experiences

The gradual development of national identities in the United States and Australia bears little resemblance to nation-formation both in older and in more recent polities. Most general accounts of nation-formation have focused on the emergence of the first European nation-states, the spread of claims about national identity as the basis of political legitimacy in Europe in the nineteenth century, and the mobilization of nationalist claims in twentieth-century anti-colonial or ethnic movements. These accounts provide little guidance for understanding how national identities emerged in the two settler countries. In old states like France, or post-colonial countries like Kenya, national identities were developed alongside new forms of political mobilization – as new bases of legitimacy for established states, or in oppositional movements for political autonomy and unity. Accordingly, studies of nationalism often explain the making of new national identities in terms of political mobilization in social movements or the state, giving the appearance of a simple association between cultural formulation and that political mobilization.

But the story is different in these settler countries. Australia and the United States both lacked strong political mobilizations around nationalism in the course of their formation. No influential nationalist movements were central in promoting the development of American or Australian national identity, and neither did any strong, long-established state promote national identity as it consolidated popular legitimacy. Certainly, some critical groups, political parties, and politicians promoted nationalist agendas: such agendas were evident in organizations and movements like the Republican Party in the United States in the middle of the nineteenth century, in the Australian Natives' Association, in the Young America movement, or in Australia's radical labor movement. But nationalism itself did not become a central political issue in either country in ways evident elsewhere. For this reason, most general explanations of nationalism have treated the United States and Australia as peripheral cases.[3] Yet, by the end of the nineteenth century, members of both countries often saw themselves as and were seen to be nations. These outcomes are not easily explained using the standard model, whereby national identities are cultivated, if not seeded, almost exclusively under the hothouse conditions of political mobilization. Instead, they are better understood as the result of a slow process of cultural innovation and diffusion, a process that looks unfocused, uncertain, and subtle – if it is even visible – when set alongside the more familiar and typical story of the creation of nationalities.

To suggest that the creation of national identities in Australia and the

United States was *more* the result of cultural innovation and diffusion than of explicit nationalist mobilization is not, of course, to suggest any absolute distinction between the two alternatives. The formulation and inculcation of national identities is always a matter of cultural production – but the question is where and how that production mostly occurs. In those countries treated as central by many studies of nationalism, either the state or an oppositional political movement was the primary site of cultural production, production which was linked directly to, if not fused with, political mobilization. In contrast, although the administrative and economic integration of both Australia and the United States was promoted by "nationalist" politicians, and these projects were supported by claims about nationality in both countries, the links between "national" political-economic projects and the creation of national identities were indirect in both cases. Creating a "national" political space is one thing; creating a national identity that corresponds with such a space is another – and in both Australia and the United States important new claims about nationality frequently arose beyond "political" institutions and organizations narrowly defined. Thus, to understand the creation and development of American and Australian national identities, it is necessary to explore a process of cultural production which has been taken for granted in the study of state-generated nationalisms and nationalist political movements.

Paradoxically, this process seemed as uncertain for the Americans as for the Australians who began to plan centennials. If it seems counterintuitive that both countries celebrated centennials – when unified independent sovereignty had been achieved a hundred years earlier for Americans but was still to come for Australians – this is because the countered intuition confuses political and cultural stories, sovereignty with the possession of a cultural repertoire enabling imagined community. Australians constantly spoke of themselves as Australians in the centennial celebrations. In the celebrations, if not yet in mundane politics, the Australian identity was more frequently claimed than any more local or more global alternatives. Forrest McDonald has spoken of the American founders as "politically multilingual"; Australians in the late nineteenth century were similarly multilingual in naming themselves, appealing to national, colonial, continental, racial, and imperial identities with little sense of contradiction. Thus, although the Australian colonies were not yet formally unified at the time of the centennial, many members were able to speak of their nation in much the same terms as Americans did. The two countries did differ, though, in the period in which they first formed around national visions, and their role in the diffusion of the "nation" idea.[4]

American nationality: innovation and uneven development

National ideas began to be relevant to some Americans a century earlier than they were relevant to most Australians. Indeed, the American Revolution (along with the French Revolution of 1789) provided an important cultural innovation for later nationalist political mobilizations. As scholars concerned with the origin of national ideas have shown, the core of any national identity involves a capacity for political action which is putatively shared by people of different status. National identity, by contrast to other identities, involves "the location of sovereignty within the people and the recognition of the fundamental [political] equality among its various strata." While it is rare to find this cultural potential fully matched by political reality, the move to ground legitimate sovereignty in "the people" offers the possibility, at least, that political voice need no longer depend on particularistic status, like membership of families or villages. All members of the new political community share a "deep horizontal comradeship" in their shared capacity to ground legitimate sovereignty. National identity begins when older public identities, based on more particularistic, pre-modern status orders, are no longer taken to be key determinants of capacities for public action. Accounts of the precise beginnings of the possibility of this "deep horizontal comradeship" differ, but scholars of very different persuasions agree that the United States early possessed this core.[5]

Indeed, the American Revolution was a crucial episode in the creation of the very possibility of the imagined community of the nation. As one of the earliest events to institutionalize and develop some core ideas necessary to national identity, the American Revolution provided important cultural resources for the later development of national identity elsewhere. National identity was increasingly adopted as the major principle of internal and external legitimacy from the American and French Revolutions onwards, and came to be associated with democratic claims. The use of nationalist claims by excluded groups against political centers developed in Europe in the nineteenth century. Movements against older political centers were more and more frequently based on nationalist claims. The national model was taken up as an active ideology in Germany and Italy, and a little later in Eastern Europe, with differing nuances.[6] At the same time as national consciousness became a basis for political opposition, public festivals organized by state elites became more and more common as tools to mobilize and constitute national identity as a ground for legitimating state authority.[7]

But despite this early and influential innovation, American national identity developed rather unevenly. The Revolution was not a nationalist revolution; and compared both to universal claims and to more particularistic local identities, national identity was not very significant. At the time of the American Revolution, and indeed for the next century, Americans still doubted the viability of national institutions. The development of a compelling and thick "American" national identity in the form we know it today might still have been arrested in the United States in the nineteenth century. Since American sovereignty began when nation-states were still new as polities, the innovative politics left weaknesses and uncertainties which made the further institutionalization of American national identity slow and halting compared with later "new nations."

Compared to the anti-colonial revolutions of the twentieth century, there was little nationalism in the American Revolution. At first, colonists rebelled in order to claim rights they understood as British; only later did they see separation as the only way to achieve those rights. Revolutionary claims were not framed in nationalist terms. Not only were British political ideas of universally shared political rights central to revolutionary thinking: to the extent that the members of various colonies recognized any shared identity, this recognition was mediated by their relation to Britain. They perceived what they had in common to the extent that they stood in the same relation to Britain, and were subject to the same influences. Indeed, it was the British who first saw, and acted upon, the colonies as a whole. In contemporary newspapers, for instance, British journalists were using the collective term "America" before the colonists adopted it. Many scholars of the revolutionary period go so far as to argue that "America was a British idea" and that to the extent the members of the different colonies shared anything at all, it was an increasing Anglicization.[8]

The American Revolution did, of course, develop and reinforce notions of shared political community. The Revolutionary War, especially, became a process of nationalist political education: British campaigning often created, directly or indirectly, the beginnings of distinctively American national identifications. But the lesson was not always deeply engrained, nor was it equally available or salient to all. National sentiment at the time of the Revolution was strongest among those who had been born or educated abroad, among "veterans of lengthy service in the Continental army," and in those areas which were militarily vulnerable. Otherwise, differences and mutual antipathies between people of different colonies remained strong, and long after the revolutionary period state loyalties were predominant. Despite the influence of the war in beginning to forge a new national identity, members of different colonies thought of themselves as more different than similar. Historian Jack Greene has concluded that "the process by which Americans began to think of themselves as 'a people' ... was still in a primitive stage of development between 1775 and 1787."[9]

Patterns of social life continued to favor identification with states over "the nation" even until after the Civil War. Although the American Revolution established the basis for national sovereignty – the possibility that political community could be envisaged nationally – and it suggested some vivid symbols to represent the nation, it left unresolved the question of who that political community included, and the symbolic representation of the nation remained comparatively weak, very localized, and quite thin. Who would shared American political community really include, and how would people participate in its representation? It took the century before the celebration of the centennial to establish the firm common ground which made answers to those questions self-evident.

Even the legitimate legal authority of the national government was ambiguous until after the Civil War. Predictions of the dissolution of the union were common from the Revolution until after the war. The political unit to which existing ideas about the nation should be applied was not self-evident: especially at first, the core "national" idea of political liberty was more closely associated with the states than the union for many people. In the first half of the nineteenth century, the underlying issue in the development of American national identity was whether liberty was to be associated with the states or with national sovereignty. On one side, the idea that states were the bearers of liberty, and the union a compact between sovereign polities, was mobilized and developed in the Hartford Convention of 1814, in Calhoun's political doctrines, and in the various debates about nullification and secession which were evoked especially by abolition and the question of new Western slave states which became more controversial from the 1830s. On the other side of the issue, the idea that the union, rather than the states, was the bearer of special political liberty was strengthened and championed: "dissolution of the Union" came to represent "loss of liberty."[10]

Despite this important ambiguity, some persistent symbols and rituals representing American nationality were established in the period before the Civil War. Most shared representations of American national identity took "the Revolutionary era as a centerpiece for public memory in the early Republic." George Washington was intensely and consistently revered as a national hero from the 1780s. Portraits, birthday celebrations, shrines, relics, books, articles, and nomenclature were so common and widespread that a visitor in the 1830s observed that "Washington, in America, is not a man but a god" (the intensity of the hagiography seems to have declined in the 1850s). Founding documents like the Declaration of Independence and the Constitution, and battles like Bunker Hill, were honored and commemorated, although to different degrees in different places and times.[11]

The Fourth of July was also widely celebrated from the late eighteenth century, with processions, bells, cannon, oratory, public dinners, church services, and, increasingly from the 1830s, more broadly appealing public amusements, refreshments, and assemblies. Interest in the Fourth of July, like attachment to Washington, decreased between the 1850s and the 1870s. For a long time, Fourth of July celebrations were organized by partisan political groups and reform movements – in some cities, early on, different celebrations would be held by federalists and their opponents; and in the first half of the nineteenth century antislavery, temperance, Sunday school, and suffrage movements often took the occasion to promote their agendas. So the Fourth of July was not "an occasion for consensus" but "frequently fell victim to fierce factional disputes." Perhaps more importantly here, there was wide regional variation in salience and style of the holiday in this period; it was most important in the north-east and, to a lesser extent, in the frontier states.[12]

In their distinctively factional character and regional variation, early celebrations of the Fourth of July were typical of most American symbols of national identity in the period. Regional and local concerns overdetermined most expressions of nationality. Fragmentation and localization were encouraged because the "invention of tradition" in the United States was unusually laissez-faire: government "scarcely considered itself a custodian of tradition at all, or even a sponsor of collective memory." Laissez-faire attitudes to commemoration, combined with stronger local identifications, led to some surprising omissions and absences in patriotic culture. For instance, celebration of the Fourth of July seems to have been lukewarm in 1837, the fiftieth anniversary of the constitutional convention; and even in 1832, the centennial of Washington's birthday, "parochial attitudes made it difficult to muster sufficient public support for an appropriate celebration." Bodnar points out in this context that "more commemorative attention was given to local, state, and regional pasts." Early expressions of national identity, then, showed extensive regional variation in significance and style. As Tocqueville characterized identity before the Civil War,

Americans therefore have much more to expect and fear from the state than from the Union and, in view of the natural inclination of the human heart, are bound to feel a more lively attachment to the former than to the latter. In this respect habits and feelings are in harmony with interests.[13]

The late nineteenth century was the period of greatest innovation in

American national identity. Most patriotic practices, organizations, and symbols familiar today date from or became institutionalized at that time. For instance, flags were not placed in schools until 1890; Uncle Sam did not come to symbolize the country until this period; and "the real story" of patriotic organizations "does not begin until after the Civil War." Thanksgiving and Memorial Day were institutionalized as a result of the Civil War. An extensive inventory of patriotic symbols and practices ranging from place names to the pledge of allegiance shows a marked period of innovation and growth in the late nineteenth century, an increase also noted in early studies of American nationalism. "Anxiety about nationality" characterized the gilded age in the United States; and public patriotic celebrations grew much larger and more centrally organized. Soon after the centennial, for example, progressive elites began "Americanization" campaigns and they attempted to reinforce an image of national unity in large historical pageants.[14]

In 1876, organizers of the centennial celebration were not on secure ground in trying to express an established national tradition in the United States. They had a comparatively tenuous basis for their claims about "the nation's" century. While they were celebrating a century of formal sovereignty, this only served to emphasize that there was no simple association between political sovereignty and national identity. Persisting local identifications and long-lasting historical ambiguities in the significance of national institutions both continued to create for American centennial organizers serious problems of national integration. As the story of the centennial will show, divisions between North and South remained particularly conspicuous. By the time of the centennial, Americans were celebrating a century of formal sovereignty, but an uneven and contested cultural unity.

Australian nationality: multiple identities, delayed sovereignty

If the uneven development of national identity in the United States does not seem to fit with the typical cases of nationalism, the development of national identity in Australia is even more puzzling to categories drawn from the study of nationalist politics. It is not clear, from that point of view, why Australians celebrated a centennial at all. The occasion of celebration in 1888 was, on the face of it, much less inspiring than the American Revolution. Perhaps even stranger, the six Australian colonies were not united in their political organization, but rather in their geographic location and geopolitical dependence on Britain. There was no formal Australian sovereignty at the time of the Australian centennial celebration.

Further, as the story of the centennial will show, a language expressing distinctive "Australian" national identity was considered entirely consistent with and even dependent on British attachments. But if the American experience shows that formal sovereignty does not automatically entail established national identity, the Australian experience shows, conversely, that it is possible to create expressions of national identity with neither unified sovereignty nor much of an oppositional nationalist political movement. As in the American case, cultural experience was distinct from formal political grounding – though for converse reasons.

It was only around the time the American colonies were establishing sovereignty that the European history of Australia began, with its invasion by an imperial British state. Captain James Cook had claimed the continent for Britain in 1770, in the course of an expedition to chart the transit of Venus at Tahiti and to map the coasts of the unknown continent. Eighteen years after Cook's visit, the British government founded a penal settlement on the coast he had claimed, its uninviting qualities being no disincentive for such a purpose. While the proper understanding of the mixed reasons for the settlement is debated, the most prominent was the need to do something about the overflow of prisoners left in Britain when they could no longer be sent to America; settlement also made sense to the British for strategic reasons. Captain Arthur Phillip, an officer in the British navy, arrived at Botany Bay, Cook's landing place, with eleven ships and just over 1,000 people, around three-quarters of whom were convicts and most of the rest marines. He soon moved to a more promising site for settlement, landing at Sydney Cove on January 26, 1788.[15]

For years the colony was tiny and precarious; the land was different from any in European experience, and the social organization of the white population first developed from the contingencies of what was effectively an empire's prison government. Free settlement, often subsidized, did not begin in any numbers until the 1830s. Different colonies were formed on the continent in the late eighteenth and early nineteenth centuries, either as offshoots of the first settlement, New South Wales, or as independent settlements. At the time of the centennial there were six Australian colonies: New South Wales, Victoria, Tasmania (Van Diemen's Land), Queensland, South Australia, and Western Australia. All colonies but South Australia were penal settlements at one time or another, but the relative importance of free and convict settlement in each colony varied. Transportation of convicts to New South Wales ended in 1840 (after some local struggle on the part of free settlers), and had ended in all colonies by 1868. Convict settlement was mostly an embarrassing memory by the centennial.[16]

Most of the vast continent had been explored by whites by 1888, but it was unsuitable for close agricultural settlement and remained thinly populated. The Australian economy was driven by a comparative advantage in a narrow range of exported primary products, especially wool, which by the 1880s made up 60 percent of exports. Gold rushes in Victoria in the early 1850s had been a sudden demographic shock with longer-term social impact, raising the newer colony to political and economic influence on a par with the first colony. In the second half of the nineteenth century, most white Australians lived in two south-eastern colonies, New South Wales and Victoria.[17]

Paradoxically, the pastoral economy supported an unusually urbanized population. Most Australians did not work the land, and most lived in cities and large towns. Whereas, at the time of the American centennial, half the workforce was still engaged in agriculture, only one in four centennial Australians worked in agriculture or the pastoral sector. Even by the time of the Australian celebration, twelve years after their own, many more Americans worked the land than Australians. A third of Australian workers were in manufacturing and construction, and another third in services. One in two Australians lived in urban areas, especially the capital cities, and the centennial decade was a period of particularly rapid urban growth. Throughout most of the nineteenth century, the Australian population was more urbanized than the American. By the 1880s, the "Australian dream" already envisioned "a small cottage on its own block of land not too far from a suburban railway line." Many Australians were also well off by international standards. By one turn-of-the-century measure, and even after a relative decline in the Australian economy, average wealth per head was still slightly higher than that of the United States.[18]

Unlike the American colonies earlier, the Australian colonies were always well integrated in, and largely dependent on, the economic and geopolitical management of the British empire. British imperial involvement in the development and exploration of the six colonies of the Australian continent was more intense than it had been in colonial America. Britain was the major export market and source of finance for Australian colonies. Different colonial identities in Australia developed within the framework of a much stronger dependence on Britain. The availability of development finance, especially, was well recognized as a crucial issue for Australian domestic politics. Economic, military, and diplomatic dependence within the imperial framework was a matter of course to most late nineteenth-century Australians. Culturally, as we will see, few Australians saw any contradiction between their British attachments and their developing "Australian" identity, and frequently, the former was an implicit premise of the latter.[19]

Political control was exercised by governors sent from Britain, but their influence lessened in the course of the nineteenth century. At first, their power was almost complete: the story of very early colonial politics is a story of successive governors, their relations to their superiors in Britain, their (sometimes conflictual) relations with their military juniors in the struggling colonies, and their interactions with the tiny gentry of free settlers. In the course of the nineteenth century, and as free settlement became typical, colonial governors from Britain became less active and less influential in day-to-day politics. Governors did link colonies with the Colonial Office in surveillance and mediation of the fairly infrequent disputes about British policies, especially where imperial and colonial geopolitical concerns did not coincide. The social displays of governors, their wives, and their imperial officers also kept the British presence symbolically powerful. Overall, the white Australian political experience of imperial administration was much more positive than that in late colonial America. Although there were a number of issues on which the Australians saw their interests as conflicting with the Colonial Office, it was willing "to allow the Colonies the greatest freedom which it considered compatible with the maintenance of Empire, and to liberalize gradually its view of how much freedom was compatible."[20]

From about the middle of the century, most of the colonies were self-governing to some extent; all but one was self-governing at the time of the centennial (the exception was Western Australia, with a population of less than 50,000). This meant that the colonies had constitutional, Westminster-style parliaments with jurisdiction over most domestic issues. Membership of upper houses was restricted, but lower houses were at the cutting edge of democratic innovations like white manhood suffrage, secret ballots, and payment of members. Although the political culture and organization of the colonies did differ in intriguing ways from American political culture, it was, as in the United States, basically liberal.[21]

In contrast to the typical American experience, colonial governments played an important role in the economy. While the leading developers of infrastructure in the United States were often private investors, the governments of the Australian colonies were central in financing development, to the extent that the political economy of late nineteenth-century Australia has been labeled "colonial socialism." For instance, during both centennials railway construction was booming; but whereas in the United States the growth took place through particularistic congressional subsidies to private enterprises, railways were an explicit government responsibility in Australia and indeed they absorbed "the bulk of government loan raising in this period."[22]

In the late nineteenth century, then, Australia consisted of six colonies, each with an independent polity operating within an imperial framework. In addition to the imperial links created by the governors, each colony maintained a separate promotional and lobbying presence in London. Developmental disparities colored intercolonial politics with policy differences. Colonies hotly disputed issues like tariffs, river waters, and railways; they acted as "rival syndicates . . . especially in the competition for loan money, immigrants, and rail freight," and there were persistent intercolonial jealousies. In the longer contemporary view, though, and in hindsight, differences were, as American philosopher Josiah Royce called them, "absurd neighbourhood squabbles" and did not exclude the simultaneous recognition of a shared identity.[23]

The name for the continent, "Australia," had been suggested first in 1814 by Matthew Flinders, whose circumnavigation had proved that New South Wales was part of the earlier-known "New Holland." The name soon came into common usage; colonial notables "began to make an ostentatious habit of signing themselves 'an Australian' without the fear of being taken for a pickpocket or a savage." As early as 1835, a group promoting more liberal policies in colonial government was calling itself the "Australian Patriotic Association." The comparatively positive connotations of the name made it appealing in battles for self-government and appealing to those in favor of free immigration; it came to be associated with ideas about the country as a "land of opportunity," and a "workingman's paradise," as well as following, in selected ways, the model of the "first new nation," the United States.[24]

Federation of the colonies, creating a united Australian state, had been considered a possibility for forty years by the time of the centennial in 1888, but for most of that time it had been "a destiny remote enough to be taken for granted without requiring any immediate effort from anyone." Federation was on the political agenda in the 1850s and again in the 1880s: the discussion mostly took place among established political elites and did not generally reflect any intensive popular nationalist mobilization. The imperial administration was generally in favor of federation and encouraged it before Australian colonists were much interested. At the time of the centennial, many people expected that the colonies would federate, and it was commonplace to speak of the time "when federation has made us a nation," though at the same time the speakers were often more immediately concerned with local and pragmatic issues and disputes.[25]

Within this comparatively uncharged context, the 1880s were a period of growing Australian nationalism: as in the United States, the late nineteenth century was an important period of national symbolic innovation and institutionalization. Australian politicians felt neglected by imperial policy in the Pacific, and a "national" interest differing from that of the empire was being defined on issues like the German presence in New Guinea and Chinese immigration. The first predominantly Australian-born generation was bringing its experience to an increasingly professionalized culture industry; the first significant generation of nationalist intellectuals was active by 1888 (though, at the most, as remote critics of the centennial celebrations). Federation was becoming more influential as a middle-class movement, especially in Victoria, where the "Australian Natives' Association" had been formed in 1871. On the conservative pole of the same political agenda in the 1880s were ideas for a larger imperial federation, a parliament of the entire British empire and a kind of worldwide British *Zollverein*. A more radical republican nationalism was promoted by a minority at the opposite end of the political spectrum, in scattered republican labor organizations and the powerful voice of the popular weekly, the *Bulletin*, which had a circulation of around 80,000 in the late 1880s. Against this background, federation gradually became a mainstream goal addressed with more practical measures.[26]

A severe depression in the early 1890s would soon add economic to geopolitical and mildly nationalist arguments for unification; and in the 1890s conventions and referendums were held to develop an Australian constitution and a framework for national government. The 1890s would also see the creation by bohemian urban intellectuals of "the Australian legend" – a nationalist mythology emphasizing "the bush," rural pioneers, and the masculine, egalitarian "mateship" of pastoral workers – the creation of an influential set of national symbols, at much the same time as a constitution was being framed. Twelve years after the centennial, in 1900, "without much fuss or enthusiasm, the six Australian colonies had voted to become a nation." Australia was formally federated in 1901; but various forms of constitutional, legislative, geopolitical, economic, and cultural attachment to Britain continued well into the twentieth century.[27]

So, although they were not formally unified, members of the different colonies in 1888 had little trouble speaking of themselves as Australians. The 1888 centenary of European settlement was celebrated as an Australian event, commemorating a century of continental exploration and development, and not the birthday of New South Wales alone. Australians also appealed to other political identities: to many, Australian identity was not conceivable without its British premises, and there were certainly intercolonial differences and jealousies in "Australian" identification in

1888. But the intercolonial differences were not critical faultlines of cultural dispute, and the British attachments did not preclude the imagining and characterization of "Australian" community. The collective identity in the commemoration was at least as strong as that in the United States; indeed, alienation from celebration of Australian identity was much less severe than the regional alienation displayed by the American South in 1876. As Russel Ward argued in an early and influential study of Australian national identity, "compared with . . . differences in, say, Canada or the USA," differences between Australian colonies were "slight indeed, tending to be *not many* differences of degree and emphasis rather than of substance."[28] Austra-*differences* lians were relatively secure in labeling themselves as Australians – among other things – while not yet unified.

Two political moves which made centennial headlines illustrate the state of play in the process which was leading to Australian federation. Sir Henry Parkes, flamboyant and idiosyncratic old leader of New South Wales, proposed renaming his colony "Australia." He was trading on discontent with the awkward and derivative name of his colony and argued (ignoring Aborigines) "we were the original Australian people." The suggestion made headlines and fierce parliamentary debates; it was greeted with "mingled mirth and anger" in the local press and in other colonies. Some suggested that all six colonies should change their names in the same way; others joked that New South Wales would be better called "Convictoria," playing on the first colony's convict origins and competition with the later colony Victoria. The idea was quickly quashed, in part with the threat that the British would take a dim view of the change. Around the same time, and on the suggestion of the (Victorian) Australian Natives' Association, all the colonies agreed, as a centennial gesture, to observe January 26 as a "national" holiday from 1888. By 1888, then, colonies were sometimes quarrelsome competitors but their quarrels took place within a framework which made Parkes's appropriation of their "collective" name shocking to many, and the celebration of a "national" holiday plausible.[29]

New nations in 1876 and 1888

In both Australia and the United States, then, a number of conditions encouraged centennial celebrations when 1876 and 1888 came around. In both places, a core liberal grounding for public action was well established, allowing the possibility of "horizontal comradeship" transcending particularistic status orders in imagined national community. In both places, too, some common symbols, language, and practices had been established which already provided ways of representing national community. By the time of the centennials, it was meaningful to speak of American and Australian nations: the idea of the nation was certainly culturally available, and its influence had been slowly spreading during the nineteenth century. Elites in both countries were also sensitive to the broader global diffusion of the discursive framework creating nations as political actors, which had been a significant development of the nineteenth century.

But some important conditions seemed to discourage centennial celebrations too, and – to outsiders – would seem to suggest that a large, ritualistic, collective representation of the imagined community of the nation would have been widely implausible. American identity was weakened by internal differentiation and conflict. For most of the country's history, local and regional identities had been more significant than national identity, and the recent past had seen severe regional conflict which threatened disintegration. Australian identity had no grounding in a formally unified sovereignty, was not clearly distinguished from British and imperial identity, and was not even at issue in any significant nationalist conflict. Each country also lacked the sort of established organizational field promoting and institutionalizing a discourse of national identity which was provided elsewhere by strong states or by popular nationalist movements.

Nevertheless, the late nineteenth century was an important period of innovation, promotion, and institutionalization of national identity in each country. The centennials were ritual events among a number of other loosely bound actions in the period, like forming patriotic organizations such as the Daughters of the American Revolution or the Australian Natives' Association, or like the adoption of the Uncle Sam symbol or the proliferation of the "Australian legend." Available symbolic representations of the nations were being consolidated in a variety of ritual and organizational practices which made ideas of national community more established, so that the imagined communities of the American and Australian nations could become taken-for-granted frames of reference, beginning to take precedence over local and supranational identities. Indeed, centennial celebrations seem to be important – and largely neglected – moments in the process by which American and Australian identities were formed.

The following chapters will show much more of how the new nations were symbolized, and how the meanings and values associated with these settler countries persisted and changed in the course of the next century. But before analyzing the cultural repertoires which made nations meaningful, what exactly people said about their nations during centennials, it is important to understand the particular contexts in which claims about national identity were made: who was speaking, and why, and to whom, and what their worlds looked like to them in the years in which the big national celebrations were planned. Since the world of the centennial celebrations seems so distant to us, particular attention to the context surrounding them is necessary to understand what nations meant to the people involved. In the remainder of this chapter, I will argue that the context of these celebrations is best captured by identifying different groups which were cultural centers and peripheries in the celebration; I will then show how the centennial celebrations were made and received, describing the public sphere within which cultural centers organized peripheries in each country.

Centennial productions: making nations norms

How, then, were ideas about national identity produced in the centennials? The cultural production of national identity has often occurred in nationalist politics: nationalist movements or states are often, simultaneously, cultural producers. But in these two settler nations, cultural production of national identity was only very loosely linked to claims for political autonomy or legitimacy. Repertoires of meanings and values formulated and reformulated in centennials were not directly mobilized in making claims for political autonomy, as they would have been in nationalist movements. And the cultural production of the centennials differed from that in officially promoted nationalisms because centennial celebrations were quite loosely and ambiguously related to state projects and actions.

The centennials were intense episodes in an uninstitutionalized and diffuse field of cultural production. They were the outcome of diverse and varying projects and intentions, and a focus for the action of people in many different social locations. Often, projects and intentions which were not primarily nationalist motivated participation in the centennial celebrations and thus accumulated national meaning – projects like industrial success or regional promotion. Meanings and values were associated with the nation in a process of cultural production, selection, and dissemination which was itself embedded in a broader public sphere. But despite the diffuse, transient, and often indirect production of national identity in the centennials, they did attract the attention of a wide range of groups, and encouraged the thickening and institutionalization of languages and practices which situated other interests and projects within the imagined community of the nation. In order to understand this development, we need to understand the role of ritual organizers and centennial promoters. What were their audiences and aims, and how did this affect what they said?

What resources could they mobilize and what constraints did they face in implementing their projects?

Centers, peripheries, and the production of national identity

The best way to understand the production of national identity in these large, diffuse, and transient events is to see them as productions by self-constituted "cultural centers" of a diffuse organizational field, cultural centers which invited the participation and affirmation of their peripheries. The work of Edward Shils on cultural centers and peripheries provides a useful analytic framework for understanding the cultural production of national identity in centennials and bicentennials. It helps understand the complex sense and the social background of the Connecticut centennial organizer's claim that "every one admits that commemorations have their uses." It also illuminates the ways cultural production influenced the particular meanings and values expressing national identity in these big ritual events.

For Shils, a cultural center is "a structure of activities, of roles and persons, within the network of institutions" distinguished primarily by an active attachment to what he calls a "central value system." A cultural center is not necessarily one united group or organization; it may be a loose network made up of various specialized or conflicting groups, roles, activities, and persons. Whatever the degree of cohesion within a cultural center, its parts will "regard themselves as participants in a center." Centers "are almost continuously oriented, subjectively and in their action, toward their peripheries; they are also oriented toward other centers of other societies." In the centennials and bicentennials, specific but transient networks of diverse actors and organizations, some more connected to the state than others, but all composed of political and cultural elites, produced and elicited claims about national identity as they tried to make plausible celebrations. They were oriented to mobilizing the rest of the country, and also, as Shils would suggest, to the perceptions held by other societies about their "nation."[30]

The periphery – or peripheries, for here, too, there is differentiation – consists of "those strata or sectors of society which are recipients of commands and of beliefs which they do not themselves create or cause to be diffused." Identifying cultural centers and peripheries means, therefore, identifying an influential relation of cultural production and dissemination which is not strongly institutionalized. This relationship is what defines the two poles of center and periphery. The regard of peripheries for centers is more intermittent and less evenly distributed among groups and individuals. The link between cultural centers and peripheries may be relatively thin, a matter of simple recognition, or it may be highly elaborated. In the analyses which follow, I focus on the groups which made up cultural centers mobilizing each celebration, but I also examine the peripheral groups influenced by their mobilization, and the groups their mobilization ignored. I ask whether different symbols of national identity were shared between members of cultural centers and peripheries.[31]

For Shils, cultural centers are characterized by their attachment to and promotion of a central value system. But recent work on culture suggests that the concept of a "central value system" needs to be revised: to label ideas and symbols promoted by a cultural center a value system is to put an unnecessary limitation on the general applicability of the framework, and to prejudge the nature of any symbolic consensus which may exist. Cognitive as well as evaluative attachments are likely to be important in any cultural mobilization. In addition, shared culture often seems to consist of inherently ambiguous symbols and practices; shared culture does not always seem to imply common values. Symbols and rituals may be more important for transcending evaluative differences than for expressing evaluative consensus. Indeed ideological ambiguity can provide opportunities and resources for contending groups, and may also be strategic in appealing to different groups. Thus, for example, David Kertzer has argued that "it is the very ambiguity of the symbols employed in ritual action that makes ritual useful in fostering solidarity without consensus." For these reasons I do not assume here, as Shils would suggest, that groups and individual actors within the cultural center share an attachment to a central value system, but rather that the common ground of mobilizing groups should be seen more broadly as a dominant cultural repertoire, which may include a variety of symbols, practices, beliefs, rhetorical tropes, and emblems, in addition to evaluations, which themselves need not be assumed to be entirely consistent.[32]

With this qualification, Shils's analytic framework has several important advantages for understanding and illuminating the production of national identity in centennials and bicentennials. First, adopting an analysis which identifies cultural centers and peripheries in the organization of these relatively fragmentary, intermittent, but intense and (ideally) inclusive events can capture the field of production of national identity in settler nations better than an analysis which assumes institutionalized, ongoing cultural production within well-defined projects with clear goals of political unification or autonomy. While states and nationalist movements can be important in these centers of nationalist cultural production, we need not assume they are important, but should open to question for each case the degree of their participation in the development of national identity.

A second advantage of this analytic framework is the basis it provides for flexible and nuanced comparison. Societies can differ in the internal constitution of their centers and peripheries, and also in the relationship between them. Center/periphery relations may also differ over time (for instance, Shils suggests that greater interpenetration of centers and peripheries is characteristic of modernity). Cross-national and historical variations in center/periphery relations will influence the production of national identity, and therefore they may have an important impact on the symbols and rituals through which national identity is expressed. But while the groups involved in the promotion of celebrations of national identity may vary considerably, their self-constitution as cultural centers is similar across cases, and we can analyze specific differences in the way the context of cultural production affects national representations without attributing them, tautologically, to national differences.

Finally, this framework also allows us to analyze variant relations between cultural centers and peripheries without assuming complete consensus or dissent in the ways national community is perceived. One important advantage of identifying cultural centers and peripheries, for Shils, was that

the conceptual schema of center and periphery makes no assumptions about the degree of substantive cognitive and evaluative consensus in any particular society, apart from the consensus – always vague and never complete – regarding perceptions of centers and peripheries.

Since Durkheim, students of ritual have tried to understand the ways it can create, express, and represent social solidarity when many rituals seem to generate as much conflict, or apathy, as effervescence. Many rituals express alternative and contesting values; indeed, they may be a direct expression of conflict. Even many rituals expressing dominant values do so in societies where, as Stephen Lukes has put it, "value consensus is manifestly absent."[33] By adapting from Shils an analytic framework which identifies cultural centers and peripheries in the production of national ritual, we can leave open for each particular case the possibility that conflict or disinterest characterizes relations between specific central and peripheral groups and actors. Therefore, we do not need to assume either maximal *or* minimal cultural integration in these events, but can analyze for particular cases the existence, extent, and nature of a cultural repertoire of national symbols and rituals. Is the cultural repertoire available for expressing national identity widespread or contested among elite institutions? Does it show variants and ambiguities as a result of this differentiation and conflict? And how does center attempt to mobilize periphery? Is the central formulation of national identity itself influenced by innovation or critique in peripheral groups? Adopting Shils's view of cultural centers and peripheries opens these questions to analysis, allowing a better understanding of consensus, dissent, and apathy in potentially integrative rituals like the centennials and bicentennials. As the stories of all these events will show, national identities are at least as much a product of dissent and reassertion as any more straightforward consensus.

So if we understand the talk of national identity in centennials and bicentennials as the outcome of mobilization by a self-constituted cultural center inviting the participation of many other groups, we can see these events as nationalist cultural productions without assuming that such mobilizations must be generated in nationalist movements or states. We can also compare the cultural centers and peripheries producing each event, identifying organizational similarities and differences – which may influence meanings and values associated with national identity – both cross-nationally and between the nineteenth and twentieth centuries. Finally, the framework allows the possibility of assessing the degree of cultural consensus and difference, similarities and differences in the meaning and importance of "the nation," between organizers and other groups.

What, then, were the cultural centers and peripheries in centennial celebrations? What did people do to celebrate centennials and who cared about the celebration? Who organized the talk of national identity in the centennials, what were their projects and intentions, to whom did they speak, what problems did they face, what did they assume about their worlds, and who did they ignore? Finally, how were cultural centers and peripheries similar and different in Australian and American centennial celebrations?

Center organization and public sphere in the American centennial

In 1876, many of the big news headlines seemed to signal serious national problems. Americans at the time of the centennial would have been warned of a depression, of Custer's defeat at the hands of rebellious Sioux, of corruption and scandal in Washington, and of continuing hostility between North and South. Despite these issues, the 1876 centennial began an important process of cultural development in which a stronger American national identity was being created and institutionalized. New Year's Eve and the Fourth of July were big days of celebration. There was a collective effervescence of fireworks, parades, hymns, prayers, gun salutes, and orations in many parts of the country on these holidays (the popularity of the Fourth of July had been declining, but in 1876 it was celebrated more than it had been for twenty years). Reports of celebrations remain from many towns and cities which at that time had little else in common: from New York, Denver, Raleigh, and Cleveland; from Indianapolis as well as Logansport, IN, from Boston as well as Worcester, MA, from Pottstown, PA, as well as Philadelphia. One collection of speeches made on the Fourth of July in all the thirty-eight states also represented, according to the editor, "the varieties of social distinction among men, – white and black, Jew and Christian, Protestant and Catholic, and even the aboriginal Red Man of the forest." This was certainly overstating the diversity of the celebration, but a huge variety of groups did do something to mark the centennial year. Centennial publications taking advantage of the commemorative market ranged from the massive volumes of prolific historian Benson Lossing, to a centennial collection of work from public schools in Des Moines, to the even more ephemeral *Ye Centennial Almanac*, from Morse Bros., Druggists, in Rutland, VT.[34]

Centennial holidays were celebrated in many parts of the country, but the central event of the year was the Centennial Exhibition in Philadelphia from May to November. Since the Crystal Palace exhibition in London in 1851, such exhibitions had become part of a familiar repertoire of national and regional events, but this was the first international exhibition held in the United States. As the president of the United States Centennial Commission (USCC), General Joseph Hawley of Connecticut, said at one of the commissioners' first meetings: "it is in full accord with the best spirit of the age that the celebration should take the form of 'an international exhibition.'" At these "cultural olympics" in 1876, most states and fifty-six foreign countries and colonies were officially represented.[35]

In Philadelphia, every conceivable product of human activity seemed to be displayed, and even some, like the telephone and typewriter, whose widespread use was yet inconceivable. Apart from the main building of the exhibition, there were official exhibit halls devoted to machinery, fine arts, agriculture, and horticulture. Adding to the somewhat overwhelming range of attractions for the visitor were a variety of lesser drawcards, including state buildings, a Women's Pavilion, and a US government building, along with restaurants, press buildings, an elaborate Department of Public Comfort, and a train which took in the major sights and carried, in all, almost four million of the visitors. A teacher visiting from Ohio expressed the general reaction when he concluded that "if a day in the Exhibition does not convince any man of his own insignificance, there is more to hope for a fool than for him." Even if visitors ignored the exhibits, there were still the overwhelming crowds; average daily attendance was over 50,000. At first, attendance was kept low by doubts about the exhibition's success, and the discomfort of the hottest summer in sixty years. Early in the summer, as few as 10,000 visitors each day strolled extensive parklands and huge exhibit halls, marveling at machines, examining foreign luxuries, and besieging iced water vendors; but over 257,000 people a day crowded the halls and avenues as summer turned to fall. Special travel arrangements encouraged out-of-town visitors; ticket agents combined to offer special low fares, and rail services were added. With a total paid attendance of over eight million, and taking into account free admissions and repeat attendances, a conservative estimate would allow that one in twenty Americans saw the centennial exhibition. Many others would have been touched by it, even in remote and lonely areas; on a Nez Percé reservation in Idaho, for example, an army surgeon's wife was pleased to receive exhibition pictures sent by her aunt in Pennsylvania.[36]

If East Coast industrial and commercial elites had not organized the Philadelphia centennial exhibition for 1876, the century since the American Revolution would have been marked by local parades and fireworks, and there would have been some talk of the founding moment and liberty in speeches and, perhaps, in histories, though little in the West or South. The century had seen the development of a number of symbols of nationality and traditions of national celebration. Nevertheless, the possibilities of imagining community would have been thin, and not much different from any other year. But a cultural center did form, a network of people and organizations which was actively attached to national ideas, which energetically promoted the recognition of those ideas, and which elicited participation in their projects from many other groups. The centennial became a much more marked enactment of national identity, drawing recognition from a wide variety of groups who themselves sometimes influenced, by their critique as much as by their enthusiasm, the formulations of national identity which were produced.

The Philadelphia centennial exhibition in 1876 was promoted and organized by businessmen, manufacturers, politicians, academics, and lawyers, a well-educated Eastern industrial elite. General Hawley, the USCC president, was a former Connecticut governor and an influential newspaper owner. The chair of the Centennial Board of Finance was John Welsh, a successful Philadelphia merchant; Alfred Goshorn, the competent director-general of the exhibition, was a lawyer and manufacturer. From 1872, these men and a number of others like them energetically set about finding financial support, inviting foreign participation, classifying displays, preparing grounds, and building exhibit halls. As self-ordained representatives of a cultural center, they also worked hard at mobilizing their periphery, promoting the exhibition and encouraging the participation of other local, state, and national bodies – like schools, state governments, and professional, religious, and industry associations – in meetings, letters, speeches, circulars, and press. They raised a good deal of financial support for the exhibition from the public. Organizers enthusiastically argued for benefits to trade, industry, and education which they hoped would flow from the international exhibition: "the proposed celebration, sir, will prove to be of national importance by its relation to the trade of the country," argued a Pennsylvanian congressman in 1871. A supporter at a National Education Association meeting in 1875 argued vividly that "until we know other people we can not know ourselves," concluding that "a great universal exposition . . . may be regarded as a school in the highest sense."[37]

Industrial and commercial elites in the East were the driving force behind the national centennial celebration; they took charge just as industry was beginning to dominate the American economy. As the centennial got underway there was a depression in the headlines – the number and the rate of business failures increased sharply in 1873 and again in 1875, 1876, and 1878 – but behind the day-to-day news there was a brighter economic prospect and a profound economic change. In the 1870s about half the working population was still in agriculture, but this would fall to 30 percent by 1910; in the same period, the workforce in manufacturing, construction, transportation, trade, and finance increased from 35 to 50 percent of those employed. Every exhibition guide book made much of Machinery Hall; a *Southerner's Illustrated Guide* was rare in taking an equivalent interest in agricultural exhibits. The claim in the *Southerner's Guide* that "Agriculture has ever formed the most prominent and attractive feature of every nation" was a minority theme in 1876 commentary. In 1870, manufacturing production was a quarter of what it would be in 1899; it was almost half the 1899 baseline by 1880. Rockefeller was in the process of making Standard Oil into a monopoly; other industrial legends were on the verge of being made, too. Excitement about industrial development and fascination with industrial processes was widespread at the time, part of the central discourse of civil society. Transportation and communications, too, were growth sectors and railways and the telegraph were opening exciting economic prospects; Oregon was the only state not yet linked in the rail network. The 40,000 miles of rail brought into operation between 1866 and 1876 was topped by the almost 60,000 new miles in the following ten years. The railway monopolies of the likes of Vanderbilt and Gould were only beginning to exercise political muscle, but railway was the glamour industry of the period. The near future would also bring the beginning of international economic influence. Per capita growth in GNP, 4.3 percent between 1870 and 1913, far outranked any competitor. The trade balance of international payments went from red to black for almost the first time in 1876. At the same time, and leaving its mark in centennial rhetoric, foreign direct investments in the private sector showed a significant increase. The centennial exhibition marked and reflected this economic transition. Where centennial discourse was at its most confident, it prefigured the economic growth, and reconfigured and invented symbolic representations of the nation to interpret it. The economic innovation was given credence by associating it with the nation – and vice versa. The agenda for this cultural work was set, if not entirely implemented, by promoters and organizers who were themselves close to the economic innovation. As Robert Rydell has argued, "patriotism was explicitly linked to the need for continued economic growth as well as political and social stability."[38]

The federal government was more notable for its absence than its presence in the centennial promotion of nationality. In Washington, serious corruption scandals, almost on the scale of Watergate (if with somewhat different substance), dominated the headlines in 1876; more significantly, the government seemed to have neither the interest nor the capacity to do much toward the centennial. Nothing is more indicative of the relative weakness of the American state in the late nineteenth century than the problems which "nationally" oriented organizers faced in obtaining federal support for the centennial celebrations.

President Grant, a Northern war hero reaching the end of his second term, took little part in the events of the year. His speech at the May opening ceremonies was damned with faint praise or worse; he sent his vice president to take his place at the extensive centennial Fourth of July celebrations in Philadelphia a few months later, and he closed the exhibition with a single sentence in an era of speeches lasting hours. The Ohio schoolteacher was among those who damned with faint praise: "a great many hard words were used in connection with the name of President Grant, on account of his refusal to be present [at the Fourth of July] but I excused him when I remembered how he was treated on Opening Day in May." Washington was preoccupied with inquiries into corruption for most of the year, and the scandals had come very close to the president. Inquiries into a "whiskey ring" showed a complex scheme of tax evasion and bribery which reached to the president's confidential secretary, who went to trial in February 1876. Another heady scandal reached boiling point in the middle of the year, when Grant's secretary of war was

anti-Grant

impeached for accepting bribes for trading posts in Indian Territory. Even his fellow Republicans all tried to distance themselves from "Grantism" as the 1876 presidential campaign developed; but after the election, national politics looked even worse. The results of the contest between Republican Rutherford B. Hayes of Ohio and Democrat Samuel Tilden of New York remained in doubt until February 1877, and newswatchers saw rounds of acrimonious challenge eliciting evidence of extensive and systematic electoral dishonesty on both sides. Hayes eventually won, but the circumstances could satisfy few except the most committed politicians of the Republican Party machine. Those who paid attention to national politics in 1876 had strong reason to take claims about shared national community with more than the usual grain of salt.[39]

Deeper weaknesses in national government affected the centennial preparations more directly, even if they did not make the same juicy headlines. From the beginning, exhibition organizers faced extremely lukewarm support from Washington. Bills supporting the exhibition were hard fought, and appropriations were defeated; a credit of $1.5 million was passed, with difficulty, only in January 1876, and government outraged organizers by demanding repayment before any other private subscribers to exhibition costs. As a lively satirical account of the exhibition put it:

Congress was naturally appealed to for countenance and assistance. Unfortunately, however, Congress, having bestowed all its material aid upon railroad and steamship subsidies, had nothing but its moral support to offer . . . The President was authorized to invite the world to the Exposition – without expense to Congress.

The federal government did fill its own building at the exhibition with exhibits from the post office, the military, the department of agriculture, the Smithsonian, and so on, items as various as guns, Washington memorabilia, astronomical instruments, Indian artifacts, and lighthouse lamps. But while the national government was active in frontier and Southern policing, and in providing technical infrastructure like mail and surveying, it had little skill and less authority to organize the centennial celebration.[40]

All states had official USCC commissioners or state boards of managers, which were appointed by the governor if the state legislatures failed to generate sufficient enthusiasm. Twenty-four states were represented in states' buildings at the exhibition, and "state days" drew big crowds in later months – in this way, ties to states were symbolically associated with national identity, and representations of the nation further strengthened. As one observer suggested, "state days" helped make the exhibition "a means of celebrating the Centennial period of our National history."

Effective state participation varied; newer states and territories had a smaller presence, and the most popular states' days were those of Pennsylvania, Connecticut, New York, and Massachusetts. Southern states were hostile to the event. But there was an "Old Time Southern Tournament" in October and a "club house known as 'The South'," receiving "strong recommendations from leading men of the South" where visitors from the South could gather.[41]

Besides states, organizations representing many different groups used the occasion of the centennial exhibition to represent themselves. The International Order of Oddfellows organized a program of speeches and ceremonies in September, for instance; bankers opened their own building with a similar program in May; Grangers organized cheap accommodation for their members; military units like the Virginia cadets made encampments in Fairmount Park during the centennial; and the B'nai B'rith contributed a statue to the grounds. Many groups also held meetings in Philadelphia to take advantage of the centennial celebration. There were meetings of the National Liberal League (critics of the Sunday closing of the exhibition), volunteer fire departments, the American Social Science Association, writers, police, and doctors, a chess tournament, and a Grand International Regatta, among many other events. Though businessmen in the north-east set the agenda for the international centennial exhibition, theirs was by no means the only collective voice heard there.[42]

Centennial participation and cultural peripheries in 1876

But of course talk and celebration of the American nation was not uniform across all sorts of social and political milieux. The point of many of the activities of central centennial organizers was to elicit more widespread participation, across the nation, in the national ritual. But they faced a number of problems of national integration, fissures in a national public sphere, as they attempted to mobilize their peripheries. Centennial entrepreneurs were strongly differentiated from their national "periphery" in several ways. Regional differentiation was problematic; high among the aims of those who organized and promoted the centennial was the integration of different regional groupings. Feminists raised a critical voice very close to centennial elites themselves. Other fissures in the public sphere were also consequential for centennial participation, but they were significant more for generating exclusion than critique. Labor, immigrant, Native American, and African American groups were not part of imagined national community in the United States at this time, and only hindsight can recognize their absence.

To central organizers of the American centennial, the biggest problem of national integration was region. Since the Revolution, the original thirteen colonies of the United States had become thirty-seven states and eleven territories; Colorado was admitted to the union as the "Centennial State" in 1876. Regional differentiation was economically and politically marked, and so too were cultural contrasts between settled East, fabled West, and troubled South. William Dean Howells, the well-known intellectual, author, and editor, reflecting on the exhibition in the *Atlantic Monthly*, found little to unite the representations of different states, and remarked that they seemed more like different countries. Eastern states were comparatively well developed, ordered, and densely settled; north-eastern and north-central states together held almost two-thirds of the population in the 1870s. All the major cities were east of the Mississippi; New York's population of two million was followed by Philadelphia with 800,000, Chicago with half a million, and Boston with 350,000. Elsewhere, only San Francisco and New Orleans came anywhere near this size. West of the Mississippi were huge, thinly settled frontier states and territories, and genuine wilderness; only a tiny fraction of the population actually lived in the West. In Southern states, agrarian economy and political alienation made for another sort of differentiation, but created equally strong cultural markers in the public imagination.[43]

Although, on the whole, Western states offered only a low profile at the exhibition, and an 1874 congressional vote on exhibition funding was lost because Western states voted against it, they did participate; among the state buildings could be found those of Arkansas, Iowa, Kansas, Colorado, and California and Nevada. The biggest frontier story of the year was the defeat of General Custer in Montana, at the hands of the Sioux. News of Custer's last stand reached the East by telegraph on July 5, when a week of elaborate centennial ritual in Philadelphia was just ending. It was seeming confirmation of frontier state fears and Eastern stereotypes of the West; but in fact, it foreshadowed an end. Development in the West was proceeding rapidly; in the sparse frontier settlements and patches of wilderness, cattle were big business, and mining was also important. Iowa already had more land cultivated with corn and wheat than the total area of smaller Eastern states. The new transcontinental railway and telegraph were encouraging a new wave of British investment in the West; and the Census Bureau would declare the frontier officially closed in 1890. But the closing of the frontier still seemed distant at the time of the centennial, and the West remained a place of fable and danger to most of the population. Of course, for those few in the West, the East was often more familiar, a source of population, finance, government services like mails, manufactured goods, and letters from home.[44]

The regional differentiation between North and South was more problematic to the creation of national centennial celebrations than that between East and West; few among the third of the population who lived in the South thought there was much to celebrate (except, perhaps, some yet undisillusioned African Americans). Only ten years after the end of the Civil War, bitterness and political tension was still central to public discourse. Although the era of reconstruction was ending, and a Democratic House of Representatives had been elected in 1874, South Carolina, Florida, and Louisiana were still occupied by federal troops in 1876. Resistance to Northern influence and aid ranged from editorial commentary to armed sniping; one man trekking the Ohio and Mississippi Rivers for the centennial was harassed as a federal spy in New Orleans. As a region, the South was much more agricultural than the North, with fewer cities, fewer railroads, and few immigrants (in Mississippi, strikingly, almost no one had been born outside the state). What was more, only a minority of Southerners saw these Northern features as progress. While some abrasive rapprochement between North and South was beginning in Congress, the South was a different land to the North economically, culturally, and politically. This important fissure in national politics was significant, for example, for encouraging the major party brawl over 1876 presidential election results; challenges to the results were made in those states which were still under federal occupation. Southern issues in federal politics also complicated final attempts to get federal credit for the exhibition; bitterness about an amnesty bill made a vote on centennial financing a close fight early in 1876, even though centennial promoters, like John Forney, a centennial commissioner and Philadelphia editor, argued that "the best amnesty bill of the age is the Centennial Commemoration, and . . . no money is half so well expended as that lately given to the Centennial Commissioners." For those who invested their energy, resources, and imagination in the centennial celebration, regional differences between North and South were very threatening to the plausibility of their imagined national community.[45]

They worried less about the challenges of women, but were forced to recognize them nonetheless. Feminist activism was growing – the National Woman Suffrage Association was formed in 1876 – and women collectively took an active public role in the centennial. The Centennial Board of Finance formed a Women's Centennial Executive Committee in 1873; Elizabeth Gillespie, its president, was widely recognized, not only as Benjamin Franklin's great-granddaughter, but as an administrator who made the committee much more than a ladies' auxiliary to the men's centennial work. Groups like the Ladies' Centennial Committee of Rhode Island energetically promoted the exhibition, fundraising and conscious-ness-raising both for themselves and for the celebration. These groups had links all over the country, too: their newsletters reported centennial news even from California. In promoting the exhibition they also promoted their own agenda, "to raise the value of women's labor" and to "open the way for women to earn their bread by other means than the needle." When planners didn't find room for all the exhibits the women's committee had solicited, Gillespie went ahead and raised money for a Women's Pavilion which became one of the more widely noticed attractions of the exhibition; she had funds left over for commissioning an opening chorus from Richard Wagner and for running a kindergarten. The pavilion showed many different sorts of work done by women; most often remarked in the general commentary, however, was needlework from Queen Victoria, and the ladylike demeanor of the pavilion's engineer. More radical feminists made a further statement at the solemn Fourth of July rituals in Philadelphia; after the reading of the Declaration of Independence, Susan B. Anthony and four others interrupted the proceedings by handing to the vice-president a Declaration of Rights for Women, scattered copies down the aisles, and moved to another platform to read it to the assembled crowd. As a result of these challenges, most commentaries and guides made passing reference, at least, to women's collective part in the nation, even if only to express doubts about the formulations presented by feminists.[46]

Whereas regional differentiation and the representation of women were central puzzles for organizers representing the nation in 1876, it takes a shift of perspective to see four other groups: labor, immigrants, Native Americans, and blacks all went largely unnoticed in the picture of the nation presented during the centennial, and were notable more for their absence than their presence in the overall cultural construction of the event. Native Americans were seen only in Smithsonian exhibits. Blacks were hardly included either, and in some incidents actively excluded. Immi-grants were little noticed, and labor less. The national celebration took so many forms that it is possible to find occasional references to these groups and their implied part in the nation; but to do so is to go beyond the rhetoric of organizers, critics, and commentators at the center of the celebration. From the viewpoint of the strongest voices in the centennial agenda, these groups were not salient in the construction of a national identity; indeed, when not ignored, they constituted an interior other to national identity.

Labor was not an important theme of talk about the nation during the centennial, even if the glories of industry were; few yet realized that labor organization and unrest would be intrinsic to the story of industrial growth. A procession in Philadelphia on July 3 included "various trades of the city," but such (little noticed) participation in city parades was a form of local collective participation more typical of the earlier nineteenth century than it was indicative of what was to come. The Knights of Labor were still a small and local organization; a group called the National Labor League also met on July 3 in Philadelphia, but they were ignored even by the minor candidate they supported for president, Peter Cooper of the Greenback Party. A "long strike" of Pennsylvania coal miners in 1874–75 had been violent and ultimately unsuccessful; trials were being held during 1876. A strike against wage cuts by textile workers in New England mills failed in early 1876. The first national strike, on the railways, was yet to come in 1877 (it was to be put down by force). Claims by workers were not considered legitimate in mainstream public discourse; the intellectuals who considered labor questions did not see any legitimacy in collective action, even when they deplored labor conditions. There were some workers' excursions to the exhibition; and occasionally, especially in the early stages of planning, organizers appealed to "mechanics and artisans" and "national pride in the certainty and reward of success of diligent labor" when they were talking up the educational aspects of the exhibition. Occasionally the centennial exhibition was seen as a benefit to labor – and Sunday closing was controversial because of this issue – but labor was neither legitimate as a part of the collective representation of the nation nor yet noticed because of the strength of its challenge, as feminist groups were.[47]

One of the less noticed exhibits at the exposition was the hand of what would later become the Statue of Liberty. In the 1870s, 14 percent of the population was foreign-born, up from 10 percent in the 1850s, and cities like New York, Boston, and Cincinnati had substantial immigrant populations. The two largest immigrant groups were the Irish and Germans, followed by English-, Canadian-, Scottish-, and French-born groups. Foreign-born citizens held reunions at the centennial; an elaborate Catholic Total Abstinence Union water fountain was quite often noticed, and associated with the Irish; and unveiling a statue of Columbus on an "Italian Day" on October 12 was a big event. But, perhaps surprisingly, immigration was not at the center of public discourse or visions of national identity at this time; "Americanization" was mostly an issue of the future, and references to immigration in the writings and rituals of the time were rare. By 1910, although the foreign-born population would still be around 14 percent, and Germans and Irish the largest groups, immigration was more diverse: the next largest groups came from Italy, Canada, Russia and the Baltic states, and Poland. It seems to have been increasing diversity of immigration, only beginning in 1876, which would soon make immigration and ethnicity a core issue in talk of American national identity.[48]

Native Americans, a tiny fraction of the total population, were closer to the public imagination than immigrants in 1876, but, more than immigrants or labor groups, they constituted an ambiguous "other" to American national identity. Expansion and settlement in the West had also meant dispossession, conflict, and resettlement for Native Americans; but resistance of the sort faced by Custer was dwindling. Public opinion about the position of Native Americans at the time ranged from fear and hostility on the part of some, like Emily Fitzgerald, the army surgeon's wife in Idaho, who commented "I wish they would kill them all," to the distant concern of liberal Eastern observers who criticized federal policy – "We make treaties . . . and then leave swindlers and knaves to enforce them." Some took morbid comfort in the view that Native Americans were, in any case, "doomed to extinction." Women publishing the *Herald of the Centennial* in Rhode Island in 1875 discussed "Indians" quite extensively and sentimentally; they reprinted a memoir from 1815, for example, observing that "it is painful to perceive . . . how the footsteps of civilization in this country may be traced in the blood of the original inhabitants." At the exhibition, the few references to native peoples were made in an extensive Smithsonian ethnological display of Native American artifacts and wax figures, and in "live exhibits" of visiting "Indians" in a small encampment on the fairground. To the extent that Native Americans were relevant to public discourse about national identity, however, they tended to constitute a negative example, "a counterpoint to the unfolding progress of the ages." As one reflection in a lengthy commentary on the centennial went, the "Indian" "exports nothing and produces nothing. He lacks the sense of property."[49]

African Americans were even more peripheral to talk of national identity in the centennial than Native Americans, although at this time more than one in ten Americans were black, and a number of African Americans made efforts at collective participation. In April 1876 Frederick Douglass unveiled the Freedmen's Memorial Monument to Abraham Lincoln in Washington; in July, he was a guest at the Philadelphia celebrations, but was almost prevented from joining officials on the platform because of his race. Douglass would spend the remainder of his life fighting a losing battle for the abolitionist version of Civil War memory. As some attempted rapprochement between North and South was beginning, attempts to enforce racial equality were abandoned; segregation was normal and blacks were losing any civic role or place in national consciousness which they might have expected. Most of the few references to African Americans in the centennial year were peripheral and ominous. Connecticut women listed in their centennial magazine a contribution of $35 raised at a "Jubilee held by Colored Persons" in Tallahassee; but attempts by black women in Philadelphia to join white women in fundraising were snubbed. At the centennial exposition, in the little-remarked education section, "colored schools of the South made a creditable showing of their progress"; but there were other minor features like a "band of old-time plantation 'darkies'" and singing black packers at "an exhibit of tobacco by a Richmond firm." In mid-July, Congress debated "the massacre of six colored citizens of the United States, at Hamburgh, SC, on July 4, 1876," who had been parading for the holiday. African Americans were not included in the centennial talk in 1876; where they made collective efforts to join the celebration, these were largely ignored, and even patronizing references to black people in the central national discourse were rare.[50]

Center organization and public sphere in Australia's centennial

The organization of the 1888 centennial celebrations in Australia differed from that of the American centennial in ways which reflected the peculiar and fluid disjuncture between imagined community and Australian sovereignty, stronger (though colonial) states, and greater metropolitan dominance of the continent. There were two periods of celebration in the Australian centennial year, the first being a week of celebrations in Sydney around Australia Day, the commemoration of the founding of New South Wales, in January, organized under the aegis of the New South Wales colonial government. Many of the nationalist themes heard in New South Wales in January were repeated during a Centennial International Exhibition organized by the Victorian government in Melbourne, the booming capital of Victoria, in August. Both events received wide notice beyond the big cities and in other colonies. The centennial was also celebrated in more remote colonies and towns, but it was celebrated more quietly, quite possibly because all their notables visited Sydney or Melbourne for the major events.

Sydney's centennial events included many speeches, sermons, ceremonies, banquets, gun salutes, processions, games, regattas, and picnics. The festivities started with the unveiling of a statue of Queen Victoria in the city, attended by 50,000; the next day, food packages were distributed to at least 1,600 poor people. Then came a series of public holidays. There was more rhetoric and ceremony at the dedication of a new park in the city (known as Centennial Park, but also labeled at the time as "People's Park" or "Queen's Park"). The same evening, 1,000 dignitaries from all colonies attended a state banquet, an occasion of toasts, speeches, and vague federalist sentiment. The official celebrations continued in the next days with a regatta on the harbour (regattas were a common form of public spectacle and celebration in Sydney), an Agricultural Society exhibition, a Trades Hall dedication and procession, a performance of a Centennial Cantata, and the laying of a foundation stone for a new Parliament House for New South Wales. Churches also held official centennial services.[51]

There had been a number of false starts and controversies over what should be done – and how much to spend – in New South Wales, and, as one almanac put it, "Disgraceful Scenes in the Sydney legislature during the debate of the Centenary Celebration Act Amendment Bill." Most significant of these false starts was a decision against holding an international exhibition in Sydney, a decision which occasioned a good deal of press criticism and embarrassment. Supporters of an international exhibition argued that they were part of a common repertoire of national celebration. Exhibitions had previously been held in Sydney in 1870 and 1879, and in Melbourne in 1880. But the Sydney facilities had been destroyed in a fire, and a deficit-conscious premier refused to build more. At this point, the premier of Victoria politely but competitively appropriated the task of holding an Australian "Centennial International Exhibition," thus establishing a claim to Australian eminence for the younger colony. A Centennial International Exhibition Commission was formed and the exhibition held in Melbourne in August 1888. As Australian notables from all colonies had trooped to Sydney in January, they took another trip, to Melbourne, in August.[52]

In major respects, the Melbourne exhibition reproduced the genre which had been developing worldwide and which was also adopted in Philadelphia. There were huge, symbolically rich, and – to contemporaries – inclusive ceremonies and banquets held for the opening and closing of the exhibition; there were exhibits from all colonies and from many foreign countries; there was an emphasis on and special fascination with technology; and there was also a special interest in the arts as the fruit of civilization. The official catalog described education, wool, and wine exhibits, as well as the courts of the various Australian colonies with exhibits of their products, industries, and resources (comparable to the state buildings in Philadelphia). Queensland, for example, sent 760 packages for their display (as the leading newspaper of that newly developed state announced proudly). There were also exhibits from twenty-seven foreign countries or regions, including German, French, British, Maltese, American, Belgian, "South American," and Japanese exhibits. A special catalog was devoted to the picture galleries and fine arts.

Particular pride was also taken in the provision of electricity at the exhibition. Daily programs put a lot of emphasis on special manufacturing displays like sausage making, an "apparatus for instantly heating water," cigar making, and felt hat manufacturing; they also announced performances like a "Grand Plebiscite Concert" in which audiences heard favorite tunes they had voted for (there had been large investment in the provision of big orchestral concerts, with a concert master and some musicians imported from Britain).[53]

As in Philadelphia, special train services and fares were offered for trips to the Melbourne exhibition. Attendance was high, around two million, or (in theory) about two-thirds of the entire Australian population. Philadelphia organizers could claim their attendance represented four in five of all people living within 200 miles of the exhibition; measured against the population of Victoria, a comparable catchment area, Melbourne organizers attracted 154 percent of their population. These comparisons cannot be fully accurate, since it is difficult to estimate repeat attendance, but they do suggest widespread success for the Melbourne centennial exhibition.[54]

Despite the different colonial governments, and reflecting rather the stronger colonial state, the organization of the centennial celebration was much more unproblematically linked to government in Australia, without so much of the independent mobilization of myriad private organizations evident in the United States. Under the umbrella created by state organizers, professional, industrial, agricultural, religious, labor, and educational organizations took their places in the parades and banquets. "Civil society" groups also celebrated the centennial beyond Sydney in January; in country towns and the capital cities of other colonies, modest events like picnics, concerts, church services, and races marked the day. The Melbourne exhibition provided an even more centralized focus than the Sydney celebrations, but it did attract many visitors and much commentary from provincial areas and from other colonies. Even in Sydney, the headline news story of August was "the exodus to Melbourne." As in the United States, too, the centennial was the occasion of many private reflections on national identity in the form of centennial histories, poems, sermons, and guide books; the flavor of some of the more peripheral of these reflections is caught in titles like The *"CENTENNIAL,"* or Simple Rhymes of an "Idle Rhymster," Celebration in Commemoration of the Centennial of Australia and the Jubilee Year of the Sisters of Charity in Australia, and *The Exhibition Historical and Descriptive Geography of the Australian Colonies,* by Mrs Savory Appleton.[55]

In the United States, the growing industrial sector, rather than the state, had sustained and promoted the celebration of the American centennial with an exhibition. Colonial governments were more important for mobilizing centennial support in Australia, but they also played a larger part in the economy, and the two celebrations were similarly oriented to economic development. As in Philadelphia, those who promoted an exhibition touted important economic and educational benefits of their project. As a speaker in an early Australian debate pointed out, "we shall bring hundreds of thousands of foreign capital into the country. Every trade will receive an impetus." The governor of Victoria, Sir Henry Loch, was repeating a platitude common to both countries when he said at the opening of the Melbourne exhibition that "we may entertain the sanguine hope that great and beneficial results will be derived by the people . . . from a careful study of the great works and industries of the world" and an earnest editorial in one of the more remote Australian cities, after recognizing that exhibitions could be viewed as "trade advertisements," argued that they must also "be viewed in the higher light of a means of instruction to Australians."[56]

Centennial participation and cultural peripheries in Australia

As in the United States, the Australian centennial exhibited fissures in the public sphere, as well as more idealistic visions of national identity. As intercolonial jealousies showed, regional integration in national identity was somewhat fragile (although it was by no means as contentious as in the United States, and differences were more easily resolved). And whereas in the United States, the challenge of women's voices was part of the national debate, but labor, immigrants, African American, and Native American voices were largely excluded or silent, in Australia, the challenge of labor was part of centennial talk but women's, immigrants, and Aboriginal voices were largely excluded or silent.

Labor had an official role in the Sydney celebrations; 13,000 unionists paraded before a ceremony in which Lord Carrington, the New South Wales governor, laid a foundation stone for a new Trades Hall. Labor organizations were comparatively strong in Australia by this time; the first Intercolonial Trade Unions Congress had been held in 1879, and there was another in the centennial year. An Australian Socialist League had been founded in Sydney in 1887. Employers' organizations were also mobilizing; an employers' union was formed in Sydney in the centennial year. Labor organizations tended to a critical republican nationalism – perhaps signified in the instructions for the Sydney parade that "Societies' bands are requested to play AUSTRALIAN AIRS while passing the TRADES HALL SITE." Just as challenges of women's groups in the United States were strong enough to give women a subtly critical voice in the dominant construction of national identity, labor challenges in Australia were strong enough to make labor heard, if not accepted, within the dominant construction of national identity. A letter in the *Sydney Morning Herald* during the Sydney celebrations, for example, even argued that employers should close for the labor demonstration.[57]

The Melbourne exhibition officially included a "Ladies' Court," in among all the displays, and it showed "a miscellaneous collection of articles, principally the work of ladies, which could not conveniently be included under the existing classification." This was not much noticed in the public discourse of the time, and most of the public events, especially the banquets, did not include women; as one newspaper noted, "ladies are not to be admitted to the galleries of the Exhibition building during the Centennial banquet." Critical women's groups were just forming in the period, and feminist voices were peripheral to public discourse. Suffrage came much earlier to women in Australia than in the United States, but culturally, "the feminine . . . [was] present as that *against which* the male national character defines himself."[58]

Cultural exclusions in centennial discourse in Australia differed from those in the United States in other ways, too. In the late nineteenth century, immigration continued to be important, and immigrants were a significantly larger proportion of the population than in the United States. But the large majority of immigrants were from England, Scotland, Wales, and Ireland. Immigration was high in the 1880s; but as in the United States, the period of the centennial was not one in which immigration was an especially critical issue on the public agenda. More significant for contemporary national identity, the first generation since European settlement in which there were more people born in Australia than elsewhere was just reaching adulthood at the time of the centennial. The predominantly British immigrants had little reason to participate as separate groups, being, if anything, more part of the cultural center than "native-born" Australians. Indeed, there were a few complaints about the dominance of an older generation of politicians not themselves born in Australia in the celebrations.[59]

The most consequential cultural boundaries drawn in the course of late nineteenth-century Australian immigration separated the Catholic Irish from other English-speaking populations, and, with a passion entirely independent of their numbers, the tiny minority of Chinese settlers from everyone else. The most important immigration issue pervading late nineteenth-century public discourse in Australia, especially in labor groups but even in high-level imperial politics, was hostility to Chinese immigration, and virulently racist discourse is easy to find in much of the centennial talk of national identity (discourse which, in the American centennial, was only heard in the Western periphery, in California).[60]

Racism characterized most late nineteenth-century constructions of Australian identity; but, in the centennial discourse, racial thought was assumed, and mostly only indirectly and infrequently expressed, in talk of the nation. Australians mostly congratulated themselves on avoiding integration problems associated with imported labor; although some "colored labor," from the Pacific, was used in a frontier state, Queensland, this was both highly contested and peripheral to Australian centennial discourse, and not so much a matter of active exclusion as for African Americans in the centennial celebration.[61]

And to whites in centennial Australia, Aborigines existed far beyond what was defined as the public sphere of the time. They were occasionally mentioned as present at or just before the British founding, as "lonely savages" – "ethnologically speaking, of a low type." Occasionally one or two sentences of sentimental pastoral nostalgia recalled and admitted the destruction of their lifestyle. The centennial included a few events like a commercial performance of a "Grand Corroboree," by "Willis and Reubens Aboriginal Troup," advertised as a "Historic Relic of a race now rapidly being civilised into oblivion," or like the marking of the celebration in one country town when "the local Aborigines were regaled with a plentiful supply of food and clothing at the public expense in honour of the Centennial"; and little remarked at the exhibition in Melbourne were native weapons collections from a frontier territory, one collection supplied by a "Keeper of Gaol and Labour Prison," and "made by Aboriginal natives in gaol." But Aborigines were not "Australians" in the sense celebrated by Australian centennial organizers; and, if they were occasionally seen as an "other" to a national identity built around racism and progress, they were not a threatening other in the way that Native Americans were to some centennial Americans.[62]

Conclusion

National identity in the United States and Australia built slowly and unevenly in their first centuries. By the time they celebrated centennials, many conditions for making a successful national celebration were in place, but "national" identity was not yet fully self-evident grounding for public claims. The centennials of 1876 and 1888 were important episodes in the process by which that grounding became more self-evident in the late nineteenth century.

In the centennials, self-constituted cultural centers energetically planned celebrations and mobilized many groups and individuals to take part in them. These cultural centers were closely associated with the two most significant colonial governments in Australia, but were much more loosely associated with federal and state governments in the United States. In the American centennial, in fact, federal and state governments were among the peripheries which central organizers mobilized, with different degrees of success, to contribute to the celebration. Commercial, industrial, agricultural, educational, and religious groups, and many other actors in civil society were also mobilized to participate in centennial celebrations, and the central promotion and organization of the centennial also evoked large popular attendance and wide notice of the celebrations.

At this time, in both countries, regional fissures in national public discourse created organizational problems; this was especially true in the United States. In the United States, some women's organizations were among the civil society interests which became attached to the organization of the centennial, and so too did a few immigrant groups. Labor, Native American, and African American groups were beyond the centennial public sphere. In Australia, some labor organizations were among the civil society interests which were folded into centennial organization; women, immigrant, and Aboriginal groups were beyond the centennial public sphere.

In these events, national identity was promoted and developed in episodic but intense processes of cultural production which were not directly associated with nationalist movements or with what Anderson has called "official" nationalism. These processes of cultural production are best characterized and compared as relations between cultural centers and peripheries. This analytic framework will be adopted again to illuminate the organization of bicentennials in 1976 and 1988; in chapter 4, we will see something of how cultural centers and peripheries had altered a hundred years after the centennials, and some ways in which these alterations themselves affected claims about national identity.

Understanding the process by which claims about national identity were produced in centennials and bicentennials helps us to understand the context in which meanings and values were associated with these settler nations. It tells us more of who spoke of the nation, what was important and problematic to them, what constraints and resources they faced, and who they were speaking to. This context of cultural production was an important influence on the sorts of things which were said in talk of national identity, and it is important to understand similarities and differences faced by centennial organizers in each country in order to understand more about similarities and differences in what their nations meant to them. Like other "production-of-culture" studies, this helps to show "how the milieux in which culture is produced influence its form and content."[63]

But there is more to the story of American and Australian national identity. Having seen how Americans and Australians came to celebrate their centennials, we can now ask what exactly they said about their nations when they did so.

3

"Our country by the world received": centennial celebrations in 1876 and 1888

In the United States in 1876, memories of the Civil War were still raw. In Australia in 1888, the six British colonies on the continent were not yet federated in a national government. In both countries, too, sheer size gave region and locality far more significance than they have today. Yet despite seemingly insuperable political, geographic, and social boundaries, many "Americans" and "Australians" organized and took part in big national centennial celebrations. Many Americans did mark, with elaborate ritual and weighty language, the hundred years since their Declaration of Independence. Many Australians celebrated in even more florid language the passing of a hundred years since the British founding of the first penal colony on the continent.

What did nationality mean to people involved in these events? How did their symbols and visions of the nation make sense to them? Organizers, participants, and critics made implicit and explicit claims about what they shared and where they stood in the world. In both countries, claims to nationhood could often transcend – if not deny – political division and international insignificance. Glorified visions of nationhood were often allowed full rein: people in each country were said to share astounding progress, incredible political freedom, and fantastic prosperity. Those who spoke for the nation claimed an honorable place in a world of nation-states. Australians were able to imagine that

> Our nation's star
> Shines clear afar
> And all the world now hails its ray!

And many Americans were comforted by the thought of

> Our country by the world received
> As high in rank, as proud in station,
> The equal of the oldest nation.[1]

There was little resemblance between the occasions commemorated in Australia and the United States, much that was different in the century since those occasions, and little similarity in the common topical preoccupations of each centennial year. Yet claims about nationality were often remarkably similar in the two "new" nations.

Reading national identity in the centennials

Centennials encouraged many people to reflect publicly on national identity. The wide variety of documents produced in the course of these massive cultural mobilizations make a fascinating record of how many members of each nation saw their national identity in the late nineteenth century. This record is no random selection of attitudes to national identity, but rather a record of claims about national identity by its promoters, and the many groups they mobilized or antagonized. As chapter 2 illustrated, the celebration of these occasions was an achievement of transient but intense mobilizations by groups which saw themselves as cultural centers evoking the participation of national peripheries. In Australia, these cultural centers were closely linked to the leading colonial states. In the United States, the association of cultural centers with state organizations was weaker and more troubled. In each case, though, celebrations were suggested and organized by elites within institutional frameworks set up several years beforehand for the purpose. In meetings, letters, speeches, circulars, and the press, they mobilized the participation of other local, state, and national bodies. Central organizations produced extensive reports on their activities, which often included minutes, debates, and elaborate descriptions of exhibitions and associated ceremonies.

Organizers addressed their peripheries in ways which would encourage national participation; those who ignored their attempts to make a celebration threatened their project of enacting national community. Many records remain, in official speeches and reports, of attempts to encourage the celebration among particular groups. As a result, professional, industrial, agricultural, religious, and educational organizations themselves took their places in the round of parades and banquets, and produced extensive reflections on national identity for the centennials, in their own reports, newsletters, magazines, ceremonies, speeches, exhibits, and poems. The occasions also prompted commentary in the press, in guidebooks and ponderous multi-volume works, and in lengthy centennial histories. More ephemeral reflections included pamphlets reprinting sermons and speeches, almanacs and yearbooks, invitations, programs, souvenir volumes, and unofficial poetry.[2]

Organizers took particular pains to address what they saw – or were powerfully reminded by their critics to see – as the major faultlines of their political communities. As we have seen, one of the most important of these faultlines was geopolitical region. Although there was at least some participation in centennial celebrations all over each country, the salience of national identity differed widely. Those who promoted national identity met many regional challenges, most importantly competition between regions in Australia, and intense Southern disaffection in the United States. Overall, regional integration was more troubled in the United States, but in both countries, regional integration was high among the aims of those who organized centennial celebrations.

In other ways, problems of peripheral integration in national celebration were more distinct in each country. Beyond the organizers at the cultural centers, the centennials became important in the agendas of rather different sorts of groups. The leading groups of critics – those who were highly engaged in the centennial occasions as vehicles for the promotion of their own critical agendas – differed significantly in each case. In Australia, labor groups constituted this engaged periphery; in the United States, feminist agendas were most clearly promoted by women's engagement in and critique of national identity in the centennial. Critical groups of this sort took an important role in the construction of national identity because their voices demanded responses from those who wished to articulate imaginary inclusion.   *and they could demand*

As chapter 2 also showed there were, of course, many groups not *further discussion here* represented in the centennial construction of national identity, sometimes because they had little collective voice and sometimes because their collective voice was ignored. Labor received little attention in the American centennial, and women little collective notice in the Australian centennial. Other groups were also notable by their apathy or absence; if their voices were raised at all, they were not heard in most mainstream formulations of national identity. Some African Americans did attempt collective partici- *unpack?* pation in the American centennial, but they were, at best, largely ignored; black inclusion was not an issue at the cultural center, and African Americans were little noticed in talk of American national identity. Immigrants, at the time of the American centennial, also sometimes claimed collective inclusion in the nation, and immigration was very occasionally formulated as an issue of collective inclusion, but much more rarely than one would expect from later American developments. In Australia, immigrants were more often part of the cultural center than they were collective groups on the centennial periphery; the main exception was the tiny proportion of Chinese immigrants, who were perceived as a threatening "other" to the constitution of Australian identity. In the cases of Native Americans and Aborigines, it is somewhat anachronistic to raise the question of even a critical inclusion, although these groups also sometimes constituted an imaginary "other" against which the nation was defined (an other which was more threatening in the American case than the Australian).

The centennials show, then, the dominant repertoire of symbols and claims about imagined national community available to those who spoke of the nation at the cultural center. To a lesser extent, they show languages of national identity adopted by those participants and critics who were mobilized and collectively recognized in the course of the national celebration. These critical and peripheral claims cannot be taken as fully representative of national identity beyond the cultural center; there is little way of knowing how representative the more peripheral records are, and some voices were not raised or were not heard even when raised. But the critical and peripheral records which do remain help assess the importance of themes which dominate the talk at the cultural center of the celebration. If critics or distant voices used the same sorts of symbols as organizers when they spoke about national identity, the wide salience of those shared elements of the symbolic repertoire makes the dominant symbols and claims all the more significant. Conversely, some symbols and claims commonly used by organizers active in promoting national identity were little used by those beyond the cultural center; thus, their place in the symbolic repertoire must be more qualified and carefully located.

Here, I take the documents which remain to us from each centennial to show what symbols and claims about the nation were plausible to those who spoke about nationality in the late nineteenth century, especially those most concerned to imagine national community. As in all integrative ritual, there was disagreement, disinterest, and active exclusion in the centennial celebrations. But the disaffected only rarely contested the claim that these were celebrations about shared nations. Many claimed or aimed to speak for the nation: what did this mean to them? And how were languages of national identity similar and different in each settler nation?

Nation and world

For organizers of Australian and American centennials, an international exhibition was the best way of expressing national identity because it invited the gaze of others, confirming status, achievement, and distinctiveness. To be recognized by others was one way of stressing what was shared by rather than what divided the country. Furthermore, other features of national identity like shared history, political institutions, and prosperity were confirmed as such by the imagined recognition of other nations. The importance of the international sphere in creating and confirming national identity was a constantly reiterated theme, not only in the talk of promoters and organizers of the exhibitions, but also as less official speakers, poets, and writers marked the occasion.

The diffusion of nationalism in the late nineteenth century has long been noted; less frequently discussed, and often taken for granted, has been the influence of national models on ways of symbolizing national identities, even in the absence of nationalist movements. When we think of nationalist symbols we tend to think of the symbolic weight of distinctive historical episodes, or the symbolic boundaries created by distinctive languages or religions or lands, and conclude that languages of nationality are necessarily those which mark distinctiveness. Even those who recognize the importance of international reference groups rarely show the complex ways in which they influence symbols of national identity. Benedict Anderson, for example, notes the significance of the international order in the construction of national identities: in "the language of many nationalists," he suggests, "'Our' nation is 'the best' – in a competitive, *comparative field*." But he does not examine the implications of the international reference group for the particular ways national communities are imagined. Arguing from a very different perspective, Liah Greenfeld goes further in articulating the importance of "reference societies" for developing national identities. But she limits their influence to cases where, she argues, a sense of inferiority poisoned the sense of national identity. Greenfeld suggests that

every society importing the foreign idea of the nation inevitably focused on the source of importation – an object of imitation by definition – and reacted to it. Because the model was superior to the imitator in the latter's own perception (its being a model implied that), and the contact itself more often than not served to emphasize the latter's inferiority, the reaction commonly assumed the form of *ressentiment*.

But what of circumstances in which relations with advanced others are not perceived as invidious, and do not lead to competition or resentment and reaction? In these accounts, international orientations were not influential in national identity formation in countries like the United States. But, at least in the restricted forum of the centennial celebrations, modeling could serve to enhance national community as much as it could emphasize inferiority. The nationalist *ressentiment* Greenfeld describes seems to be only one of a number of ways perceptions of "the other" have been influential in national identity formation.[3]

For many of those who organized centennial celebrations, the recognition and participation of other nations was crucial. When they spoke of the nation, they constantly spoke in the same breath of the recognition of other countries. When they spoke of what characterized their nations, they imagined other countries recognizing and applauding these features. For Australians and Americans in the late nineteenth century, an important part of what made them nations was their position in the world, often conceived as their likeness to or their recognition by powerful others.

National identity in the world's gaze

Official appeals and arguments during the rocky early years of the Philadelphia exhibition were filled with claims that a true, unified nationality itself depended on the exhibition's international character. It seemed crucial that foreigners would see "a century of greater progress and prosperity than is recorded in the history of any other nation." News of promised foreign participation was discussed in great detail in almost all the literature and the debate produced around the occasion; the foreign nations to be represented became an important argument for holding a celebration. Fears that the exhibition would fail lead to talk of "the humiliating position we are in before the world"; and when the time of the opening ceremony finally arrived, the president of the Centennial Board of Finance felt that "the assemblage here today of so many foreign representatives uniting with us in this reverential tribute is our reward."[4]

Pleasure in cosmopolitanism was reiterated in both official and unofficial American sources. Bayard Taylor, the author of the centennial ode performed on the Fourth of July, in a review of the exhibition for the *New York Tribune*, cited approvingly its "broad cosmopolitan stamp which extended even to details." Women's fundraisers included International Assemblies, which were made up of "highly decorated tables, representing the different nationalities of the world," in which "the lady aids wore the costumes of different nationalities." Alfred Goshorn, director-general of the exhibition, was praised because he was "presentable before the nations of Europe ... We have no persons who would make a better impression on foreigners."[5] Such explicit and implicit affirmations of the significance of "our country by the world received" were constantly made, not only in official arguments and symbolism but in almost all the textual traces left by the American centennial. Medallions, certificates, decorations, poetry, and all the ceremony of the year appealed to the vision of America welcoming the world, and the world welcoming the United States. On the official certificate issued to exhibition subscribers, "America [was] represented as welcoming the representatives of foreign nations." The symbolism also appeared in obscure locations, like the privately exhibited "Centennial Vase" which showed America welcoming Europe, Asia, and Africa. Rarely far from ideas of welcoming others were ideas of eliciting their admiration; a speaker for the B'nai B'rith was one among many who thought the centennial celebration would "illustrate America's triumph that challenges a world's applause."[6]

Similar sorts of rhetoric appeared frequently in Australia. As one politician said in debates about what to do for the Sydney celebrations: "we shall have the eyes of the world on us, and we shall be bound to carry out our celebration in no niggardly way." Part of what was taken to characterize the Australian nation was a people "in sympathetic touch with the best of the old world civilization . . . with all the modern political developments," according to the final report of the Melbourne exhibition commissioners. Like the ceremonies of the Philadelphia exhibition, the symbolism of the opening ceremony of the Melbourne exhibition in 1888 was international. In a building decorated with the "names of the principal cities of the world," and "shields of all nations, with the name of each," an arch proclaimed "Victoria welcomes the world." During the opening ceremony, as in Philadelphia, the orchestra played the "national air of [each] nation represented." Prayer, song, and speeches welcomed visitors, related gratitude for other countries' interest, and expressed the hope that "the Centennial International Exhibition of 1888 may conduce to the credit of Australasia."[7]

The international theme was not confined to talk of the Melbourne exhibition. In the Sydney celebrations there was a lot of talk of the way "our nation's star / shines clear afar" too. In January, at the opening of Centennial Park, the leader of the government in New South Wales, Sir Henry Parkes, spoke of "this interesting occasion," "when we commence . . . a new century, which will lift us to the first rank of nations. (Renewed cheers.) . . . at the end of another generation we shall be able to hold our own against the world." And just as the Philadelphia director-general, Goshorn, was praised for being presentable to foreigners, Parkes was praised for his international profile: "certainly no Australian has received greater recognition than [sic] as a statesman beyond the limits of Australia than our present Premier."[8]

International recognition was important to Australians who expressed national identity unofficially as well as officially. Sermons, poetry, guidebooks, and the press all emphasized the theme. As one discussion put it: "just now the eyes of England and the world are on us. We are compassed about with a great cloud of witness." Newspapers in remote cities discussed the international importance of the celebration: "the Australians will call the world together to witness an experience in colonization unparalleled in history." Hyperbole along these lines typified even obscure poetry of the occasion:

> And million voices gladly hail
> Australia, her flag unfurled,
> Proud sovereign of the southern world.[9]

Identification with other nations

Other nations could be important for imagining national identity in several ways. Often, recognition was important: the "eyes of the world" were something of a cliché on these occasions and it was common to frame the celebration as some sort of demonstration to the world. Sometimes other nations were used to point up a flattering or hopeful comparison, to add weight to claims of national identity. But the international dimension of national identity was sometimes even stronger, a direct identification with powerful others. This important theme can be missed when national identity as a cultural repertoire is seen through the lens of nationalist political mobilizations. A direct identification with Britain was predictably strong in Australia, and seen as consistent with a meaningful Australian identity. Less well recognized has been British and Anglo-Saxon identification among East Coast elites talking about their nation in the United States. American identification with Britain was certainly weaker and more socially circumscribed than that in Australia, but it was frequently expressed in some circles on the occasion of the American centennial.

British identity was crucial at the cultural center of the Australian centennial. Just as six separate colonial polities did not seem to present much problematic inconsistency with a more general identification as Australian, an identification with the British was an important part of what it was to be Australian. As Sir Henry Parkes said at the state banquet in Sydney,

I will seek to maintain our position in the future as a thorough Australian, and being a thorough Australian a most consistent and patriotic Briton.

And when the chairman of juries spoke at the closing ceremony of the exhibition in Melbourne, he spoke in revealing categories of the "diversified character of the exhibits displayed throughout the British, Foreign, and Colonial Courts." Whatever Australians were, the British were not foreigners. All the symbolism and speeches of the ceremonies of the centennial loudly proclaimed a British identification.[10]

Sometimes the importance of Britishness in Australian national identity was understood in terms of filial loyalty. Sometimes this filial loyalty extended to the proud vision of Australia becoming another Britain. Sometimes it was understood as membership in worldwide empire. All these understandings shaded into explicit statements of pride in commonality of political heritage, or of race (and often political heritage and "Anglo-Saxon" race were conflated). This understanding allowed the occasional extension of Australian identification to the United States, too.

A common understanding of Australian history saw the pioneers as "sturdy sons of Britain," "worthy of their British name," as in the Centennial Cantata performed at the opening of the exhibition. Several poems carried expressions of filial loyalty to an extreme: as one put it, "never before more stupendous ovations, / Were ardently, lavishly poured on the throne." A rare argument in the mainstream literature criticized these frequent extremes of loyalty, suggesting that Australians should be grateful for their inheritance from Britain only in the sense that contemporaries in Britain should be grateful for their own heritage; but even this author concluded:

The blood that runs in our veins is the blood of the men who for centuries have fought the battles of British freedom against the forces of despotism and tyranny . . . The race that built up one great nation in the northern sea and planted another great nation beyond the Atlantic need not shrink from the task of establishing yet another in these islands of the south.

And this author was typical, too, in his appeals to freedom, race, and similarity to the United States.[11]

Liberal political norms and practices were understood as British: "to-day we have . . . a basis broad and firm, on which rests our British Constitution, secure as the everlasting hills, and with it peace and contentment – the envy of the civilized world." This political interpretation of Australia's Britishness was important, but perhaps even more common in the grandiose imaginings of the occasion was the imagined connection to world empire. Reflecting conservative enthusiasm for imperial federation, just fading from the political agenda at this time, several official speakers in January in Sydney imagined imperial identity: Australia would become "one solid block in the structure of that great Empire which encircles the globe."[12]

Another important variant of Australia's identification with Britain was racial. Racial categories and explanations were common sense, and overlapped with other sorts of identifications. In an essay on Australia's progress, for example, the commissioners of the Melbourne exhibition wrote of the difficulties of early settlement and the progress since, in this way: "the indomitable courage and endurance characteristic of the Anglo-Saxon race eventually triumphed over all obstacles, and the result is the Australia of to-day." Against this background of racist common sense, the sophistication of Japanese exhibits in Melbourne surprised many and provoked a revealing sort of praise: "the growing intelligence of the [Japanese] people is incontestably proved . . . by the increased demand for Anglo-Saxon literature in the country."[13]

The racial element of national identity, along with the themes of political freedom and progress in Australian national identity, allowed the grandiose vision of Australia as part of a world empire to fade easily into a sisterly identification with the United States. After praising an imperial, liberal, and Anglo-Saxon Britain, one writer spoke of "America, her eldest born, exalting in her separate life, but proud of her lineage . . . and Australia as some fair daughter." To Australians, there was no contradiction in extending their British identification to the United States, too. The American Revolution had been unfortunate but justified, and Australia was luckier: the Australian colonies had been given autonomy in their internal affairs and the political freedom which they claimed as their own they considered an important part of being British. Thus, it was possible to write in praise of a local military turnout that the soldiers

are of the stuff that won England her battles in the past . . . the same bone and sinew in our citizen soldiery as fought at Bunker Hill or Lexington, as drove out tyranny from that other England now gone, and let in freedom and a great destiny.

The easy grouping of British and revolutionary soldiers may have seemed foreign to many Americans, but it made sense to Australians because of their identification with Britain along political and racial lines.[14]

The identification of Australian with British identity was distinguishable from, though certainly strengthened by, colonial dependence. The Britishness of Australian identity was perhaps most strongly asserted by members of political elites, and sometimes loyalty to and identification with Britain was stated in the same breath as perceptions of pragmatic economic, political, and geopolitical dependence. But the Britishness of Australians was a claim expressed even in the absence of the explicit recognition of dependence, and it carried an emotional resonance which was far more than pragmatic. It would remain emotionally compelling long after the distinct political identity of the unified country was formalized with federation in 1901; if anything, it was even more evident in federation celebrations.

The link between national identity and British "inheritance" was not unique to Australia; it could be heard, though much less pervasively, in some American discussions of national identity too, along with a general consciousness of the heritage of European civilization. An identification with Britain – a mix of political, historical, and racial associations, as in Australia – was important to Eastern elites during the centennial. It was not often directly expressed in official sources, but it did appear in sources which were otherwise close to the cultural center. It was evident in worries about offending the British in holding the celebration, in commentary surrounding the exhibition in Philadelphia, in the emphasis and praise given to British participation, and in histories which saw American identity as developing the best in its British antecedents.

Early in debates about the Philadelphia exhibition, one senator had suggested that "England would resent being asked to participate in a celebration of her own humiliation and defeat." This suggestion seems to have made many organizers unduly nervous, if the number of rebuttals they left is any indication. The secretary of the USCC, John Campbell, a professor from Indiana, argued, for example, that "we remember now less of our trials and more of the blessings of our common Anglo-Saxon family." John Forney, active in promoting the exhibition in Europe, thought that British interest provided "an example which cannot fail to act magically at home." Quite a few writers singled out British interest and participation for special praise; Bayard Taylor observed that "Great Britain has shown, by her contributions, that she is still nearest and knows us best." The women's organizations fundraising for the centennial often reserved some of their warmest interest for the participation of "the land we love to call our mother country." After the Exhibition, another women's newsletter reflected hopefully that "our English Cousins who visited the great Exposition must have been filled with honest pride as they looked upon the numberless fruits of industries grown from seed sown by England." The special significance of the relation to Britain was also evident elsewhere: for instance, an advertisement for Webster's dictionary on a poster at the centennial based its claim to eminence on extensive quotations of British praise and evidence of British use. And a clergyman writing for a journal published by college students over the centennial summer made an invidious comparison of contemporary Americans with heroic forefathers because "a hundred years ago . . . our white population was homogeneous, of the Anglo-Saxon stock."[15]

Preoccupation with the relation with Britain became in some more reflective American writing an identification with Britain, possible because both countries were taken to share Anglo-Saxon political values and race.

Identifying liberty with Anglo-Saxon identity, as Australians did, one poet wrote of how

> diamond flames
> Spell all the best and greatest names
> Of men by whom God's work was done
> Like England's Alfred and our Washington.[16]

And in what was perhaps the most extensive and reflective account of the exhibition, the chief of the Bureau of Awards, like other commentators, frequently praised British participation with a warmth not extended to other nations, and accounted for his praise on racial grounds. Thus, on exhibition judging, he wrote, "Especially did the judges from the north of Europe, and pre-eminently those from the Teutonic nations, come most handsomely up to the high standard . . . The bearing of the English judges in this respect, was above praise." The achievements of the Japanese puzzled the racial categories of the Americans as well as the Australians. As with the Australians who measured intelligence by the number of English-language books imported, a racist identification seemed to be behind the assessment of the medical director of the Philadelphia exhibition that, "in marked contrast to the unhealthfulness of the Japanese colony is to be placed the excellent sanitary conditions of the cottages for the employees of the British commission" – especially in the light of his careful statistics, which seemed to indicate that he had quite a few more English patients than Japanese.[17]

An anxious and flattered response to British recognition was fairly frequent in reflections by Eastern elites in the American centennial. An identification with British history and Anglo-Saxon character was somewhat less frequent; and explicit comments indicating identification along the lines of race appeared only rarely. Identification with Britain was less common in the poems, ceremonies, speeches, and reports of groups beyond the cultural center, and there are indications that the "Anglo-Saxonists" may have met some opposition if their identifications had been more widely broadcast. Such opposition is hinted in a satirical account of fireworks on the Fourth of July in Philadelphia, which interpreted one display with an anti-British twist which radical Australians would have enjoyed: "The Lion and the Eagle Lying Down Together – Symbolic of the peace 'twixt England and America. NB. The Eagle is Inside of the Lion."[18]

So identification with Britain was not a widespread theme of American national identity, but it was surprisingly important to some – and they were near the cultural center. The Australians showed a general consciousness of the importance of world recognition to their national identity, but the British part in their vision of themselves was more frequently claimed and carried more emotional weight. The reverse was true for the Americans: the importance of the general international gaze was paramount. But for both countries, an integral part of imagining themselves nations in the late nineteenth century was imagining their place in the world. These visions were often carried to the point of identification, but they were always at least a concern for recognition. Concern for the recognition of other countries, and identification with Britain, were threaded through all the talk of national identity which was evoked by the centennials in both countries. Often missed by those who analyze national identity from the vantage point of an interest in nationalist politics, these dimensions of national identity were nevertheless integral to the way national community was imagined. Talk of other nations was often a precondition of talk of other aspects of national identity. For example, international identification was a part of the way the past was imagined, as in the Anglo-Saxon virtue of the founding moment in the history above, and international recognition helped define the progress which was also celebrated during the centennial.

Shared experience and imagined community

The nation in time

As Benedict Anderson argued, a sense of shared experience through time is an important dimension of a sense of national identity. He suggested that this leads to the construction of a shared past and future. In languages of national identity, a version of the past and a vision of the future are developed – from many possible alternatives – to represent the nation and its unity. Although their national histories might have been seen as very different, Americans and Australians followed surprisingly similar patterns in formulating their nations' shared experience through time. They emphasized founding moments and progress in the century since their foundings; and they could envision that progress continuing into the future. Within this shared framework, perhaps the template for "new nations" of the late nineteenth century, they differed in their emphasis.

Shared identity in both countries was partly built around those "founding moments" which were the occasion of celebration. For the United States, as we might expect, the founding moment of the revolutionary period was crucial, and the Declaration of Independence carried special symbolic weight. The Australian "founding moment" was much less glorious: the beginnings of a penal colony and a life remote from anything Europeans valued. But this made surprisingly little difference to the language of national identity; the founding moments took on about equal *[handwritten margin note: Founding moment, progress (hope)]*

weight and salience in each centennial. In both countries the founding moment was important in national identity, and not merely the excuse or occasion for celebration. In both countries, too, progress was also an important theme in national identity. Accounts of the nations' histories were told as stories of progress, and progress was a template which could be applied to many different aspects of each history. The two countries differed most in their confidence in the future. Despite Anderson's suggestion that an imagined future is part of the discourse of national identity, there was comparatively little talk of the national future in the American centennial, and what there was often revealed the hopes of those who saw contemporary problems. It was not, as in the Australian case, talk of progress into a grand future.

Founding moments

When the mayor of Philadelphia welcomed the commissioners of the USCC to their first meeting, early in 1872, in Independence Hall, he talked at length about the sacredness of the venue:

> how fitting is it that your mission should be sanctified at its very outset by the holy influences that prevail within these walls, and that you should receive from the Father of his country, whose portrait now hangs before you, the injunction so well imparted by his majestic presence, to spare no pains.

His theme was taken up by many others in many different ways. Images of the liberty bell, Independence Hall, George Washington, and Benjamin Franklin were scattered through all sorts of ceremonies, buildings, and documents. The Revolution was used as a touchstone in the way organizers talked about the exhibition and a rich source of national symbolism.[19]

Revolutionary history was an important theme in the ceremony of the occasion. The Declaration of Independence was taken as constitutive of the nation; at the Fourth of July oration in Philadelphia, for example, one speaker introduced a rare but rhetorical counterfactual question: if there had been no Declaration, he asked, "who can be bold enough to say when and how independence, liberty, Union, would have been . . . assured to this people?" At this ceremony, "the faded and crumbling manuscript . . . was . . . exhibited to the crowd and was greeted with cheer after cheer," and it was then read by a "grandson of the patriot of the Revolution." (According to one report, though, "the enthusiasm of the crowd was too great to permit them to listen to it quietly," – and according to the satirical *Humorous Account*, "the soda-water fountain was much patronized during this portion of the ceremony.")[20]

The importance of the founding moment in national identity extended to quite a popular level, and may have been as strong there as among groups at the cultural center, despite the popularity of the soda fountain during the reading of the Declaration. References to Washington and the revolutionary period appeared in most of the unofficial literature of the centennial, in guides, almanacs, poems, and speeches. This historical identity was not always the dominant theme of the unofficial literature, but it was very common. A midwestern schoolteacher visiting Philadelphia thought it worth recording that, in the obscure Wagon and Carriage Annex of the Centennial Exhibition, "Gen Washington's old yellow coach was also on exhibition, but, aside from the name of its illustrious owner, I think it would attract but little attention." A centennial almanac produced by a pharmacist in Vermont included small sketches of everyday life in 1776 (though it was quick to note that "in our Stock of Goods, however, we have not had the same regard for the good old times").[21]

The revolutionary era also provided a widely used basis for claims to inclusion in the nation and for claims critical of the national community. Writers and speakers in a wide range of groups used a link with the founding moment to legitimate their centennial participation. The founding moment was also used to appeal for the integration of the South in the centennial celebration. And critical groups themselves used the founding moment to ground the legitimacy of their challenges.

Some groups used a link to the founding moment to establish the legitimacy of their participation in the celebration. The Catholic Total Abstinence Union built an elaborate water fountain at the centennial grounds; a speaker at the ground-breaking ceremony developed the theme that "catholicity is friendly to individual freedom and promotive of national Independence" by referring to founding moment heroes: "Side by side with Franklin was priest Carroll, found most faithful among the faithful in assisting to establish that independence which the layman had declared and signed." Likewise, a centennial ceremony for bankers was introduced with praise of "Robert Morris, the Financier of the Revolution." And the writer of "Iowa's Centennial Poem," uneasy that her state was not one of the original thirteen, claimed nevertheless a "priceless heritage," because "they were our ancestors who fought / when liberty with blood was bought."[22]

The founding moment was almost always used as the basis of a claim about shared national identity by promoters of the celebration when the issue of participation by disaffected Southern states was relevant. Appeals to a shared identity in the Revolution were often made in the official statements of organizers and promoters when they claimed that an

group interest

exhibition would "reunite all the elements of this nation into one grand whole." As one supporter from North Carolina said:

If there is any spot which should be consecrated by such an occasion, that spot is here in Philadelphia, where American liberty was born; and upon such an occasion the people of all parts of this country can drown out the memories of our late unfortunate struggle with the more glorious memories of the struggle in which our forefathers engaged.[23]

The point was fairly widely understood. But Southern critics of the Philadelphia Exhibition also appealed to national identity in the founding moment to undercut the claims of its promoters. A senator from Georgia argued against funding the centennial exposition on the grounds that such funding was unconstitutional: "I concede that the United States are a nation . . . we have to look to the Constitution to find the power which we as a nation can exercise in celebrating our Declaration of Independence." A less reasoned appeal to founding moment symbols in criticism from the South was made in a vituperative verse from Virginia, referring to the design of the official centennial medal:

> The US design
> Of medal and sign,
> Of Washington, 'tween Lincoln and Grant in relief,
> Find parallel fact
> To counsel the act,
> Of Christ crucified by each side a thief.[24]

With quite different agendas, other critics of the establishment mobilized the same sort of claim. A Centennial Congress of Liberals, opposing religious influence in law and national ritual – such as in the closing of the exhibition on Sundays – like the Southerners, criticized current practices for the way they fell short of the founding moment ideals which supposedly constituted national identity, arguing "we feel ourselves to be, in a peculiar sense, the heirs of the originators of American Independence." And feminists used similar sorts of appeals; they hoped to "show to the world that the women of 1876 have signed their own Declaration of Independence."[25]

In many different ways, then, Americans used a "founding moment" history when they came to imagine what constituted their shared identity. It remained a touchstone of historical common sense. Of course there was little talk of the conquest of native peoples in this founding moment vision, and neither was there much of the founding of the country in first settlement, especially the settlement of the Southern colonies with indentured labor which had some small parallel in Australian convict founding. There was also little of opposition to and lack of enthusiasm for the Revolutionary War and the Constitution. In the centennial, as in many other expressions of American national identity, the founding moment of the American Revolution became a robust element of the symbolic repertoire which provided resources for nationality claims, a symbol impervious to the vicissitudes of more critical discussion. It was, indeed, more valuable to critics than vulnerable to criticism.

The revolutionary period had indeed seen genuinely innovative politics, with worldwide consequences, and it had been, among other things, the forging of an identity in conflict. It thus seems quite natural that the Americans developed a "thick description" of their shared identity in a founding historical moment. By contrast, all the Australians had to claim was a disreputable event in which, as Australians, they took no part. Yet, counterintuitively, centennial Australians too made constant references to the "founding moment" of British settlement in almost all of the official and unofficial records they left of Australia's centennial year. Australian founding moment symbols were, in the end, less robust in the face of critical reflection than American ones, as the bicentennials would show – and even in 1888, Australians invested most of their national pride in progress, rather than their founding (as a minority of Americans did). But though they only rarely expressed pride in their founding, they did refer to it almost all the time as part of the national identity they were celebrating.

How did Australians in 1888 understand their "founding moment"? There were two ways they found to talk about it, despite the difficulty of glorification. Sometimes they made their talk of the founding moment very vague, framing it as an episode of heroic settlement rather than the founding of a penal colony, the extrusion of oppression by a powerful state. They sometimes carried this vagueness to the point of simple denial of the facts of 1788, though they still chose to speak of some imagined founding. Second, and this was the most common strategy at the cultural center, they spoke of the hopelessness, insecurity, and oppression of the founding moment, but contrasted this with later history. These were important ways of building an understanding of the founding moment into their shared historical identity, just as, in a different way, the Americans did.[26]

The official centennial ode, written for the Sydney celebrations in January, took the first tack of vague euphemism. Australia was first imagined as "peacefully sleeping among ferns and flowers." The scene then shifted to a "Chorus of Sailors, who having discovered the Land of the Southern Cross, take possession of it by hoisting the British flag, which proclaims Australia a land of freedom." The Centennial Cantata performed later in the year at the opening of the Melbourne exhibition also envisioned the beginning of history as a "Solitary Past":

> O'er all perpetual solitude doth brood
> Save where the savage stalks in search of food.
> A land by civilization's step untrod
> Alone with Nature, and with Nature's God.

The cantata then moved on to talk of the first "Pastoral Pioneers." Both poems showed a typical blindness to the Aboriginal people, and the impact on them of European occupation.[27] But uneasiness about convict settlement, not invasion, was the real sticking point. In the permitted vagueness of grand poetry, it was better to ignore the distasteful realities of first settlement – to imagine sailors proclaiming freedom (quite an ironic imaginative leap), or pastoral pioneers. Nevertheless, despite the strong reasons to ignore invasion and penal settlement, some founding moment vision was necessary in imagining the national past.

A very common way of developing a "thick description" of the founding moment was to focus on the "discoverer," Captain Cook, rather than the "founders," Captain Phillip and the convicts, despite an anachronism of eighteen years. Cook was the true hero of the celebration, especially in Sydney. His portrait appeared more frequently than Phillip's, in history volume frontispieces, on elaborately engraved invitations, and in the stained glass windows of the Centennial Hall. The New South Wales pavilion at the exhibition in Melbourne in August included "a tableau of Captain Cook landing at Botany Bay, and many interesting relics of the great navigator" – but no apparent reference to Phillip's first settlement. The emphasis on Cook over the actual convict settlement could even end in some confusion about the occasion, as it did for the newspaper in a more remote city which announced inaccurately that "the centenary of the landing of Captain Cook at Botany Bay will be celebrated tomorrow throughout Australia."[28]

Anachronism and amnesia allowed talk about the "founding moment" in the celebration. They appeared more frequently in unofficial sources distant from the cultural center of the celebration. The other way to talk about 1788 was to face the facts more squarely, even to exaggerate how bad things were. Many speakers and writers were not afraid to do this during the centennial, and this tended to be the official way of imagining a shared past. It allowed greater emphasis on a grandiose vision of the century's progress which was a matter of more pride in the Australian vision of history than the founding moment itself.

One of the most extensive confrontations with the problematic founding

occurred in a speech of Sir Henry Parkes. At the centennial banquet
including representatives of all colonies in Sydney in January, he went
further than most speakers by arguing that Australians should not be
ashamed of the "criminal" in their founding. He spoke in detail of the First
Fleet, the "helplessness of the founders of this great Empire," of "Captain
Phillip and his band of exiles" and argued (against the grain of contemporary public opinion):

We have no reason to blush, or for a moment to desire to avoid comment upon
those early years of exile; and I venture to say that during those early years many
heroic things were done which go intimately into the foundation of nations . . .
Many a man was sent here for offences which could hardly be said to affect his
moral character.

He even admitted that "the early years of toil and hardship witnessed
brutality and wrong upon the helpless."[29]

Sometimes the hard times became a part of national identity without the
convicts who first lived them. Perhaps because of the competition between
New South Wales and Victoria, and resulting official delicacy, the
organizers of the exhibition in Melbourne told a "hard start" story without
mentioning the convicts. Of course, settlement was "begun under circumstances of great difficulty" when "ships which carried the first settlers, to
the number of 1,030, anchored in Sydney Harbour, and the pioneer
colonists of New South Wales landed and took possession of the soil." But
the story they told was one of land settlement and development, not penal
settlement.[30]

The founding moment of British settlement was important in the way
Australians imagined their shared history in 1888. It was sometimes
imagined rather vaguely, and often told as a time of hardship. But it was
part of what national identity meant; it was mentioned in almost all the
celebratory talk, and it was not just mentioned as a necessary part of the
rhetoric of the occasion, but accumulated a density of meaning. It was
mentioned in more remote colonies, and in unofficial as well as official
sources. And as in the United States, the Australian founding moment
became a symbolic ground for competing political claims. The lively
populist journal, the *Bulletin*, ran a detailed series on the convicts and the
brutality and oppression of the settlement, and its editorial on "the day we
were lagged" argued that there was little cause for exuberance in the
celebration. (These and other contributions were only part of an intelligent
and relentlessly pursued anti-British and populist agenda.) A cartoon
summarized the critical position – "The Same Old Tune (And a Bad One at
That)" – by showing a "1788" convict dancing to the tune of an imperial

soldier, and an "1888" figure representing New South Wales manacled by imperialism and dancing to the tune of a grinning John Bull. The weekly also published a poem against a proposed statue of Governor Phillip, full of vivid and melodramatic images of the convicts' hardship, concluding "ghosts shall mock to see how humors can / Out of a tyrant carve a noble man." Australians might have seen more to be ambivalent about in their founding moment, but even where they were critical, it was, as it was for the Americans too in the late nineteenth century, an important part of their identity in celebration.[31]

Visions of progress

In both countries, the celebration of national identity also evoked talk of the meaning of shared history beyond the founding moment. Almost always, the story of the century was told as a story of progress. The ubiquity of the idea of progress in nineteenth-century European culture paradoxically encouraged its use to characterize the supposedly unique history of each nation. As Kenneth Bock has pointed out, the idea of progress at this time entailed that "where progress did occur it always followed the same path." Indeed, just as some Australians saw aspects of the American example as illustrating their future, Americans could occasionally see something of themselves in Australia's future; the *New York Tribune* critic discussing Australian exhibits at the Philadelphia exhibition spoke of "somewhat the same process of growth as we ourselves have gone through" and predicted a similar future. This did not mean that in either nation they saw progress as any less their own. Overall, though, visions of progress were much more breathless and more widespread in Australia than in the United States.[32]

In Australia, contrasting images of "then" and "now" (which the *Bulletin* turned to critical use in their image of "the same old tune") were commonly used to express this sense of shared progress in national history. An official regatta program showed contrasting images of Sydney Harbour; newspapers used "then and now" cartoons of the sort the *Bulletin* parodied. Most verse adopted this structure, opening, for example, with European discovery and moving to a climax in which Australia was crowned with the Southern Cross by other nations.[33] Talk of the dreary founding moment was almost always a prelude to references to the progress since, and progress talk sometimes appeared even without the founding moment. In this sense, progress was more integral to Australians' image of what they shared than was their problematic founding moment, although that provided an invaluable benchmark. At the centennial banquet in

Sydney, for example, the "gratifying work of the past century" was the subject of extensive self-congratulation. And after a vivid picture of the hardship and suffering of the early days under a "well-meant but vicious system of government," a sermon for the opening of Centennial Hall spoke of "steady amelioration," with free immigrants, exploration, settlement, gold discoveries, agricultural development, cities, commerce, communication, and "the general diffusion of the conveniences and comforts of life."[34]

In Melbourne in August, all the talk and symbolism took up a theme of progress. The official report of the commissioners contained a lengthy historical essay entitled "A Century's Progress," and their catalog commented that "the rate at which the resources of Australia have developed is marvellous." On the cover of the daily exhibition program, a draped female figure held up a lighted (electric) bulb labeled "PROGRESS" amid symbols of plenty. Speeches and histories did not leave the meaning of progress to the imagination; they were filled with elaborate detail. They usually offered many facts about economic development, but political development was also mentioned frequently: "on the political and social sides the manifestations were equally distinct and congruent, and equally encouraging in their results."[35]

As in Australia, national identity in the United States was often seen as characterized by progress at the time of the centennial. Much of the nationalist point of the international exhibition in Philadelphia was to make a show and a celebration of progress. As the USCC put it in their mobilizing circulars: "one of the leading objects of the Exhibition . . . is a comparison between the evidences of our progress in a century and that of other nations," for "we have a hundred years of progress to celebrate such as history has not recorded of any other nation." When promoters of the celebration spoke among themselves, they almost always spoke of the progress of the nation as an important part of shared history to be celebrated. At an early meeting of the USCC executive committee, one speaker imagined a successful exhibition showing "that our country in a hundred years has planted more mile stones on the highway of progress than any other country in the world (Applause)." The theme was a governing one in almost every official pronouncement of the time. Progress sometimes seemed even more important to exhibition promoters than the founding moment, though it was often linked to founding stories.[36]

Emblems of progress appeared everywhere too; on the stock certificate issued for funding, for example, an image of the signing of the Declaration was flanked by images of "Progress – a busy manufacturing city in contrast with a neglected windmill" and "Civilization – combining the railroad, telegraph, steamship, and reaping-machine, in contrast with a conestoga

wagon, mail-rider, sailing-vessel, and a laborer with a sickle." Among the
images of the founding moment on the centennial vase displayed at the
exhibition were panels which represented "genius, ready to inscribe on the
tablet the progress made in literature, science, music, painting, sculpture,
and architecture" and "the advancement in commerce, mining, and
manufactures." An engraving of the new Star Monument was entitled
"The Memorial of a Centuries' [sic] Progress" on a flyer issued when
Congress visited the exhibition preparations in 1875.[37] Progress also
provided a framework for the commemorative histories and detailed
historical talk of the centennial. For example, a fairly serious volume on
The American Centenary: A History of the Progress of the Republic devoted
each chapter to an illustration of progress, using "model establishments
and associations" so that "the contrast between them and their predecessors may be made more conspicuous." And a contemporary account of
a fireman's parade in Philadelphia observed that "The Centennial year has
been prolific with parades of different societies which have been formed
since the settlement of the country, and, perhaps, no better mode could be
adopted to show the progress of the nation."[38]

But although progress was one theme of talk of national identity in the
American centennial organization, especially in official speeches, emblems,
and histories, the theme was less often stressed in the unofficial poems,
critical arguments, and more popular guides and speeches beyond the
cultural center. An attachment to the idea of progress was watered down, if
it appeared at all in more peripheral American sources, to something less
grand, a catalog of facts about changes in everyday life. In contrast to
Australia, progress appeared, overall, less frequently than founding
moment history, and, also in contrast to Australian national identity,
founding stories of the nation could appear independently of progress
stories.

Manufacture and industry was the model of progress used by those
promoting the Philadelphia exhibition; they extended their perception of
this sort of progress to provide a general picture of progress as part of the
history the nation shared. Unlike the vision of history as founding moment,
this was a vision which did not seem to resonate in other social locations.
The Civil War was still a very prominent part of the nation's history, which
fit badly a story of progress. The significance of the Civil War as
counterargument to progress becomes evident in differences in the way
Australia and the United States imagined their national future.

The glorious future?

Surprisingly, Americans talked very little of their national future in the centennial. From any stereotype of secure and self-satisfied Victorian culture, or indeed of the gilded age, grandiose visions of the future would seem natural, and certainly they were implied by ideas of progress. Australians talked of the future constantly, as a simple extrapolation of the progress they saw as characterizing their history, in this predictable way. Americans did not, and the little talk of the future in the American centennial was often provoked by (comparatively rare) references to an unstable past and hopes, rather than expectations, for a better future. Compared to the constant imagining of national identity in the international gaze and the founding moment, and, less widespread, the construction of national history as progress, the future was of little salience in the American centennial. Whereas talk of the founding moment and the international gaze appeared in almost all the speeches, reports, magazine commentary, and poetry occasioned by the centennial, talk of the future was much less frequent. Though elites managed to transcend the implications of the Civil War when they spoke of the progress of the country, the war left its mark in a comparative lack of confidence in the future. The Australians had no such chastening experience of disunity to make them doubt the efficacy of progress toward a shared future, and the significance of that future.

The rare talk of the future in the American centennial took place in two contexts. First, when elites were thinking of progress in manufacturing specifically, there seemed much surer ground for extending progress into the future. Second, when the view of history as progress was not adopted, and integration problems were recognized (problems like reintegration of North and South, and women's political equality), talk of the future saw the resolution of these problems in a better future after a difficult past.

It was only when progress was conceived in terms of manufacture, invention, and commerce, or the effects of the exhibition itself were being promoted, that the future was imagined as an extrapolation of past progress. A Philadelphia commissioner very concerned to promote the economic advantages of an international exhibition made one of the few specific suggestions about how the future would be when he suggested that the permanent buildings of the exhibition

should be so managed that when our posterity comes to do honor to the close of the second century of American civilization they will find in them trophies of the hundred years which will terminate July 4, 1976. In each succeeding year let us place in these permanent structures the peculiar American discovery or improvement of that year in every imaginative and substantial production.

The Pennsylvania manufacturers and merchants who were early the most enthusiastic organizers of the celebration wrote, in a funding appeal for a building to the Pennsylvania governor, that "the unborn millions who will celebrate the second centennial of American Independence may esteem it as one of their chiefest treasures." When progress was conceived largely in terms of manufacture, commerce, and invention, talk of the future seemed on surest ground.[39]

The other context in which talk of the American nation's future emerged was when the past was criticized and the speaker could only hope that the future would be better. This happened in several of the more organized political claims made around the centennial, and where the dissent of the South and poorer Western states was recognized. The National Liberal League, taking the occasion of the centennial to press their claims for a more genuine separation of religion and state, imagined the people of 1976 looking back to their critical vision: "if there is to be one far-seeing man in those shadowy millions, he will point back to a . . . visible germ of the greatest movement of the incoming century." Similarly, the women involved in organizing for the exhibition aimed to improve opportunities for women's employment in the future. They hoped that "women, led to earn their livelihood in branches of business yet unknown to them, will have reason to bless the organization known now as the Women's Centennial Executive Committee." Their envisioning of a future was captured in their centennial newspaper's title, *The New Century for Women*.[40] Finally, there was a vein of talk of the future which hoped for the healing of Civil War divisions:

A revival of a just and noble national pride will be a renewal of national character . . . The greatest and happiest result of the Centennial years will be promotion of a new era of national feeling.

A turbulent past was recognized in this vein of talk, and the future was imagined in terms of reconciliation and, sometimes, the economic development of the South. Indeed, there was at least one account of such an experience of reconciliation, though it was isolated in the commentary on the occasion. During the official New Hampshire visit to the exhibition, some Virginian cadets offered an escort to the Northern delegation, and this impressed them and offered them hope for the future. "This distinguished courtesy," they reported, "reminds us again of a country re-united and at peace, in the glory of which the sons of Virginia and New Hampshire are to share in the future as they have in the past."[41] But such visions were rare in the centennial talk, and in general, Americans did not find it easy to speak of the future when they spoke of their national identity in 1876.

For the Australians, on the other hand, their understanding of their nation's simple progress from the founding moment allowed them a rosy and sometimes grandiose vision of their future: as Parkes claimed in his banquet speech, "as surely as the sun rises upon the first day to-morrow of another century, so surely at the close of that century we should be one of the greatest people on the face of God's earth." Australia was, to the writer of the official centennial ode, a "young nation awakening on the Centennial day to a sense of its real power and future destiny." Australia's future seemed guaranteed by its kinship with Britain: Australia was "the Britain of the Southern Hemisphere," or "the new Britannia of the world," and

> her strong-limb'd race
> Will help Australia "hold its pride of place"
> In the great world – as with her parents' sway,
> "*Eastward* the course of Empire takes its way!"[42]

Sometimes, too, Australians appealed to their perceived kinship with the United States in projecting their future from past progress.

When they thought of the future more specifically, as they often seemed to do, Australians thought in terms of economic development and prosperity, institutional development, political union, freedom and justice, and international greatness. More commonly than in the American talk, they imagined how things would be at the bicentennial. Growth and prosperity in the future was a theme which was often discussed in quite specific terms. It was Parkes's belief that "at the end of that hundred years the population of this country will be at least 60,000,000 of souls," and one poet imagined a pastoral idyll in which immigrants from Britain would

> make bright homes, and till the pristine soil,
> And grain their labour crowns, with golden spoil,
> And soon the lonely forests joyful ring
> with mirth and laughter.[43]

Political themes were also strong in the way Australians imagined their rosier future. Most speakers and writers assumed the likelihood and desirability of political union in the future. Federation was thought to be "one of the established common-places in the public mind," and exhibition commissioners were pleased by "the spectacle of Australian unity of aim presented by the exhibiting colonies." Some also described the future in terms of political values. A moral about political values was drawn by commentators on the opening of Centennial Hall in Sydney: "if, indeed, the crowning fact of freedom be a freeman's vote – if citizenship makes all men equal in their civil and religious liberty – . . . then no citizen should have come away from yesterday's ritual without having caught glimpses of his great privileges and touched some chords of the future."[44]

Visions of history were important in the ways Australians and Americans shared much in the way they thought about their nations in their centennials, and their visions were in broad respects remarkably similar. For both, founding moments had great symbolic power, and progress provided the thread of history; both themes were important in characterizing what members of the nation shared. But the nuances in the use of these elements of similar symbolic repertoires were different. From a disreputable founding moment, Australians could construct a version of history as progress into a greater future. Americans focused more on their founding moment when imagining the history their nation shared, and progress was a less widely compelling theme. The two countries differed most in their understanding of the future: Americans had less to say about the shared future of their nation than Australians.

For both countries, too, these histories were part of what the international gaze should recognize, and historical strengths were often attributed to Anglo-Saxon influence. Claims about international gaze, international identifications, founding moments, progress, and the future existed as elements of a symbolic repertoire of imagined community to which members of both nations could appeal, and build into speeches, ceremonies, poems, emblems, arguments, and histories in different ways. But they had more symbolic resources to hand, too. Speakers in both countries also appealed to political identity and prosperity, and, to a lesser extent, their lands, in characterizing what the contemporary community of the nation shared.

Shared qualities of imagined community

Past, progress, and future were often important features of imagined national community in the centennials, symbolizing shared experience. When people in both countries imagined shared qualities which bound their communities, they also thought frequently of their political values and institutions, and prosperity or a close analog of prosperity: wealth, resources, productivity, or development. Political identity and prosperity were core ways of characterizing the nation both in the United States in 1876 and in Australia in 1888. They were important in the way organizers and elites spoke and they were also important beyond the cultural center. These themes were closely associated with talk of international recognition and shared history; liberty and prosperity were what the international gaze would see and what the result of history had been. Though appearing less widely than liberty or prosperity, the theme of the land was also available to characterize shared qualities of imagined community in the centennials.[45]

Although themes of political identity, prosperity, and the land were shared, there were also some differences between the countries in the ways they expressed imagined community. For the Australians, political values and institutions were associated with their identification as British; this was only a rare association in the American talk. For the Australians, British political identification shaded into a clear understanding of national community in terms of race, an understanding which was much less evident in the United States. Notions of prosperity differed a little too: prosperity was seen mostly as a matter of resources and land development in Australia, and a matter of wealth and industry in the United States, although both nuances in the interpretation of prosperity existed in both countries. And their land, and the continent they shared, seemed slightly more important to Australians than Americans, at least at the cultural center of the centennial celebration.

Shared political values and institutions

Of all the qualities centennial Americans attributed to themselves, they were most secure in their claim to share political values and institutions. Perhaps the clearest indication of this came in a rare discussion of immigration. Compared to the pressing problem of regional integration, challenges to American national identity which would be raised by increasing ethnic diversity were little recognized at the time of the 1876 centennial. Immigration was an issue of the future, and almost entirely neglected in the official literature; only hindsight would notice the few portents of "Americanization" issues which appeared in the unofficial literature and ceremony. But one unusual reflection did notice diverse immigration, and was remarkably prescient in the way it used symbols of national identity to resolve the possibility of future cultural difference. Students of Boston and Harvard Universities producing the *Centennial Eagle* during their summer at the exhibition wrote on "prophetic elements of the exhibition." In the exhibition crowds they noticed "not merely the descendants of American [sic], but also those of Germany, Ireland, and Africa"; but concluded

this fact need not awaken regrets in patriotic hearts. Among the people there will ever be a community of interests; and when such does not exist in an immediately acknowledged form, the modifying power of our suffrages will shape it out of the conflicting elements of the times.[46]

They appealed to distinctive political institutions to overcome threats to national identity posed by cultural difference. In so doing, they were making use of one of the most common qualities attributed to the national community during the exhibition. Americans in 1876 saw their community as bound together by a commitment to liberty. Almost every writer and speaker, whatever their particular agenda, appealed to this value. Claims about national identity almost always involved claims about liberty and its variants – independence, opportunity, political, civil, or religious freedoms, republicanism, self-government, or democratic institutions. Liberty was linked to a vision of history as progress from the founding moment (where progress was claimed): political values and institutions which dated from the founding moment created the basis for subsequent progress. Further, world recognition should be founded on the nation's liberty. In an early appeal for exhibition support, the USCC argued that the exhibition would "make evident to the world the advancement of which a self-governed people is capable." As one writer reflected: "What justifies the existence of the United States as a nation? . . . The establishment and maintenance of a democratic form of government."[47]

Liberty was often used to characterize the nation in a simple and abstract way. The theme was not highly elaborated at the organizational center of the celebration, but rather appeared frequently in the quick descriptive phrase of official speakers, as well as in official emblems. According to General Hawley, speaking when he was elected president of the USCC, the purpose of the celebration was "to take measure of the growth of a free nation"; formal presidential statements referred to "the growth and progress of a nation devoted to freedom," and "a free and independent people"; and the vice-president, speaking on the Fourth of July in Philadelphia, made his theme American citizenship and the "spirit of American fidelity to the cause of human freedom."[48] Many of the official symbols of the celebration invoked liberty (along with prosperity or industry). The motto from Leviticus, "proclaim Liberty throughout the land unto all the inhabitants thereof," appeared on the seal of the USCC with an image of Independence Hall. It also appeared frequently in other literature of the centennial, along with an image of the Liberty Bell. Official "centennial medals" showed a figure representing the "genius of American independence" surrounded by the motto, "These united colonies are, and of right ought to be, free and independent states," and a figure representing the "genius of liberty" who "extends a welcome and a chaplet to the Arts and Sciences assembled." A figure representing "America," or "The Genius of Liberty," was included on the complimentary passes printed for the exhibition. And in at least one Philadelphia ceremony, schoolchildren were given a commemorative medal with the image of a "head of Liberty."[49]

Appeals to abstract or personified freedom or liberty were made in almost every centennial poem, official and unofficial. Freedom or liberty was mentioned in every second line of the hymn, "America," sung at the ringing of the new Liberty Bell – "Sweet land of liberty . . . Let Freedom ring." In some poems the theme structured the verse, as in this 22-page poem in which a personified liberty was addressed:

> Hail, goddess, dear! whose quenchless strife
>   First won for us the right to be:
> We thank thee for our birth and life,
>   And for thyself, sweet Liberty![50]

The theme of liberty was a robust one, and just as the founding moment was a useful symbol of national identity even for critics, political values and institutions were often taken as symbols which could ground oppositional and critical claims. Southerners criticizing the exhibition, the National Liberal League criticizing Sunday closing, and women making claims for national inclusion all claimed a shared *political* national identity. In one of the more striking examples, a savage and amusing tract on women's political and legal incapacity, Celinda Lilley of Vermont said that "as a loyal woman of America, devoted to the cause of freedom . . . I will endeavour to furnish the Commission . . . a description of the type of self-government which predominates." She went on to observe that "it is no vain boast that every man in the State is a sovereign, for ignorance, imbecility, and depravity are no hindrance to a man's becoming a legislator and a jurist."[51] The perception that political identity was a crucial part of national identity could be vague or concrete – framed as "Liberty" or "republican institutions" – and it could be a cause for grandiloquence, a handy emblem, or grounds for critique. Whatever the context, it was one of the most frequent and pervasive claims about what the American nation shared.

Surprisingly, Australians also saw their political identity – their "independence and civil and religious liberty" – as a significant quality of their community. References to democratic sympathies, to the colonial constitutions, to responsible government, to "liberal and enlightened political institutions" and to political heroes unknown to later Australians were common in speeches and poems. Speaking both officially and unofficially,

Australians characterized themselves with achieved freedom and enlightened political institutions. One review of Australia's history spoke of earlier agitation to end convict transportation as creating "a national public spirit": "it led to a united struggle for free institutions (a constitution), and again victory crowned justice." One of the reasons for national gratitude discussed in an Australia Day sermon in Victoria was "the formation and establishment of responsible government in 1843, and the consequent contentment within our own borders," and the speaker noted that "legislative assemblies on a popular basis . . . are a special feature of Australian statesmanship." Many claims to political freedom took a more poetic turn, too:

> A land of freedom, free in church and school,
> Where freemen choose from freemen who shall rule;
> Where neither priest nor king dares dominate,
> And brains, not birth, breed rulers for the State![52]

Whereas for Americans their political values and institutions were associated with their founding moment of separation from Britain, for Australians, their kinship with Britain was mostly a condition, rather than an impediment, to the political qualities they cherished. Political identity was linked to the way they saw themselves as British for "the colonies are also indebted to the parent country for the liberal and enlightened political institutions which they enjoy." But sometimes political identity was also used to mark distinction from the British. In the Australia Day sermon, for example, the speaker pointed out that the "legislative assemblies on a popular basis" were "free from class legislation which mars the statute book of the mother land." If Australia was thankful to her British inheritance for her free institutions, the nation had increased that inheritance, too.[53]

In the United States, in one of the rare discussions of immigration, political institutions had offered symbolic resources to resolve perceived problems of national integration across cultural difference. In Australia as well, immigration was not generally an issue for expressions of national identity, but one reflective article in Australia's *Centennial Magazine* on "Australia's Mission and Opportunity" offers intriguing parallels to the American suggestion that political institutions would resolve cultural difference due to immigration. The context was Australia's much more directly racist hostility to Chinese immigration and fear of "Asian invasion," an issue high on the contemporary political agenda in a way comparable only to the Californian experience and not to its relevance for American centennial organizers. Although the political context was different, the issue of cultural difference in the future was resolved by appeal to national political values as it had been in the American *Centennial Eagle* talk. Asian immigration should be minimized, the author said, "in order that, in their interest and in that of the world, a free and equal common-wealth may be firmly established with our laws and civilization supreme." He imagined "an empire which embodies the divine ideas of justice and freedom." National political values were a potent symbolic resolution of problems of immigrants' cultural difference. But unlike the American students, this author saw exclusion as a way to preserve the shared political community he valued, and did not see political institutions as offering resources to unify threatened national community.[54]

Mostly, the political identity of Australians – as free and just – was a theme emphasized by elites, and less frequently voiced on the margins than it was in the United States. But as in the United States, political identity could be used as the basis of criticism. A *Bulletin* cartoon, for example, contrasted images of the few political heroes acceptable to their anti-imperialism, who were praised, for example, for "sturdy democracy," with covered images of other well-known political heroes, with shameful labels like "bought with a title," "advocate for colonial peerage."[55] As in the United States, though to a lesser extent, critics promoting their agendas during the Australian centennial could occasionally appeal to putatively shared national political qualities in voicing their criticisms.

National prosperity

Freedom and benign political institutions were seen as important and distinctive qualities shared by members of the nation in both Australian and American centennials. Prosperity (or wealth, civilization, or resources) was another important characteristic of national identity, and often a matter for elaborate self-congratulation. Very often, distinctive political values and institutions were seen as the cause of material prosperity and progress.

In the United States, centennial organizers, especially, staked their claims to national celebration on material advancement and prosperity, and saw this as intrinsically linked to America's political identity. A memorial certificate drafted for visitors to the Philadelphia exhibition on the "Anniversary of the INDEPENDENCE OF THE UNITED STATES OF AMERICA," claimed the exhibition was "the illustration of their progress in the Arts and Sciences, in Wealth and Material Resources and of their success in the practical application of the principles of FREE REPUBLICAN GOVERNMENT, ESTO PERPETUA." A promoter spoke of the next generation's "great heritage of liberty, prosperity, and power"; promoters also argued that the exhibition would "test the relative advantage of a government by the people over imperial governments, for the successful development of the great works of peace" and that "by this test we shall discover the true value of our national experiment of self-government." The causal association of political institutions with progress or prosperity was often made in the context of imagining what the world would see when they saw the nation.[56]

The linking of liberty and prosperity was also a common way of characterizing the American nation in less official texts. The publishers of one of the major descriptions of the exhibition spoke of the exhibits as "the fruits of prosperity and peace, and in our case certainly due in no small measure to the high civilization which our glorious institutions secure." And a writer for a gazetteer of 1876, reflecting on the country's "Resources and Prospects," thought that the future would

prove beyond controversy the superiority of a republic to every other form of government, and the value (not the theoretical but the practical value) of free institutions to assist and to direct the development of the resources of the country.[57]

Australians reflected in perhaps even more elaborate terms on their national prosperity during the centennial; the imagined community of the Australian nation was said to share astounding material development and increasing prosperity. Histories, speeches, and centennial symbols dwelt on the development and products of the land, the mineral booms, the cities, and a sense of growing prosperity; "development" statistics were part of the repertoire of the occasion's celebration. The development of the cities was a frequent emblem of advances in Australia's wealth, and comparisons of grand buildings were common. In Australia, enthusiasm about prosperity and development was not confined to the official talk and was a common theme of more peripheral discussions of national identity during the centennial. A small almanac for an area near Melbourne, for example, even went so far as to claim (along with supporting statistics about railways, crops, and so on which were common in the discourse) that: "In material wealth Australasia . . . can be described without exaggeration as among the richest countries on the face of the globe . . . everywhere growth is rapid, continuous, and sustained . . . the general view is one which may well excite feelings of pride and gratulation [sic]." Indeed the topic was so common and extensively discussed that it ended by boring one contemporary writer as it tends to do the twentieth-century reader (his reaction, though, captured well the sense of excitement evident in Australian visions of prosperity):

The unbounded resources of Australasia, her inexhaustible stores of hidden wealth, the resistless torrent of prosperity that must flow when these resources are developed and this wealth made accessible – all this has been so long the theme of profuse congratulation on the part of enthusiastic visitors, and no less profuse self-congratulation on our own part, that it is, I think, justifiable to look on the topic now as a rather threadbare one.[58]

Prosperity was a key national quality to Australians at the time of the centennial. As in the United States, though to a lesser extent, free and benign institutions could be seen as the cause of progress, or at least as in compelling association; "political events," the Melbourne commissioners observed, "have no doubt in many cases been potent factors in determining the progress made, and in directing the energies of the people." And in one of Sir Henry Parkes's centennial speeches, he pointed out that

our riches are so boundless, and our application of power is so completely in our hands, that if we do not become rich and prosperous, as well as free, the fault will be at our own doors.[59]

For Americans, liberty was a core and widely claimed aspect of national identity; prosperity was important too, but more frequently claimed by centennial organizers than others, and justified by its association with liberty. Australians appealed to the same symbols of shared national qualities, but their relative salience was somewhat different. Political freedoms were more a theme of the cultural center and their symbolic mobilization less widespread in claims about national identity, whereas prosperity and development were unqualified and widespread qualities associated with national identity. In both cases, though, national elites organizing the celebrations saw a crucial link between political identity and material success.

The land

One other theme emerged occasionally when there was talk of imagined community during the centennial years: sometimes, what was taken to characterize the nation was the land or the continent. Investing national identity in the land was a minor theme at the cultural center in both countries, compared to position in the world, history, or freedom and prosperity. However, talk of the land was one way of making claims about freedom or prosperity more concrete. Although its use was comparatively rare in both cases, Australians tended to utilize the land as national symbol slightly more than Americans.

Although, for Australians, the land was not a central claim about national identity in official talk, it could be important in the poetic imagination and in heroic history, more important than for many Americans writing on the centennial. Australian speeches and poems imagined in detail "this great island continent," and sang "the song of our beautiful land," "our sunlit, sea-girt home." Land was sometimes associated with liberty – Australia was a "sunbright land of liberty" – and was constantly associated with progress and prosperity:

> And where the lonely savage, hungry, prowl'd,
> The wild cat litter'd, and the dingo howl'd,
> Wide waving corn all greenly-golden grows,
> And the "lone wilderness blooms like the rose!"[60]

The heroism of the explorers was often celebrated in poetry, and, much more frequently than in the United States, history glorified the exploration and pioneering of the continent. Histories were written as histories of exploration, as well as political and material development. In such histories, explorers took their place with political figures as national heroes. In the *Centennial History*, for instance, the first few chapters treated early continental discoverers, geography, fauna, and flora; and although in remaining chapters political issues and progress dominated the narrative, continental exploration was also treated in detail. Another centennial historical review devoted most attention to the exploration of the land because "the history of . . . Australian Land Exploration furnishes remarkable proofs of the heroism, foresight, and perseverance of the men engaged in it . . . and prepared the way for pastoral occupation and industrial settlement which, in a few decades of years, covered the plains with flocks and herds." This romantic view associating the land with development was not without challenge from the relentless *Bulletin*, however:

> Farewell the crystal streams,
>   Welcome the drains that stink;
> Farewell poetic dreams,
>   Welcome the skating rink.[61]

In the United States, perhaps surprisingly considering the energy in frontier expansion, the land was not a central national symbol for centennial organizers either, but again the theme appeared fairly frequently in some minor ceremonial occasions and in centennial poetry. A (token) South Carolina speaker at the Oddfellows' day at the exhibition, for example, was eloquent about the land: "the United States has increased from its comparatively small dimensions . . . until it reaches from the hyperborean mountains of Maine to the tropical fields of Texas, from the shores of the Atlantic to those of the Pacific ocean." In "Iowa's Centennial Poem," the poet began with a reflection on the land, using much the same language as Australians would do:

> A hundred years ago today
> A barren wild our borders lay;
> Our stately forests grandly stood
> Wrapped in majestic solitude.

Very occasionally, speakers extrapolated the taming of the land to a sort of imperial vision. The Californian representative at the Oddfellows' ceremonies, for instance, spoke of the closing of the frontier, but could see "no reason why the aegis of our liberty should not spread over all, bounded only and on all sides by the waters of the great deep."[62] But such imperial visions were much rarer in the American talk of the nation during the centennial than they were for the Australians (who had the possibility of imperial federation in mind), and the land, though it was claimed as part of national identity by some poets and non-official speakers, was not a dominant theme of national identity at the cultural center.

Repertoires of national identity in the late nineteenth century

Australia and the United States were unusual places in the late nineteenth century. They had comparatively little history as geopolitical units, and they had little experience of either state-run or oppositional nationalist movements. As actual or prospective nation-states, they still seemed to face serious problems of regional integration. Nevertheless, ideas of nationality were becoming more and more compelling experiential frameworks all around the world, and they made sense to important groups in each country. Members of each country, and especially elites, saw themselves as distinctively "new" nations, by comparison to the European models with their Asian and African dominions and dependencies. Centennial celebrations in each country were episodes of widespread cultural mobilization which promoted national identities and gave them elaborate symbolic specification.

In these events, national identity was constituted within a discursive field which had two dimensions: geopolitical relations, and shared national qualities or experiences. Claims about position in the world and shared qualities and experiences made claims to nationhood plausible. In the absence of envisaged relations with powerful others, and shared qualities and experience, there would have been nothing to celebrate; these two cultural constructions made nationality matter. In their absence there would have been no grammar for talk of national identity to make sense. This discursive field was the basis for national identity in both Australia and the United States.

Relations to the rest of the world defined national identity in two ways in each country: the world's gaze confirmed distinct national identity, and an identification with other powerful nations also strengthened it. The world's gaze was more salient to Americans, and identification with powerful others was more significant to Australians, but both themes helped build national identity in each country. Ideas about world opinion could take on shades of identification in the United States, and shades of display in Australia. The imagined community of the nation – what was shared across geopolitical and cultural faultlines within the country – was constructed partly in the imagining of the opinion of other nations and identification with other nations. Ideas about the country's place in the world were very important to elites making the celebrations in both countries, and strongly linked to other ideas about what the nation shared.

Shared qualities and experience were also a constitutive part of national identity. Those who spoke of the nation during these celebrations envisioned a shared historical experience of founding moment and progress since. The founding moment was more relevant to Americans, and progress to Australians, but a history of progress since a founding moment was common to the national identities expressed in both countries. Occasionally in the United States and frequently in Australia, visions of a shared future extended this experience of imagined community in time.

Shared collective qualities of the contemporary community were also a constitutive part of these national identities, ideas of what was shared across internal social and political boundaries. Political values and institutions were important shared characteristics claimed in both the United States and Australia; so too was prosperity. In the United States there was more widespread plausibility to political qualities, and in Australia to prosperity, as characteristics of national identity worthy of centennial fascination; but both were important in both countries. Sometimes, and more frequently in the United States, political qualities were thought to be the cause of prosperity. The respective nations were also sometimes characterized by their lands; this was not an important symbol to official speakers in either country, but more evident in unofficial talk and more widespread in Australia than the United States. It was more common in Australia to associate the land with freedom, prosperity, and heroic history.

The international gaze, international identifications, founding moments, progress, the future, political values and institutions, prosperity, and the land: these were the elements of symbolic repertoires of national identity in these "new nations" at the end of the nineteenth century. If the discursive field made talk of national identity possible, these symbolic elements made it concrete. They were elements of a symbolic repertoire which could be put together in different ways according to circumstance: who was speaking, whether they were speaking in official, critical, poetic, narrative, ritual, or emblematic genres, and how conspicuous historical problems meshed with constraints of the discursive field of national identity. There was significant variation in the ways these symbolic elements were synthesized within each country; there were also broad variations in salience and emphasis between the United States and Australia. So, for instance, East Coast elites in the United States might talk of Anglo-Saxon heritage when they spoke of the founding moment, a symbolic association which would not be made by other groups; or Australians celebrating their centennial would speak more of the future than would their American counterparts. Each symbolic element could be used independently, but there were different patterns of emphasis and association characteristic of different groups within each country, as well as characteristic of each country.

Within this symbolic repertoire, some elements seemed more highly elaborated, and more likely than others to be adopted by peripheral speakers and to be used in oppositional claims. In the United States, international recognition, the founding moment, and liberty were the symbols of nationality most highly elaborated, used most widely and in the most varying contexts. In Australia, on the other hand, British heritage, progress, and prosperity were the strongest symbolic elements in claims about nationality.

For historians familiar with either country, this comparative picture invites many questions and suggests further explanations of national identities in each country. Here, I reserve more detailed discussion for chapter 5, in order to examine something of how each national identity changed. A hundred years later, the two countries would celebrate their bicentennials in very different circumstances. Different international contexts and different integration issues would face those who would speak about the nation in what were in themselves somewhat different celebratory genres. How robust were the old symbolic repertoires, and the discursive fields which made national identities meaningful, to a hundred years of change? What changed and what persisted in American and Australian national identities? And was there convergence or differentiation between Australian and American nationalities?

4

"To remind ourselves that we are a united nation": bicentennial celebrations in 1976 and 1988

When the United States celebrated the bicentennial of the Declaration of Independence in 1976, and Australia commemorated the bicentenary of its European settlement in 1988, ritual and symbol were mobilized once again to characterize the imagined community of the "nation." Many of the challenges to national integration which had once worried centennial organizers had been overcome. Regional political differences and geographic dispersion were no longer critical problems for claims about shared national identity. National political institutions, national markets, and international position were all better established than they had been in the centennials, in both countries. There had been significant growth in the capacity of the American state in the intervening century, as well as expansion and consolidation of the national economy, and the acquisition of a central geopolitical role. In Australia, formal federation had created the Australian state, an industrialized national economy had grown, and links with Britain had been attenuated by other geopolitical alliances and somewhat more diverse immigration. Further, patriots in both countries could draw on defining moments and formative experiences unknown in the centennials, like Gallipoli in Australia or the Cold War in the United States. But to organizers of the bicentennials, their tasks did not seem any simpler. In 1876, many Americans had hoped that the centennial would bring "the revival of a just and noble national pride." By 1976, that revival seemed necessary again. "Amid the dissension that sometimes amounts to hate in our country today," Americans were warned as their "Bicentennial Era" was launched on television in 1971, "it behooves us to remind ourselves that we are a united nation."[1] Centennial organizers might have said much the same thing.

As in the centennials, large organizational efforts were devoted to making celebrations which could properly express national identity. Ritual and symbol were invoked to characterize the nation in ways which would invite identification while discouraging dissent. As in the centennials, organizers of both bicentennials shared similar cultural tasks: characteriz-ing shared horizontal links between members of the population in ways which plausibly transcended salient cultural and political differences, especially those differences which were faultlines of current political claims. And as in the centennials, they thought of their nations along two dimensions: place in the world and shared experience.

But despite established national institutions, similar ritual organization, and the same discursive field, what it meant to be Australian or American could not be fixed or final. Some meanings and values associated with national community did remain the same, but some differed, and there were new themes addressing new concerns about national integration. Where similar themes persisted in events a century apart, it was because they remained plausible ways of transcending difference in the context of new debates in cultural politics. Typical of the problems organizers faced, and their solutions, was the formulation of one Australian publicist: "What does it mean to be Australian? It's a $64,000 question with 64,000 replies but easily answered by a spectacular 14-minute video shown in the Exhibition's big top theatre."[2]

Reading national identity in the bicentennials

As in the centennials, reflections on national identity in the bicentennials were the products of transient but intense mobilizations within an organizational field dominated by central bicentennial organizations which encouraged the participation of many other groups. The goals, organiza-tional forms, and methods of American and Australian ritual planners were similar, partly because of the comparable political organization of the two countries and partly because of a demonstration effect. In both cases the organization was intensive and extensive, and left many and various public records of contemporary formulations of national identity.[3]

Overall, center/periphery relations constituting the public sphere within which national identity was enacted in the bicentennials were like those in the centennials. Central groups, organized specifically to commemorate the occasions, planned and promoted activities and events which linked and encouraged the activities of many other groups. Bicentennial organizers directed their mobilizing efforts to other national organizations, regional groups and governments, professional associations, corporations, educa-tional institutions, other interest groups and organizations, and to "com-munities." Many groups were active in the celebrations: they created rituals and reflections on national identity which responded to or were attached to the framework created by central groups.[4]

There were also two significant ways in which the organization of the bicentennials differed from that of the centennials, in both countries. First, federal governments were more active at the center of the organizational field creating the bicentennials than they were in the centennials. Bicentennial organization in Australia was no longer hampered by the institutional divisions between different colonial governments which had presented challenges in 1888, and in 1988 the Australian national government provided the umbrella for bicentennial planning. In the United States, the 1976 celebration was encouraged from Washington, not Philadelphia, and unlike the centennial it addressed more directly the concerns and problems of Washington constituencies. A second development in national ritual organization was more subtle: by contrast with the centennials, the central promotion of the events at a vernacular, community level was more intense in the bicentennials. Central organizers cast their net as widely as possible. They saw their role as one of promotion rather than direction, but they did touch local community celebrations more than they had done a hundred years earlier (perhaps confirming Shils's judgment that the link between cultural centers and peripheries becomes tighter with increasing modernity).

National planning for the American bicentennial began when the American Revolution Bicentennial Commission (ARBC) was formed by Congress in 1966. The ARBC was relatively weak and poorly funded, and faced a variety of controversies and criticisms in Washington in the early 1970s; for example, the event was tagged the "Buy-centennial," and the *Washington Post* did a series of critical articles in mid-1972, which prompted widespread press discussion and congressional criticism. Planning became more intensive in 1974, when, in the face of the disaffection and dissent, the ARBC was replaced by the American Revolution Bicentennial Administration (ARBA) under the leadership of John Warner.[5] ARBA relied on similar organizations in every state and territory: most of these had been formed by early 1970, and organizations in Massachusetts and Philadelphia had begun planning much earlier. There were a number of nationally sponsored activities, such as the popular parade of "tall ships," "Opsail '76," and the Festival of American Folklife. Most federal government departments and agencies listed extensive bicentennial programs, like the Department of Agriculture's production and distribution of "over 40,000 copies of a brochure entitled *Let's Plan a Party* to local communities." There were more than 300 corporate and other private sponsors for various projects, and ARBA instituted a number of "alliances" of various types of organizations like "ethnic/racial" or "business" alliances. Membership in such alliances was earned with programs which "encouraged members, affiliates, or employees to become active in Bicentennial efforts." Most national entertainment events – such as the Academy Awards, the Miss America pageant, and the Rose Bowl – were staged with a bicentennial theme. An extensive public relations effort included bicentennial media kits, feature article series, public service campaigns, recorded and filmed announcements, photo sheets and slide series, and information clearing-houses. More than 300 media organizations were recognized by ARBA for their special bicentennial features, public service efforts, and sponsorship.[6]

The Australian Bicentennial Authority (ABA) was formed in 1980 after discussions between national and state governments from 1978. Among the objectives of the authority were "strengthening national pride, identity, and purpose," "involving all Australians in the Bicentennial programme," "offering educational and cultural programmes to help Australians toward a clearer appreciation of their origins, the present, and the future," and "achieving international participation in the Bicentenary." Among the most prominent of ABA activities were a number of national spectaculars like a Parade of Tall Ships in Sydney Harbour on Australia Day, and a traveling exhibition. From the early 1980s, on the prompting of the national government, states were forming their own bicentennial organiz-ations and collecting suggestions about activities. Elaborate programs addressed and encouraged the involvement of schools, teachers, youth, "older Australians," the disabled, unions, ethnic groups, sporting groups, and church groups. The ABA endorsed many privately planned activities, and from 1985, corporate sponsorship of bicentennial projects was encouraged, at both national and state levels. As in the United States, promotional and public relations campaigns were important and, in general, there was an intense, though often forgotten, effort of national mobilization.[7]

So federal governments were more active at the cultural center of the mobilizations around bicentennial celebrations than had been possible during the centennials, in both countries. There was a further difference in center/periphery dynamics in the organization of the events a hundred years apart. In contrast with the centennial celebrations, there was no central focus like an international exhibition for the bicentennials: rather, celebrations in local communities were actively promoted from the center. In the United States, after early and large plans for another Expo in Philadelphia and for a system of national "Bicentennial Parks" lost favor, "emphasis was redirected toward encouraging, assisting, and coordinating Bicentennial projects, activities, and events at the grass roots level."[8]

Consequently, a central program in both American and Australian bicentennials became a "Bicentennial Communities Program." These programs linked central organizations with local events through promotional activities, registration, and recognition. Cultural centers were thus addressing and encouraging peripheral enactment of national identity in more widespread and more systematic ways than they had been in centennials.

Beginning a process typical of this more systematic attempt to mobilize and recognize local bicentennial enactment of national identity in the United States, the ARBC sent "invitations to 40,000 localities" in 1973. Communities were instructed about forming local bicentennial committees, which were to be "broadly representative of all segments of the community." Moreover, they were told that

recognition [from ARBC] will be facilitated if the activities which form the program necessitate widespread citizen involvement. Be as innovative as possible in devising and selecting the activity. We suggest that certain groups be designated as sponsors for the specific activity. This means all elements of the community, such as, but not limited to, civic associations, service clubs, the Chamber of Commerce, youth groups, societal organizations, parochial organizations, ethnic units, educational instrumentalities, etc. Leave room for the individual because our Nation's bicentennial should have a place for everyone.[9]

Forms for registering local bicentennial activities and events "were distributed widely to Bicentennial program planners, primarily through state Bicentennial organizations and ARBC regional offices." Central organizers suggested, for example, that "exciting Bicentennial Community activities can inspire citizen support and involvement." Along with ARBA recognition, local organizers were encouraged in promotional and organizational meetings and ceremonies, and provided with resources like idea books and bicentennial manuals.[10] More than 12,000 communities ultimately received official recognition under the Bicentennial Communities Program. According to ARBA's 1976 report, these included

municipalities, counties, and various types of incorporated and unincorporated places from every State in the Union and the Commonwealth of Puerto Rico. More than 182 million citizens, almost 90 percent of the Nation's population, were affected by or embraced within this program. Included are all 156 cities with populations in excess of 100,000, every State Capitol [sic], 1,800 counties, more than 8,000 communities with populations under 10,000, and 38 Native American Communities.

More than 66,000 community events and activities were registered in ARBA's "Binet" database.[11] In Australia, mobilization of community activities and events for the bicentennial was also important, and similarly organized. "Bicentennial Community Committees" were established in most of Australia's 845 local government areas from 1982, with the majority established by 1986. The committees received "publications and manuals . . . certificates and bicentennial flags" and were responsible for organizing and promoting local events, as well as for liaison with "Australia-wide projects." Over 24,000 activities and events were registered with the ABA; most of these were locally organized.[12]

Through the communities programs, central organizers formed more systematic connections with vernacular or spontaneous celebration of the bicentennials than had been envisaged in the centennials. Historians of American national identity have pointed out that, especially in the nineteenth century, American patriotic ritual and collective memory has been particularly distinctive for comparatively weak official involvement and stronger private and vernacular participation than in most other countries. John Bodnar has suggested that vernacular traditions have remained relatively independent of official ones in the United States; Michael Kammen has argued that collective memory has generally been more private than official in the United States. But Kammen, Bodnar, and others have also suggested that the official state role in promoting national identity increased in the United States in the course of the twentieth century; the evidence from the bicentennial confirms this change, and suggests more about its nature. While vernacular patriotic traditions probably remain stronger in the United States than elsewhere, the development of a deliberately syncretic organization by ARBA for the 1976 bicentennial made connections between vernacular and official celebration which were a channel for official mobilization and guidance across the country. So, for example, whereas in 1876 a small town might have held spontaneously an elaborate centennial Fourth of July parade – or not, depending on the town itself – in 1976 the same town's bicentennial events and activities would have been encouraged and recorded by ARBA.[13]

The influence of this change in center/periphery relations in the organizational field within which national identity was produced should not be overstated; it probably affected formulations of national identity at the center more than it did at the vernacular level. The framework provided by ARBA for regional and local participation in the bicentennials allowed extensive local differentiation in patriotic themes. Although my concern here is primarily with the themes developed and promoted in the central organization, it is important to note that the bicentennial records of patriotic themes in community celebrations showed some significant differences from those emphasized by ARBA. Further, local response to central encouragement was frequently syncretic and pragmatic, and existing local events were often given the added weight of bicentennial representation. As Bodnar also concluded,

the celebration of . . . the American Revolution Bicentennial in 1976 [was] heavily influenced by government officials who urged widespread citizen participation . . . and loyalty to the nation . . . [but] Ordinary people continued to use them for entertainment, for the celebration of a past that was mostly local, ethnic, or personal, and for other unintended purposes.[14]

Differences between official and vernacular celebration were similar in the Australian case.

So stronger center/periphery links in the bicentennials did not necessarily mean that a specific, official patriotic ideology was being spread and enforced more firmly; for bicentennial organizers, sheer participation, not any particular representation of the nation, was the goal. Indeed, to take an Australian instance, the ABA noted in 1985 that the local committees were "planning activities that reflect the interests and priorities of the localities they represent." Encouraging widespread community participation meant that central organizers made their claims about what exactly the nations were less specific, more diffuse, and more inclusionary; the process encouraged "ideological ambiguity." As the following analysis shows, greater ideological ambiguity could be seen in many of the newer themes of national identity in bicentennials compared to centennials. This official ideological ambiguity was, in the more innovative American case especially, partly a consequence of the greater official connection to vernacular and community celebration by central organizers. So, for example, American organizers crafted ambiguous criteria for community participation upon which diverse and conflicting meanings could be projected. They suggested in their guidelines for community recognition that

Festival USA is firmly focused on people, the sights and sounds of the people – all the people – the multiplicity of their ideas, their expressions, their interests which best convey the diversity of our culture, the warmth of our hospitality, the vitality of our society, the tradition upon which we draw and the traditions we create.

Missing in such carefully crafted statements to communities was the political and historical specificity of earlier characterizations of "Festival USA" – characterizations not directed to communities – as celebrating "Our Freedoms," "Our Founding Fathers," and "Our Form of Government." So the effect of tighter central mobilization of peripheral celebration in the bicentennials was paradoxical: in order to encourage community

participation, central organizations were more ambiguous in their statements of what national identity was. In expanding their promotion of
national identity during the bicentennial, organizers traded some thematic
definition for the possibility of claiming widespread participation.[15]

Their formulations of national identity were also influenced by their
critics. In both countries, bicentennial planners recognized sources of
potential conflict and organized to pre-empt criticism. The pre-emptive
strategy in both cases was deliberate. Both American and Australian
organizers shared the fear that the celebrations would be more notable for
conflict than consensus. However, American organizers were more influenced by this fear than Australians, because their bicentennial took place
sooner after the height of the activism of the 1960s and early 1970s. Just as,
in the centennials, "imagined community" seemed more distant to many
Americans than Australians because of the Civil War, internal divisions
seemed more threatening to many Americans in their bicentennial than for
Australians by 1988.

American organizers seriously doubted the success of the 1976 celebration, and expressed a much greater sense of possible failure than did
Australians. Indeed, the politics of the bicentennial celebration are a
neglected aspect of the way in which the critical movements of the 1960s
and early 1970s were – depending on one's point of view – defused or
transcended. So, for example, the introduction to the application for
registration with ARBA as a bicentennial community was highly defensive:

> Though this Nation is now troubled by both ancient and modern problems of
> human society, the ARBA first urges an examination of our country: its heritage
> and values . . . Neither the President, the Congress, nor the ARBA would represent
> that the programs the ARBA supports, endorses, or activates can provide a
> panacea for all the ills of our society.[16]

ARBA devoted the entire first chapter of their final report to the heated
political divisions in the United States during the 1960s and early 1970s,
asking "after a decade of racial tensions, assassinations, scandal, rising
inflation, embattled campuses, and eroding public trust, what was there left
to celebrate?" (though by the time of that final report, in 1977, they felt they
could conclude "there was plenty").[17]

Because of their fear that political divisions would lead to the failure of
the bicentennial, American organizers held meetings with groups of their
critics among youth activists, feminists, and ethnic and racial minorities in
the early 1970s. Strong and radical challenges were expressed at these
meetings; organizers responded by expanding representation on boards
and initiating new campaigns in attempts at greater inclusion. Typically, a

pre-emptive concern about criticism was followed by meetings which led to an expansion of formal inclusion in organizational branches and policies and the fading of more substantive oppositional claims. For example, contesting by ethnic and racial groups was one of the biggest worries of organizers: ARBA called a meeting of "representatives of ethnic and racial groups . . . to insure their participation in the planning for the Nation's 200th Birthday." This led to a larger "Bicentennial Ethnic and Racial Conference" at the beginning of 1975. In turn, a high-level advisory committee and a bicentennial alliance of ethnic and racial organizations was formed.[18]

Ultimately, there was less criticism of the American bicentennial than organizers had expected. The main national opposition faced in 1976 came from the People's Bicentennial Commission, which had been founded in 1971 by New Left activist Jeremy Rifkin; "at the height of its activity, it had local chapters in the majority of states and claimed a paid membership of over 10,000." In addition to organizing a variety of demonstrations, debates, and historical re-enactments (like "a 'Boston Oil Party,' . . . a protest against the marketing practices of major oil companies"), the PBC provided widely distributed alternative bicentennial publications, like *Commonsense II: The Case Against Corporate Tyranny*, and an alternative celebration planning guide.[19]

Twelve years later, at the time of the Australian bicentenary, the concerns which mobilized social critics of the 1960s and early 1970s in both countries had largely receded, and some political claims of the period were quickly recognized as relevant to organizers' construction of nationality. In particular, as the ABA reported in 1983, "the Government . . . asked that special attention be given to the concerns of women and Aboriginals." ABA's "Women '88" program aimed to address feminist concerns by making grants to national and community organizations, giving achievement awards, promoting women in sport, and supporting books, film, and television about Australian women. ABA ultimately claimed that these activities allowed women to "participate under the woman's umbrella in addition to their participation as members of a family or community."[20]

But the major public issue faced by Australian organizers was Aboriginal opposition, which was generally and early recognized as a problem for those who planned for the bicentennial. Early ideas for the bicentennial year included a historic treaty with Aboriginal peoples (which did not eventuate). Historians planning for a series of bicentennial histories argued in 1980 that in treating 1788 they shouldn't give undue emphasis to Europeans, and in the ABA's first report, they envisaged that the bicentenary would be "much more than a commemoration of the arrival of the First Fleet." Bicentennial plans continued to be influenced by the fear of Aboriginal protest. For example, early plans for the authority to sponsor a re-enactment of the First Fleet's voyage were abandoned in the face of fears of extensive Aboriginal protest, in favor of the ideological ambiguity of the pure spectacle of a parade of tall ships in Sydney Harbour. The re-enactment was privately organized anyway, and the ABA did contribute some funding, but it was never their centerpiece, although it rated some space in annual reports and newsletters. The ABA constantly used language which reflected their worries about finding "a communications strategy to ensure that all Aboriginal Australians are provided with information on the Bicentenary in a relevant and culturally sensitive format," and they formed a National Aboriginal and Torres Strait Islanders Programme which funded community and cultural centers, sports and recreation facilities, publications, films, and plays, and promo- tional "goodwill" activities. Most bicentennial historiography and re- gional programs also made attempts to focus on Aboriginal perspectives and activities. Despite all the attempts to pre-empt or mute Aboriginal protest, Australia's bicentennial year saw boycotts, continued activism, and increased discussion of Aboriginal issues.[21]

So central constructions of national identity, in the bicentennials as in the centennials, were created within an arena of oppositional cultural claims, and bicentennial organizers were influenced by some of these critical claims as they tried to develop languages of inclusion, as their predecessors in the centennials had been.[22] As in the centennials, national divisions seemed more immediate and more threatening to the project of American organizers than to Australians. But, compared with the centen- nials, criticisms of bicentennial national identity came from different directions. Whereas in the centennials regional divisions were most critical to organizers, bicentennial organizers tended to worry most about critical claims from ethnic and racial groups. The claims of feminist critics were also relevant to bicentennial organizers, more than they had been even in the United States in 1876 and certainly more than in Australia's centennial. US organizers were also faced with strong critics among New Left youth activists.[23]

Like the centennials, then, the bicentennials encouraged many and various reflections on national identity in both the United States and Australia. Although they were quickly forgotten, they left a surprising number and wide variety of documents, expressing both the organizational and the symbolic dimensions of a massive cultural mobilization around claims about national identity. Like the records of the centennials, these documents are no random selection of reflections about national identity, but rather they represent claims about national identity made by celebration promoters, and the groups they mobilized or antagonized. In analyzing national identity in the bicentennials, I followed a strategy which maximized the comparability of claims and symbols used a hundred years apart (though the extended comparison will not be drawn until chapter 5): I examined most of the records of central bicentennial organizers, while also assessing the mutual influence of central claims and those of critical and peripheral groups. ARBA and the ABA left behind an enormous amount of documentation, including extensive records in many reports, minutes, promotional materials, newsletters, databases, and videos. Beyond these central organizational records, I also drew on publications of other groups participating in the activities of the year, publications of critics, and records of community celebrations.

To pursue the comparison with centennial nationalities, then, I focused on the ways the nations were imagined at the cultural center of the celebrations, but did not assume these formulations as "common culture," but rather as organizers' best efforts at finding symbols plausible to very differentiated and sometimes critical audiences. Where alternative and oppositional discussions of national identity were available, they suggested more of the context within which dominant formulations of national identity were constructed, and whether the dominant themes were widely shared. Where themes were similar, they gave added weight to the importance of symbols adopted by bicentennial organizers; where alternative and oppositional groups did not seem to share themes with organizers, the examination of expressions of national identity beyond the cultural center suggested that the importance of central symbols of national identity should be qualified.

Although records available from the nineteenth- and twentieth-century celebrations are comparable as records of attempted cultural mobilizations, and I drew from the full range of records left by the bicentennials, bicentennial records also allowed more systematic sampling than did those left by centennial organizers, and I took advantage of this development. Both ARBA and the ABA published newsletters to promote the celebrations, and while all these newsletters were among the full range of bicentennial documents I examined in drawing the thematic comparisons, my conclusions about dominant repertoires of national identity in bicentennials are also supported by a more systematic examination of themes of national identity in a random sample of stories from 1976 or 1988 in these newsletters. Both newsletters were promotional in tone, and written for the public. The American newsletter, the *Bicentennial Times*, was a monthly, 12–18-page publication with a peak circulation of 400,000. The random sample of seventy-eight stories represents about 10 percent of the stories in the year's issues. The Australian newsletter, *Bicentenary '88*, was a quarterly, 20–40-page publication, with stories a little more in the genre of news-magazine articles than the newspaper articles of the *Bicentennial Times*. Its circulation (or, more circumspectly in later reports, "print run") reached a peak of 130,000 in 1988. It was distributed free to "libraries, historical societies, service clubs, companies, tourist bodies, interested individuals, and mayors." The random sample of forty stories from the 1988 issues which forms the basis of the comparison represents a sample of slightly under 20 percent of the stories for that year.[24] In analyzing the newsletter stories I identified the themes which implicitly or explicitly provided the basis for the story's relevance to the celebrations, assessing the grounding of claims about imagined national unity of past, present, or future. Newsletter stories often made several different implicit or explicit claims about national identity, and so I also examined how different symbolic representations of the nation were linked. I also compared the way stories on the same topic were framed in each country, the different sorts of rhetorical appeals, and the way the topics were developed.[25]

But while the sample from bicentennial newsletters allowed some more systematic examination of bicentennial themes by comparison with the centennials, the stories in the newsletters were only the tip of an iceberg of materials. They drew their concerns and their topics from much broader programs, and their language was amplified in pamphlets, videos, speeches, and reports. This full range of bicentennial reflections remains important because it is more comparable to the range of documents reflecting centennial concerns, and because it gives more insight on the context within which central themes of national identity were formulated in each country. It also shows more about similarities and differences between Australian and American bicentennial national identities. I turn to the full range of documents produced on the occasions of the bicentennials to point to possibilities in each country's language of national identity which did not become the dominant themes they were in the other country. In many instances, a theme or symbol of national identity stressed by organizers in the United States was available but infrequently used in Australia, and vice versa. These "recessive" themes did not appear often enough to be sampled, but they are significant for what they show about the alternative possibilities in each language of national identity. When similar symbols are available, what makes some more appealing, plausible, or meaningful than others? The comparison of national identities expressed in American and Australian bicentennials, drawing on a wide range of documents produced on each occasion, is a further step in answering this question.

How, then, were international position, national histories, and shared community foundations imagined in these bicentennials? How did bicentennial national identities compare, and how had they changed since the centennials?

Nation and world

Imagining the recognition of other nations was an important part of the way organizers framed their idea of the nation in both countries during the bicentennials. Thus, Australia's governor-general said of one celebration that it "expresses our high resolve for our nation's future as Australia enters its third century as part of the world community of nations." And in their last newsletter, American organizers quoted President Ford's claim that the bicentennial "became a joyous reaffirmation of all that it means to be Americans, a confirmation before all the world of the vitality and durability of our free institutions." The rhetoric differed in some significant ways, but the point of mentioning the nation's place in the world was the same.[26]

In the centennials, envisioning membership in a world of nations had been a crucial dimension of the discursive field within which national identity was constructed. Australians thought frequently of the way "our nation's star / shines clear afar" and Americans of "our country by the world received." Both countries had organized international exhibitions as one established form of national celebration. International exhibitions demanded attention to the rest of the world; was the importance of international attention in cultures of national identity an artefact of this form? Would international attention have been less important if some other form of national celebration had been adopted? Of course, neither country needed to have chosen to hold an international exhibition in the late nineteenth century, and the fact that they did so (in the face of many problems) goes some way to confirming the importance of the international sphere in talk of national identity. Further, international attention was widely imagined in reflections unconnected with the exhibitions. But even more confirmation of the significance of the international sphere, independent of nineteenth-century exhibitions, emerges in the bicentennials. For organizers of these twentieth-century events, discussion of national identity still entailed reference to international standing. Achieving the recognition of other nations was part of the cultural task organizers of bicentennials in both countries set themselves, even a century after the big exhibitions.[27]

So the international confirmation of national identity was still an important aspect of the national imagination a hundred years after the centennials. The forms in which this was articulated were quite different: florid poetry, classically imagined emblems, and long speeches gave way to snappy headlines, gifts, and performers' tours. The symbolic repertoire available to express this dimension of national identity thinned too; there was no longer any talk of identification with other nations, identifications which had been crucial in the Australian centennial and important at the cultural center in the American centennial. International confirmation of national identity was imagined only through recognition, and no longer by identification.

There was also an important difference in the salience of international regard for national identity between the United States and Australia. Whereas in the centennials, this aspect of national identity had been equally important in each country, though in slightly different ways, international recognition was much more significant to Australians than Americans organizing the bicentennials. International recognition became a core part of Australian national identity as it was organized in the bicentenary, a theme governing the relevance of other themes; in the United States, it was simply part of the appropriate ritual. Despite these differences, an international theme, a theme of self presentation to and recognition by other nations, remained a feature of organizers' promotion of the commemorations in both countries.

In both bicentennial newsletters, international gifts, events, performances, and commentary were enthusiastically noted. Some typical American stories are captured in the symbolically busy headlines "Japanese Bonsai Trees Gift: Living Works of Art," "Brass Bands from Britain End US Tour," "Lincoln Honored in Cantata Offered as Argentine Gift for Bicentennial," and "Bicen Communities Asked to Honor German City That Helped Wm Penn." Similarly Australians noted Britain's gift of a "sail-training brigantine, the Young Endeavour," and the "$US5-million USA Gallery – America's national Bicentennial gift to Australia." Smaller marks of recognition were noted too, like stamps of "tiny Caribbean Isles" or a book written by a Sri Lankan diplomat about links between his country and Australia. Both countries also noted international participation in major patriotic events. In the tall ships spectacular on Sydney Harbour on Australia Day "in a breathtaking climax to an historic voyage, Poland's sail training vessel *Dar Mlodziezy* made a dramatic entry ... under full sail." And the "mammoth Fourth of July 'Parade of Sail' into New York Harbor" took place against a "magnificent backdrop of sixty international naval review ships."[28]

But international recognition was given added weight in the rhetoric of the Australian organizers. In the Australian rhetoric, international participation added extra status to the celebration of national identity. As the final annual report revealingly described the many projects endorsed by the ABA: "quality and variety was in evidence too with a complete range and high proportion of international projects and events." The international dimension seemed to guarantee the quality and variety. And a sort of status anxiety was let slip in a minor pamphlet about an International Mathematical Olympiad: "Australia is more than qualified to play the role of hosting international events." Recognition was sought, too, beyond normal diplomatic arrangements. For instance, in one major national program – headlined "Top Artists Take Oz To The World" – "international tours by twenty-one of Australia's top performing companies and artists . . . [were] taking place at major festivals and special seasons planned for the United Kingdom, North America, and Europe."[29]

The American *Bicentennial Times* occasionally noted activities overseas, but rarely were these activities of Americans: rather, they were stories of foreigners marking links, as in the story "Brazilians Join in Salute to US" describing "an exhibit in the heart of Sao Paolo . . . [in which Brazilians] emphasized American history, culture and technology, and highlighted the many links between Brazil and the United States." Recognition was not so much sought, as it was in the Australian arts program, as offered. And the few stories featuring the activities of Americans overseas discussed military bases, as in the "military community of Kitzingen in West Germany" which "conducted a Bicentennial hike" and "issued Bicentennial medals commemorating Mount Rushmore" – "with the participation of their German friends." Themes of recognition were not generalized, as they were for the Australians, but invoked only where they were clearly politic. Further, international links were predominantly a theme of central organizers, and not at all a part of the celebration as seen by critics and in communities. Events with an international tone did occur locally – Raleigh, North Carolina, registered as a bicentennial community activity "The British are Coming! British Military Band Performance," for example – but they were rare.[30]

The different salience of the quest for recognition in the "World Community of Nations" is suggested, then, by the way the meaning of international recognition was conveyed by commemoration organizers: simply as news appropriate to the event, in the United States, and much more frequently and anxiously, in Australia. The quest was more conspicuous in Australian national identity than in the talk during the American bicentennial. This is part of the explanation for an odd difference in the celebration of the two bicentennials: sport was both rhetorically and organizationally important in the Australian bicentennial, but it was almost entirely absent in the official organization of the American bicentennial.

Sport was an important topic of Australian bicentennial newsletter stories, and rated a special ABA program of events and promotions. Early on in planning for the bicentenary an "International Festival of Sport" was mooted, a festival which would "attract a medley of international sporting events with strong spectator appeal to Australia in 1988." By the end Australian organizers touted their SPORT '88 program as "attract[ing] the best athletes in the world" and as allowing sports organizations to show their capabilities to "the rest of the world." Almost every newsletter story about sports emphasized international prestige, describing international events in a variety of often obscure sports organized on the occasion of the bicentenary: "World Series Draws Top Cyclists" ran a typical headline. Along with news of competition conditions and performance found in any sports report, there was sometimes a claim about the link between sport and national identity: "The Australian Socceroos' surprise triumph over favourites Argentina . . . brought an enthusiastic and revitalised interest in the sport and national pride in the local team." But very often, sports stories elaborately described imagined international recognition with scarcely any reference to Australia itself. To central organizers in Australia, it seemed to be the existence of international sporting competition, rather than Australian superiority or even Australian performance, which made sport relevant in their expression of Australian national identity.[31]

By contrast, American bicentennial organizers hardly ever mentioned sports. The only mention of sport in the American newsletter sample was made in a minor way in a story about the celebration of the Fourth of July in "Bicentennial Communities." In this story, among references to various spectacles, parades, exhibits, citizenship events, and religious services, ARBA rather ambiguously noted that "Fourth of July sporting events are being planned all over the country, although ARBA's information would indicate otherwise [sic]."[32] The absence of sports stories in the American newsletter is puzzling at first: sports seems a vernacular interest which may well have proved as useful a vehicle for talk of the nation in the United States as in Australia, and American nationalism has been evident in international sports competition such as the Olympics. Of course, the most popular American sports are probably even less internationally widespread than Australian ones. Perhaps more directly influential in this instance, a prohibition against directly commercial promotions in the use of bicentennial symbols, and the commercial basis of most American sporting organizations, encouraged this absence, disallowing an organized program of bicentennial sporting events of the sort that was important in Australia.

But the framing of most Australian sporting stories so definitively as instances for international regard also further reinforces the fact that although international relations were important in defining national identity in both countries, this dimension of national discourse was much more important to Australians.[33]

The elaborate description of imagined international recognition, with scarcely any reference to Australia itself, was evident in other sorts of stories too. Like international sporting competition, international conferences were noted by Australian bicentennial organizers, rating a separate section in ABA annual reports. They noted, for example, the "International Fire Science '88 Conference," describing speakers from NASA, Northern Ireland, Paris, Hong Kong, Denmark, and New Zealand, and concluding: "these and other speakers will give the bi-annual conference . . . extra oomph for the Bicentenary." And they noted, too, a tourism conference which "has ensured that the 1,500 delegates from forty different countries will return to their homes with vivid impressions of Australia." Their concern with international regard is epitomized in a story about the visit of a sail-training ship from Colombia ("More Tall Ships Fever in Sydney"). Much of the story was devoted to the ship's voyages and purposes. A couple of paragraphs described a "Bicentennial message from Colombia's President." The only references to Australia came in mentions of the popularity of the ship (as in the headline) and in the Colombian message itself. What is reported of this message seems particularly diplomatic: "even young nations like Australia offer valuable contributions to the inheritance of civilization." It was a reassuring message, one which there is a lot of evidence to suggest the Australians wished to hear. As Australian celebrity historian Manning Clark put it in a nationwide bicentennial broadcast at New Year, "I believe we Australians can make a contribution to the conversation of humanity."[34]

A hundred years earlier, talk of position in the world had expressed national identity in both "new nations." International recognition was more important to Americans, and identification with powerful others more important to Australians, to ground their national identities, but both elements existed in both symbolic repertoires available to talk about national identity. By the late twentieth century, identification was not, in general, a plausible way to talk about national identity in either country. But some expression of place in the world still seemed intrinsic to the organization of celebrations of national identity, and this took the form of claims about international recognition. "Reference societies" remained important in grounding expressions of national identity.

While the international dimension of expressions of national identity remained significant in both countries, it was much more salient to Australian than to American bicentennial organizers; there was much greater differentiation in the use of symbols of international attention in each bicentennial than there had been in the centennials. The symbolic resonance of the recognition of other nations was dampened in the United States while it remained powerful for Australian organizers. In the century between the events, Australia had been formally federated as a nation, and its close colonial relations with Britain had gradually attenuated; but it remained economically and geopolitically semi-peripheral within the world of nation-states. The United States, on the other hand, had moved from a comparatively marginal world position to a more independent economic and geopolitical position. The differing relevance of international recognition suggests that the nation's place in the world is indeed a matter of greater concern where it is in some sense a dependent one. Similar differences in the importance of other nations to national identities have been found by Lipset in comparing Canada and the United States; evidence from decolonizing nations, like mid-century Burma and the Solomon Islands more recently, also seems to confirm the importance of international regard for claims about national identity.[35] If commemoration organizers in Australia found international recognition a more plausible way of imagining unity than their peers did in the United States, then, this was partly because they had more reason to wonder about their self-presentation.

The United States seems unusual, in 1976, in the culturally thin way it thematized international recognition. Recognition had been much more important a century earlier; and it remained much more important to Australians. Relative world position had shifted. But for organizers of the 1976 celebration, there was also a more immediate concern: internal political fissures which seemed to threaten the very possibility of claims about shared nationality. In the American bicentennial, issues of internal weakness were more conspicuous than international strengths. These threats to cultural integration demanded elaborated reflection about shared history and about community foundations.

Shared experience and imagined community

The nation in time

"Rhode Island, Alive with Colonial History, Begins Colorful Celebrations in May," the *Bicentennial Times* recounted. The long article described a variety of events – races, re-enactments, balls, and visits – with many historical allusions to the symbols, relics, and events of the revolutionary period:

Newport, Rhode Island's colonial capital, will be the scene of a re-enactment of the famous Stamp Act Riot on May 1 in historic Old Colony House, the nation's second oldest capitol building where such giants of the Revolutionary War as Washington, Jefferson, Count de Rochambeau, and the Marquis de Lafayette were entertained.

In the same genre, Australia's *Bicentenary '88* noted the marking of the bicentenary on Norfolk Island, introducing the story with a historical reminder:

Forty-one days after Arthur Phillip strode ashore at Sydney Cove and established the first British settlement in the Antipodes, Philip Gidley King rowed into Sydney Bay, Norfolk Island, and established the second.

This version of history was woven into stories of the legacy of the celebrations too; the American newsletter told of a "program which will encourage public review of the most significant achievements of the Revolutionary period," and in Australia a story about a new Parliament House which would be "a place of inspiration to all Australians" referred to "the first reactions of Europeans to the appearance of the land, and the hopes and aspirations of the early settlers."[36]

As in the centennials, talk of shared history was an intrinsic dimension of the affirmation of national identity in the bicentennial commemorations. Compared to the centennials, though, the symbolic repertoires in which history was expressed showed important differences, and greater divergence between countries. In neither country was there much talk of progress or the future; these no longer seemed plausible ways of grounding shared nationality in either country in the late twentieth century.[37] And the two "new nation" histories were imagined much more differently in the bicentennials than they had been in 1876 and 1888.

Founding moments and critical claims

Historical experience was more salient in the American bicentennial; and to American organizers and their critics, their "founding moment" remained a robust symbol grounding claims about national identity, as significant in 1976 as it had been in 1876. History was more frequently mentioned by American bicentennial organizers because they took every opportunity to mention the "founding moment" of the revolutionary period. Stories of the late eighteenth-century history were most typical in organizers' historical view – stories of George Washington's letters, revolutionary militia, or Italian influences on Jefferson's architecture. Even when newsletter writers selected community history as their topic, it was often history from this period, as in a story of the restoration of a colonial courthouse in York, PA. And for the American organizers, the founding moment became a central theme which could ease the introduction of other topics, such as the recognition of international or minority contributions to imagined community. The "Revolution Inspires Winners of France–US Art Contest," it was claimed, and "Stamps of Tiny Caribbean Isles Honor US Founders, Including Black Hero."[38]

For Australians, on the other hand, the power of "founding moment" formulations had evaporated, and most historical references by Australian bicentennial organizers appealed instead to the two hundred years since the first British settlement. There were innumerable variations on the reference to revolutionary history of the Rhode Island article; the reference to Captain Phillip's first settlement was rare, and even in that story there was a quick transition to a more diffuse historical review. Australian organizers introduced historical allusions only casually; for them, the reference to history seemed just a part of the cultural task of the celebration, whereas for the Americans, it was independently significant.[39] What accounts for the dropping of this historical formulation from the Australian repertoire of symbols of national identity, and, equally important, the persistence of the American founding moment symbols?

Certainly, the founding of Australia as a British penal colony was inglorious, but it might have been too embarrassing in 1888, too, particularly because, at that time, the fact that the first settlers were mostly convicts was still humiliating.[40] In the Australian centennial, the founding moment was often mentioned despite its problems, and it developed many symbolic resonances for all sorts of speakers. The centennial formulations were still used in the sesquicentenary in 1938, in which a central focus of the celebration was precisely the heroic vision of the founding, along with the glory of the progress since. In 1938, the "founder" was imagined speaking his vision: "I see the inhabitants of this great country of the future reflecting with pride and gratitude upon the era of progress of which we this day lay the foundation." This heroic vision was strongly linked to imperial attachments in the minds of sesquicentenary organizers.[41]

Even in 1988, there were still ways the Australian organizers might have spoken more frequently of their founding moment. When, very occasionally, official speeches and broadcasts demanded some mention of European settlement in 1788, they adopted what had been the dominant image at the time of the centennial: they noted the fragile beginnings of the country, the harshness and uncertainty of life, and contrasted it to the achievement since. As a nationwide broadcast on January 1 concluded,

We began as a dumping ground 200 years ago. It wasn't glorious. There was no milk and honey, no promise of streets paved with gold, no dream of a better place to live. Never was a country founded in so much pain . . . But even in the midst of so much loneliness, so much suffering, the stirrings of independence and pride began.

And there were other ways available to commemorate the founding moment, though these too were rarely adopted and little noticed. Speakers could also integrate the founding moment in Australian identity by referring to European settlement as one among successive waves of immigration. This convenient cyclical framing, although diffusing somewhat the impact of European settlement, made room for mentioning early Aboriginal and later non-British immigration, and it drew resonance in association with talk of diversity and multiculturalism.[42]

Another available formulation was illustrated in one very obscure event of 1988, a 250th anniversary marking the birth of Captain Phillip, the leader of the First Fleet and founder of the first convict settlement, or as the private organizers of the event described him, "the Father and Founder of Australia." (This was listed as an endorsed activity in the huge compilation of bicentennial events by the ABA but received no other official notice.) Phillip's personal heroism was praised, and, addressing a prominent contemporary issue, it was noted that he worked unsuccessfully for a treaty with the Aborigines. As the organizers told it:

Phillip founded a Colony that has grown into a great Nation, with competence, ability, compassion, and understanding. He tried to help and understand the Aboriginal People . . . and tried in 1793, on his return to England ill and emaciated, to get a Treaty for the Aborigines. Sadly the dream was not realized.

The anniversary service, which involved "nearly five years of planning," was solemn, nationalistic, and strongly focused on the founding moment of European settlement. Although it should not be taken as either representative or consequential in its reassertion of a traditional Anglocentric view of Australia's founding, this obscure ritual commemorating the personal heroism of the insignificant European invader further illustrates that the Australian founding moment was not, in principle, unspeakable by 1988. It also indicates, though, why Australian organizers did not adopt this language.[43]

Australian organizers avoided talk of the first settlement they were commemorating because they feared, from the beginning, the opposition it would evoke from Aboriginal activists and their supporters, who called

Australia Day "Invasion Day" and demonstrated accordingly. Contemporary critics gave Australian organizers good reason not to make too much of the founding moment. Events like the Captain Phillip anniversary and the First Fleet Re-enactment were privately organized and sponsored, and treated just as any other event among the myriad activities different groups had organized for the year: if organizers had made them central events, they would have been lightning rods for even more dissent by Aboriginal critics and their supporters than the bicentennial did ultimately attract.

But whereas Australian organizers quickly abandoned a founding moment vision of history in the face of critical claims, American organizers clung to a founding moment vision as they faced their critics, and it provided the grounds for some of those very critical claims, too. When anti-war and racial conflicts were at their height, youth activists meeting with worried bicentennial organizers in 1971 charged that "there is nothing to celebrate" (and also that the organization "was not representative of the American people," that it "should disband," and that "all efforts should center around wiping out hunger").[44] In the face of dissension like this, some organizers argued for an even greater stress on founding moment history than the national group ultimately adopted. California bicentennial organizers argued early on, for instance, that "there is a need to restore the patriotic feeling in children through original historic documents of our Country and not the interpretation of these." They suggested a touring exhibition of "paintings of the American Revolution," and the propagation of copies of historic documents. National history was very assertively imagined, even by elites in California, as that of the Revolution and the founding fathers, in the face of national dissension. Indeed, the California organizers were worried that the commission in Washington was watering down the national identity they wanted to claim: they feared that "the national American Revolution Bicentennial Commission is giving consideration to plans which either minimize or bypass . . . [these ideas]" and tried to put things back on the right track with their suggestion about reprinting documents of the founding moment and the founding fathers.[45]

And one of the most active critical groups of the 1976 bicentennial appealed as much to founding moment history as organizers did. Jeremy Rifkin, of the People's Bicentennial Commission, argued, for instance, that "what we need in this country is a new patriotic movement to restore the same kind of spirit that our Founding Fathers employed 200 years ago against the wealthy aristocracy, against the privileged families and wealthy institutions." As titles of PBC publications and activities, like *Commonsense II* and the "Boston Oil Party," indicate, the PBC relied extensively on founding moment symbols to make their critical claims. The PBC urged people to reclaim these national symbols: "to challenge the official Bicentennial observance . . . with the words and deeds of the American revolutionary patriots." Their alternative guide to bicentennial celebration gave elaborate recognition to founding moment symbols: "the Fourth of July may be a Bob Hope Special now, but once it was a truly revolutionary holiday . . . a *true* People's Patriotic Celebration might be . . . a chance . . . to celebrate a common heritage, a colorful and theatrical presentation of the Revolutionary principles of 1776." They recommended celebrating Tom Paine's birthday, the Boston Massacre, Patrick Henry's "give me liberty or give me death" speech, Thomas Jefferson's birthday, the battles of Lexington and Concord, the Declaration of Independence, Sam Adams's birthday, and the Boston Tea Party, as well as "days when something of historical importance happened in your community." This group of critics appealed as much to founding moment history as did the organizers of the 1976 celebration.[46]

Two hundred years

So founding moment history remained a strong symbolic ground for critical as well as for dominant claims in the American bicentennial, as it had been in the centennial. Australian organizers, on the other hand, downplayed the founding moment, even though this had been an important mark of national identity in their centennial. When they spoke about history, Australian organizers referred more casually to a variety of symbols drawn from the entire two hundred years of European settlement. A story about a "Facelift for Historical Sites," for example, alluded to hunger marches of the Depression, to an old trade route, and so on, as well as to Sydney's founding. Similarly, the story of a historic records search mixed references to politicians, singers, a goldfields rebellion, an exploration journal, and women in history with the brief mention of a hero from the founding. This vision of history was eclectic, simply part of the cultural task of the celebration: many of the infinite possible historical allusions would do to define a commonality. Even more typical was the use of a reference to history as a rhetorical device in a story of a different sort; an anthology of Greek writers prompted reference to Australia's history of immigration, for example, and news of an air race noted pioneer aviators in the outback.[47]

There were few references to the actual occasion of commemoration in the Australian celebration, but neither were there other central historical moments defining national identity. Most referents were not specific to any aspect of the two hundred years, and others invoked many various sorts of history. The Australian bicentennial story had to be told with history; imagining a shared past was part of the cultural task involved, one dimension of the discursive field within which claims about national identity were shaped. But no episode was particularly conspicuous in that history, and the choice of histories was governed not by national identity itself but by which *other* stories there were to tell.

If Australian organizers tended to avoid their founding moment, American bicentennial organizers were comparatively silent on the two hundred years since the Revolution. They did occasionally refer to aspects of the nation's history beyond the founding moment, as the Australians did: there were reports on "colorful garage-door paintings depicting symbols of the nation's 200-year history," for instance, and about how "Texas Panhandle Recalls Story of Pioneers," and reports of a ceremony celebrating General Greeley, who "supervised the massive extension of military telegraph lines in the West in the 1870s." But these general invocations of history as part of the celebration of national identity were less important, and less frequent, than references to the American founding moment. Two hundred years was worth mentioning sometimes, but it was far less significant than the revolutionary period to organizers of the American celebration. Even taking for granted the power of the Revolution in American collective memory, this absence seems worth noting. As historian John Bodnar has observed in another context, "ARBA treated the American Revolution as the end of history."[48]

Yet the framing of history in Australia – with no focus on a particular period or group – was a theme with vernacular appeal available to American organizers. In the decades before 1976, as Michael Kammen has shown, there was increasing grassroots and vernacular attention to local history and preservation in the United States, and vernacular history was widely celebrated in local bicentennial celebrations. The "general" and local history more typical of the dominant Australian construction of national identity was more common in the way the American communities chose to celebrate the bicentennial than celebrations of the founding moment. In the centennial, there was some evidence that the salience of the founding moment extended to quite a popular level. The evidence from the bicentennial suggests, by contrast, that local communities paid much less attention to founding moment history than did organizers or their activist critics. Almost twice as many themes in ARBA newsletter stories as in community activities seemed to develop founding moment history; almost twice as many symbolic appeals in community activity listings as in ARBA newsletter stories made other sorts of historical references. Different sorts of histories seemed to be celebrated in local communities. Historical themes of community activities were local and, as a consequence, less periodized: the celebration of the nation was marked by a history of a school district, a memorial trail, an "old settlers' fest." The differences in symbolic history were no contradiction of ARBA aims: indeed, they were, to some extent, encouraged. But there was no intrinsic reason why historical symbolism could not have been more deeply shared: if Riverbank, CA, could hold a "Paul Revere Ride," similar possibilities were available to other communities. The differentiation in constructions of history between cultural center and periphery in the celebration was marked; and critics were closer to their opponents than to local community celebrations.[49]

In the bicentennials as in the centennials, shared experience over time was an important part of what it meant to be a nation. Symbols of history and claims about historical experience were frequently mentioned in talk about what members of each nation shared. There was some persistence in the sorts of national symbols which could express shared history, but also several important changes in symbolic repertoires. In both countries, there were few references to progress compared to the centennial; this was no longer a plausible way of imagining historical experience. Also lost were visions of the future, which had been powerful in Australia in 1888 and important to some in the American centennial.

The symbolic power of the American Revolution has long been noted, and it was mobilized for imagined unity once again in 1976, with the spin of contemporary claims – to include "lesser-known women of the Revolution," and "black hero[es]." Symbolism of the revolutionary period seemed as compelling to bicentennial critics as to organizers. American history since the late eighteenth century had little resonance with bicentennial organizers, though it was more important than founding moment history in local communities.

Australians no longer talked much about their founding moment; in comparison to the American Revolution, it did not have enough symbolic power to resist critical claims. As Chilla Bulbeck has shown in studying Australian monument construction, "challenges to orthodox history" had been leading to a "reorientation of Australian history from the deeds that won the empire or nation to the activities of ordinary men and women and the history of local communities." But general and local history had also been re-invigorated in the United States in the period before the bicentennial; and, on the other hand, there were heroic framings of the Australian founding moment available, if not politically feasible. Founding moment claims could not be mobilized by Australian bicentennial organizers in 1988, because, in contrast to the American bicentennial in 1976, these claims could no longer mediate official and oppositional views, and fell to Aboriginal critique. A similar weakness in the appeal of this sort of founding moment also became evident in the attempts to commemorate the Columbian Quincentenary in the United States.[50]

Many students of collective memory, recognizing what Barry Schwartz has called the "social context of commemoration," have debated the extent to which the past can be reconfigured according to contemporary issues and concerns. Much evidence exists to show the constant reinterpretations and frequent elisions in collective memory: yet some also argue that the past is not made anew, and search for the conditions which encourage the persistence of some symbols of shared past over others. The persistence and importance of the American Revolution as historic symbol of shared national identity, especially in official and critical discourse among elites, seems to suggest that this historic symbol is powerful and persistent because it provides grounding for critical as well as official claims about national identity: it can cross important political divisions at moments when claims about sharing are appropriate. The Australian founding moment, by contrast, while it was symbolically powerful in the late nineteenth century (despite the embarrassment it also created then) because of the importance of links to empire, could not survive the onslaught of critical claims in 1988.[51]

Shared qualities of imagined community

Inventing shared community, the organizers of these patriotic celebrations also reiterated foundations of national identity which were relatively abstract and nominally inclusive. International recognition and shared historical experience helped ground claims about nationality; but there were also ways of symbolizing more directly what "we" could be claimed, with least quarrel, to share. Shared horizontal links between members of the population, which could most plausibly transcend notable differences, included political values, the land, diversity, and the spectacle of the celebration itself.

In the centennial celebrations, the two countries had both claimed to be free and prosperous; liberty and prosperity were frequently contemplated and elaborated as collective qualities of both "the United States" and "Australia," and devices by which community could be imagined across internal boundaries. Liberty had been emphasized more in the United States, and prosperity in Australia, but both themes were widespread in both countries. The use of "the land" as a way of symbolizing national identity was less frequent in the centennials than symbols related to liberty or prosperity, but occasionally evident in both countries and slightly more frequently mentioned in Australia.

Appealing to imagined community foundations, general and inclusive qualities which all citizens could be said to share, remained important in the bicentennials. The symbolic repertoire expressing community foundations changed significantly in both countries, though, and more significantly in Australia than in the United States. By the time of the bicentennials, the two countries were more differentiated in the ways they could plausibly express imagined community foundations. In neither country was prosperity an important symbol of national identity; like progress, this was no longer a plausible way to talk about what members of each nation shared. The theme of liberty, so important in a number of variants in both countries in the late nineteenth century, was still important to American bicentennial organizers, but political values and institutions no longer provided compelling grounds for claims about imagined community in Australia. References to the land as characteristic of the nation became central in Australia; they were not relevant to American bicentennial organizers, though the land was important at the local level in the United States. And two new ways of symbolizing what "we" share entered the vocabulary of celebration organizers in both countries; they appealed to symbols of diversity, and to the experience of the celebration itself.

Shared political values and institutions

In the bicentennial as in the centennial, the United States was, to celebration organizers, the "sweet land of liberty." Australian organizers, though, no longer spoke much of "a land of freedom, free in church and school," as they had done in 1888, and might have continued to do. Comparative studies of "settler nations" have sometimes inferred differences in national identity from differences in political culture. Political values have frequently been seen as constitutive of American national identity, and the centennials and bicentennials confirm their symbolic power for American ritual organizers aiming to mediate diverse particular identities. But the bicentennials also suggest that evidence about political culture relevant to discussions of American national identity may be misleading for understanding of national identities elsewhere, even in similar countries: political culture should be conceptually distinguished from national identity in public cultures. The comparison also suggests that national identity should not simply be equated with what Greenfeld saw as the crucial defining characteristic of nationalism, the perceived absence of status orders formally relevant to political community. While national community could not have been imagined without the capacity to imagine political equality, this was not particularly salient to Australians. Shared political values and symbols are not always or necessarily adopted as defining features of the "imagined community" of the nation, even though they may be a formal condition of that imagined community and even though, as the United States shows, they may become significant in some circumstances.[52]

American bicentennial organizers often spoke of activities expressing liberal political values when they spoke of the bicentennial. Liberal political values were taken to characterize the national community, as in this story of a challenge to register more voters ("New 'Votingest City' Challenge Goes Out"): "Join us, challenge us. Celebrate the heart of the American experience – a free nation governed by free people casting their free vote." There were many other bicentennial activities concerned with liberal political values which the *Bicentennial Times* found worth noting, like a public service information campaign on privacy rights – "although the Constitution did not mention the term 'privacy,' a constitutional right to privacy has long been implicitly accepted" – and other education and discussion activities – "'Original States' to Probe Constitutional Application," "Town Meetings Undergoing a Revival." Citizenship weeks and ceremonies were also treated as bicentennial observances. Political themes also appeared frequently in other stories of celebration. Communities were urged to join a bell-ringing ceremony "to let the sound of every bell ... ring out to declare our freedoms and signify our unity." And organizers claimed that "permeating the unprecedented surge of celebrative activity is a strong spirit of renewal and appreciation of the principles set forth in the Declaration of Independence, the Constitution, and the Bill of Rights."[53]

Such claims to found unity on shared political values often coincided with expressions of the imagined recognition of other countries. They were also closely linked with a view of history emphasizing the founding moment of the Revolution. As in the centennial, and like founding moment history, shared political values made core symbols for organizers of the bicentennial, and they were important for critics too. Early in bicentennial planning, indeed, the working title of the celebration had been "Festival of Freedom"; but this title, too rich a ground for critical claims, became more ambiguous as plans developed. (As the minutes of the California Commission recorded one worried member noting, in 1970, "the title should be 'Festival of Liberty' ... the Founding Fathers emphasized liberty, which refers to the spirit rather than freedom.") The People's Bicentennial

Commission made as much of appeals to founding political values in their critical claims about national identity as it did of appeals to the founding moment of the Revolution.[54]

There is less evidence, however, that political values and institutions were core symbols of national identity in more local celebrations. Listings of community activities and events seemed to show little of the preoccupation with political values evident in the writings of national organizers and their critics. No doubt, some such events existed, and no doubt, too, political identity was expressed in some events listed with other themes. Indeed, *Bicentennial Times* writers tended to select for national reporting some localized activities with political themes – like New York students meeting to rewrite the Constitution, for example, and a Wisconsin poll to find out what citizens think of government. Political themes were also relatively frequent in schoolchildren's bicentennial essays. But the organizers of the bicentennial were making no random selection from community events when they noticed such activities, because in community celebrations, political values and institutions were not emphasized as frequently as they were by bicentennial organizers and their critics.[55]

Although Australians in the late nineteenth century considered themselves among the most politically advanced nations on earth, and political identity was then a frequently reiterated part of their national identity, political values were not relevant to bicentennial organizers in Australia a hundred years later. They hardly ever referred to national political values and institutions. Very occasional claims about national political values were made in a few major speeches, in some comments by foreigners and immigrants, and in bicentennial videos produced for schools. But such claims only illustrated that languages were available in which the Australian national identity might have been characterized in political terms; in fact, in 1988 Australia's national identity was not grounded in its liberal political values or institutions. Epitomizing this absence was a report by bicentenary organizers on the opening of a new Parliament House in Canberra in 1988, a new and distinctive political center. The Australian Bicentennial Authority's report of the opening – which was not a particularly popular or well-attended event – provided one of the few occasions on which organizers mentioned political values, and even then their reference was cursory. In an American context, a story about a new legislative center, planned since nationhood and planned to last another two hundred years, would have been filled with claims about the political foundation of the nation.[56]

The land

Instead of political values and institutions, the opening of Australia's new Parliament House evoked for Australian bicentennial organizers reflections about the land. Reporting the opening, an ABA publicist reiterated geographic themes. She quoted an "eminent historian": "the building emerges from the land of Australia. It rises up out of the land and the people." How it was "integrated into its site and surroundings" was a topic for detailed comment, and in the art commissioned for it, "the theme of the land is prominent, beginning with the pivotal Aboriginal mosaic in the Forecourt . . . [which] depicts a meeting place and is intended to symbolize the continent of Australia."

It was characteristic that these references to the land should be so frequent in a story about Australia's new political center. As those who reflect on Australian national identity have long noted, symbolic geography has been a central theme of reflections on what it means to be Australian. References to geography and the environment were much more common in the Australian bicentennial talk than they were in the American bicentennial. For Australian organizers, the continent, the land, its extent, and its inhospitability became foundational in the way political values were in the American organizers' vision of community.[57]

For instance, the land was an important part of the answer to the "$64,000 question" put by one bicentennial publicist: "what does it mean to be Australian?" The video suggesting answers to this question was "set against the awesome backdrop of the Australian landscape," and "viewers glimpse[d] the dry beauty of the bush, Sydney's busy harbour, and the clean lines of the sort of wave which made Australia's surf beaches famous." The land was taken to be an important part of what Australians shared with Americans, too:

We want to point out the similar origins of our two countries: both were vast, sparsely inhabited territories with long-established native populations, settled by migrants who had travelled thousands of miles in search of a better life; both offered great natural hazards of climate and terrain to be overcome; and both were separated from "home" by thousands of kilometres of water, which could only be crossed by sailing ship.[58]

It is hard to see an American writer, offered the same topic for reflection, coming up with the same sorts of ideas.

For Australians, an important part of the meaning of being identified with the continent was, paradoxically, to stress the maritime, as the story above illustrates. Among newsletter stories with a geographic theme, stories of arduous ocean voyages were quite common. Sometimes, it seemed, the repressed founding moment was displaced into more neutral stories of an endless repetition of ocean voyages. But equally typical was a story about a "GE Bicentennial Around Australia Air Race" – in which "Australia's vast red outback had definitely provided the extraordinary navigational challenge central to the event's success." Many special bicentennial activities called for epic and unlikely circumnavigations, voyages, and journeys, and these seemed thought to be, in many different contexts, a suitable way of marking the occasion. Among only the highlights of the year noted by Australian bicentennial organizers were: "Police Overland Expedition . . . gruelling 117-day trek from Darwin to Adelaide," "1961 De Havilland . . . flying 13,000 nautical miles in two months from Britain," "Macassan Prahu . . . sailing from Indonesia," "30-strong International Friendship Ride . . . five-month journey from England," "the 6,000-km, fly–drive Flag Inns Bicentennial Balloon Challenge," "Great Australian Camel Trek . . . on an epic 3,200-km journey," "the last great cattle drive, sets out on 2,000-km trek," "Around Australia Yacht Race . . . 7,000-nautical mile circumnavigation of the continent," "legendary bushman R. M. Williams opened the 5,000-kilometre Bicentennial National Trail," and "Australian Bicentennial Exhibition . . . 20,000-kilometre, history-making journey around the nation." References to the land appeared in almost all the other materials evoked by the celebration of the bicentenary, too. A new epic ballet, for example, commissioned for a bicentennial tour, "in its three parts encompassed Australia's sea, coast, red centre, and cities."[59]

Epitomizing the symbolic resonance of the land in the Australian bicentenary was a chain of "bicentennial beacons" around the continent. This event was unofficially organized but officially endorsed, and unlike the obscure 250th anniversary of the "father and founder," it was widely promoted by the ABA. Bonfires were built at 30-kilometer intervals around Australia's 15,000-kilometer coastline: according to the ABA, these bonfires became a focus for community activities. The first beacon was lit at sunset, and was the signal for the next; the bonfires moved around the continent until they returned to their starting point at dawn the next morning. Planners of the event hoped that "these Birthday Beacons will fittingly symbolise the unity of all Australians."[60]

By contrast, American bicentennial organizers only rarely referred to their land in symbolizing national identity. When they did so, the land was subsidiary to some other major theme, and the stories were predominantly stories of more vernacular, community celebration. There was occasionally talk of particular restoration projects, the renaming of a Colorado mountain, fields planted in patterns to resemble the American flag, and so on, in newsletter descriptions of local enactment of the bicentennial. And occasionally geography was used to characterize region: "The rolling prairie, dotted with cattle, an occasional windmill and beautiful wild-flowers, is what greets the eye during a visit to the Texas Panhandle." But these were rare exceptions: in the way central organizers of the American bicentennial characterized imagined community, symbolic geography was almost non-existent.[61]

There is some evidence, though, that symbolic geography was much more important beyond the cultural center of the American bicentennial celebration. The few ARBA references to the land mostly came in stories of local activities; and symbolic geography was important in local bicentennial celebrations. In the complete listings of community activities, events, and projects frequently referred to the land, to geographical and natural symbols, and the environment, and local communities often marked the American bicentennial with tree plantings, park restorations, studies of topography, conservation projects, neat lawn competitions, and so on. Historian John Bodnar has shown that a focus on the land, and heroic pioneers, has been popular in vernacular US midwestern commemorations since the late nineteenth century; the bicentennial also suggests that symbolic geography characterized American national identity much more at the vernacular level than it did at the cultural center of the national celebration.[62]

In the centennials, political values and prosperity had been important ways of symbolizing imagined community in both countries. Relatively abstract and inclusive links shared by all members of the nation were quite similar in each country. Symbols available to represent this dimension of national community altered in important ways by the time of the bicentennials, and altered more in Australia than the United States. In both countries, shared prosperity was no longer much remarked; as with the historical vision of progress, this no longer seemed a plausible or appropriate theme for national self-congratulation. Shared political values and institutions remained as important for American bicentennial organizers as they had been in 1876; there are indications, however, that these were less commonly mobilized symbols of the nation on cultural peripheries. Australians no longer spoke of political culture and institutions in their bicentennial. In the centennials, the land had been a minor theme of national identity; in the late nineteenth century, symbolic geography was only occasionally used to characterize the two countries, but it was slightly more common in claims about Australian national identity. By the time of their bicentenary, Australians had adopted symbolic geography as a major way of talking about national identity; it played the same central role as themes of political identity and prosperity had played in the Australian centennial. For American organizers, the land remained a minor element of their symbolic repertoire of national identity, as it had been in the centennial, but there is some evidence that this theme was much more significant beyond the cultural center of the celebration. Geographic distinction was not important to organizers of the American bicentennial, and political distinction was not salient to Australian organizers, but vernacular interpretations of national identity in the United States seemed closer to those of the Australian cultural center than to those of American organizers.

Both political and geographic themes provided relatively abstract and inclusive ways in which bicentennial organizers could express the links which bound imagined community in the celebrations. Programs and activities which expressed these links were important in the way organizers chose to describe their bicentennial years. Both sorts of themes created a basis for an integrated national identity which could be imagined to transcend problematic difference. There were two further ways to represent imagined community in the bicentennials; in talk of national diversity, and in talk of shared spectacle.

Diversity as national community

An important device for creating imagined community in both bicentennials was the explicit recognition of potentially problematic difference. Organizers adopted rhetoric and programs which claimed diversity as characteristic of national identity, and addressed especially those groups from whom they feared criticism. As an ABA report boasted, there was "a wide range of programs which recognized the special interest and aided the participation of different sections of the community." Similar talk of diversity and programs addressing particular groups was important in the American celebration: bicentennial organizers drew more and more, in the early 1970s, on the symbolic resources foreshadowed in a 1969 speech by President Nixon: "We have forged one nation from an extraordinary diversity of people, cultures, and traditions . . . All of this is part of the rich treasure of experience on which we must draw for the Bicentennial."[63]

In both cases, characterizing the nation as diverse was a central rhetorical strategy for representing unity across difference. It emerged in the United States in characterizing ethnic and racial differences, but spread easily both to the characterization of other collectively recognized and vocal subdivisions in the national population, and also became a central

Connect to local

theme in the different political context existing in Australia. Talk of diversity coded the recognition of women, youth, the aged, and the disabled, and regional groups, as well as ethnic and racial groups. There was little difference in the frequency with which organizers in each country adopted rhetoric stressing diversity, despite the comparatively greater diversity of the American population, and the longer American experience with diverse immigration.[64]

Activities by and for different ethnic groups were often worth reporting in both countries. For example, American organizers described how: "approximately 10,000 Estonians are expected to participate in the week-long 'Estonian Salute to Bicentennial '76,'" providing "treats for connoisseurs of ethnic cuisines," and "opportunities to delve deeply into all aspects of Estonian culture." The relevance of this diversity theme was sometimes stated more explicitly: organizers commented, for example, that Japanese–American participation in the Smithsonian Institution's bicentennial "Folklife Festival" "did much toward stimulating a broader appreciation of cultural diversity in the United States." The Smithsonian took – with ARBA's help – "the craftsmanship and cultures of many nations to cities and communities around the nation with corresponding ethnic populations." Diversity was constantly mentioned as a minor symbol in bicentennial talk with other themes, too; even a description of a re-enactment of Paul Revere's ride in Boston noted that his route would now take him through a variety of ethnic communities. This rubric was particularized at the community level in activities like a Mexican–American Friendship Week in San Antonio, and an extension of a Native American museum in Oklahoma; but overall, "diversity" themes were mentioned much more frequently in ARBA newsletter stories than in listings of community activities.[65]

Claims about ethnic diversity were similar in Australia: Australian organizers claimed that the bicentenary "increased knowledge and appreciation of the nation's rich cultural diversity." And Australians were reminded that "Australia has been influenced and largely formed by the millions of immigrants who have made their homes here over the last 200 years." Ethnic diversity was often absorbed into imagined community in stories about performance, art, and literature, or in stories about activities organized by ethnic organizations themselves.[66]

Newsletter stories about groups defined by racial difference – African Americans and Native Americans in the United States, Aborigines in Australia – dealt with activities and events which were produced by others, more than the groups themselves. There was little news of more popular participation along the lines that white ethnic community participation was *myth of racial harmony* (handwritten annotation)

presented. For instance, projects recognizing African Americans tended to be more centrally organized than vernacular in any way. Nevertheless, the *Bicentennial Times* made a point of noting, for example, that "Black History, Contributions [Were] Brought into Sharp Focus During the Bicentennial." Using the rhetorical device Roland Barthes called inoculation (the recognition of problems before claiming success), they observed first that "blacks justifiably harbored many reservations about celebrating" but went on: "The sufferings and contributions of American Blacks were highlighted in new museums, exhibitions, books, music, and drama on a scale that reached virtually every interested American." Bicentennial organizers often emphasized the role of African Americans in the Revolution. Other bicentennial projects included a midwestern tribute and forum on the contributions of black women, a booklet on African Americans in Congress, and a sculpture of Martin Luther King, Jr., in Dallas.[67]

If African Americans were often linked to the past in the rhetoric of inclusion, stories about Native Americans were focused on the future:

The Bicentennial has provided a new focus on the status and problems of Native Americans. It is hoped that the impetus provided by the celebration will extend beyond the bicentennial year to more substantial areas of concern that will have the effect of improving their quality of life.

Inclusion of Native Americans was most often discussed in describing projects concerned with improving living conditions, creating employment, and preserving heritage in Indian communities. This reflected the direct and pre-emptive outreach, mobilization, and funding effort on ARBA's part, a pragmatic emphasis not evident in responses to other groups. Curiously, much more effort seems to have been devoted by American bicentennial organizers to assuaging Native American critics than to programs and talk integrating African Americans.[68]

In much the same way as American organizers approached the problem of the national integration of Native Americans, Australian organizers also created a special program for native peoples in the hope that it would "restore a future to the past." This program funded community and cultural centers, sport and recreation facilities, and publications, films, and plays. Commissioned books concerning Aboriginal history, culture, and society seemed especially notable: these books, "told from an Aboriginal perspective, are among the legacies of the Bicentennial Aboriginal program that will help bridge gaps and counter-balance a lack of Aboriginal historical material." And the emergence of Aboriginal movements on the mainstream agenda was one of the unintended consequences of Australia's bicentenary; criticism from Aboriginal points of view was widely reported as the bicentenary developed. The rhetoric of inclusion could extend even to this, and in a startlingly cooptive move Aboriginal demonstrations ultimately seemed to be numbered among the myriad activities of the year:

We could see the entire, diverse Australian community – including Aboriginal people, many of whom did not celebrate the Bicentenary but whose successful march on 26 January showed the world that their spirit had survived 200 years.[69]

And just as plausibly imagining community meant, for bicentennial organizers, that ethnic and racial minorities should be explicitly seen to be participating, other groups were also mentioned: women, the aged, youth, and the disabled. Imagining the nation as diverse became a useful formulation about national identity applicable in a variety of contexts. Mostly, activities and events specifically planned for these groups were the subject of comment. Similar associations – with history, art, performance, and (in Australia) sport – were the devices of inclusion. Thus, in Australia, a commissioned book on women's culture was described in a story titled "Into a Woman's World. It Could Change a Man's Life." And Americans suggested that "Lesser-Known Women of the Revolution [Were] Brought to the Fore by the Bicentennial."[70]

In the centennials, the reconciliation of ethnic and national identities had not been salient; regional differences were far more worrying to centennial organizers.[71] When strong cultural differences evident in immigrant groups were recognized in the centennials, political values and institutions provided resources for the projected symbolic reconciliation of intra-national difference. In this language of assimilation, diverse groups were expected to lose particularist identities in the course of adopting "traditional" American political values and practices; the symbols and meanings of this "Americanization" were drawn from the founding moment of the Revolution. This symbolic reconciliation in assimilation was the first of three ways of dealing with difference adopted in the United States in the course of the century. In the second language of the "melting pot," promoted from the time of the Progressives, diverse groups were presumed to adopt dominant American values and practices, but in the course of this process to enrich and alter that tradition. In the third language, of diversity, becoming common by the time of the bicentennial, the differing identities of diverse groups were themselves claimed to characterize American national identity, and their representation was encouraged. Appeals to national diversity became more and more plausible in the course of the critical politics of the early 1970s, and they were adopted and promulgated by organizers in the American bicentennial partly in response to fears that the celebration would otherwise fail.[72]

The political context of Australia's adoption of diversity rhetoric was somewhat different, but the cultural logic was the same. Until after the Second World War, immigration in Australia was much less culturally diverse than it was in the United States. Racist immigration policy continued until the 1960s, and so too did the use of assimilation as a dominant trope for inclusion of difference. But variants of "multicultural-ism" in policy and cultural claims emerged from the 1960s. For instance, sociologist Jerzy Zubryzycki argued at a Citizenship Convention in 1968 that Australia should "accept migrants' retention of their ethnic identities ... and reject attempts to promote amalgams of cultures, assumptions of Anglo-Saxon superiority, and demands that ethnic minorities conform to English-oriented cultural patterns." Australian bicentennial organizers quickly adopted "diversity" language, which was readily available, at least to elites, by the time planning for the Australian bicentenary was underway. In Australia as in the United States, what Australian critics labeled a "tactical pluralism" led to programmatic recognition and inclusion of difference on the part of bicentennial organizers, and the use of symbols of diversity in characterizing national identity.[73]

Shared spectacle as national community

Another type of symbol celebration organizers could use to express imagined community transcended the painstaking inclusion of problematic difference. Sometimes, talk about the imagined community of the nation involved appeals and activities which implicitly stated, but did not characterize, national identity. These symbols were abstract yet emotional: they involved the bare assertion of the existence of celebration, references to abstract symbols like the flag, and the ritual use of spectacle as expression of social bonds, allowing organizers to assert the existence of what Durkheim might have called "collective effervescence." Appeals to national spectacle and symbol could seem to transcend difference to create the sort of imagined community bicentennial organizers wanted to claim.[74]

Thus, Australia's *Bicentenary '88* introduced a special section, "A Nation Entranced," complete with glossy photos, in this way:

Two million people can't be wrong. That's how many converged on Sydney Harbour for the magnificent finale of the Bicentennial Tall Ships event, the Parade of Sail, which formed the centrepiece of a fantastic day of celebrations on Australia Day, 1988. As well as the vast throng in Sydney, people around Australia made the event the success it was, an unforgettable experience.

And American organizers told a similar story, "National 21-Day Salute Starts June 14: Opsail Spectacular to Draw Millions in NY" which later continued: "well over 7 million spectators ashore and more than 20,000 spectator craft are expected to turn out for the July 4 event while additional millions will watch the extensive television coverage being planned."[75]

The celebration itself became the basis of imagined community, a topic for enthusiastic description and exhortation: "The Celebration is Everywhere!," "Flying of Flags Urged," "Beacons Unite a Nation." Such references to the bicentennials were reiterated constantly in implicit claims about community in celebration not associated with further characterization of the nation. President Ford asserted – in a quotation with no other symbolic development – that the bicentennial "reaffirmed what it means to be American," and organizers made much of events like a flight carrying a flag from Guam to Washington on the Fourth of July: "Sailor Brings Flag That Saw a Bicentennial Dawn."[76]

In curiosity stories from organizers, the possibilities for inclusion extended even to animals: "Arcadia, Cal., Bicentennial Commission Extends Membership to Horse." Souvenirs could make the basis of claims about shared identity too: thus, there was an Australian story of "the most enduring of all Bicentennial mementos – the Bicentennial Bricks," which "will celebrate the firm foundations of Australian society." For organizers, the nation was imagined as sharing all the detail of the spectacle and celebration in the process of creation. Spectacle and celebration were forms of the expression of national identity which also had wide vernacular usage, of course. Unlike themes of political values or of the founding moment, for example, organizers and local bicentennial communities in the United States used this sort of appeal about equally. Thus, the residents of Hardy, Illinois, registered as a bicentennial activity the creation of an "avenue of flags" along the main street; Portsmouth, Iowa, the decoration of rural mailboxes in bicentennial colors; Grangeville, Idaho, a "Bicentennial day with festival, bbq, kiddie parade, and rodeo"; New York an exhibition of the history of the flag; and in San Diego, the band of the Marine Corps performed a "Salute to America."[77]

Like diversity claims, claims about shared spectacle as grounding imagined community were very similar in both countries.[78] And like diversity claims, shared spectacle as ground for shared national identity was new to the symbolic repertoire of celebration organizers since the centennial. There is little doubt that spectacle and abstract, emotional symbolism have always been popularly compelling; records of Fourth of July celebrations, or the sheer overwhelming scale of exhibitions or the bunting and glitter of Australian parades, show the importance of this sort of contentless effervescence in national celebrations in the nineteenth century. What seemed different by the time of the bicentennials was the representation of this experience in claims about national identity from the cultural center; this sort of vernacular experience became something to be claimed by promoters of celebrations of national identity. In the centennials, speakers at the cultural center of celebrations did not speak of the shared experience of Fourth of July parades, the flag, or the exhibitions as part of national identity, even though these may have been appealing vernacular grounds; rather, such "national" experiences were themselves represented as expressing more weighty national qualities, like liberty or progress. While bicentennial organizers could still refer to substantive national characteristics, they allowed themselves more license to ignore substantive claims for appeals to ritual experience itself. In this, discourse in both bicentennials reproduced the ironies of broader changes in the public sphere in the course of the twentieth century; while claims were no longer so limited in their circulation by geographical or hierarchical boundaries, they became less substantive, less consequential, and less open to reasoned challenge. Appeals in the bicentennials about the shared experience of celebration were more like advertisements flashing attractive images than ones listing product benefits.

This "postmodernization" of imagined community was most evident in talk of spectacle by bicentennial organizers. It could also be seen in some of the more symbolically thin claims about the diversity of the nation, and in Australians' eclectic appeal to historical experience, although where these themes were elaborated, they became more substantive dimensions of imagined community. The symbolic repertoire with which celebration organizers represented the nation did not lose all substance, though: if it had, national identity in the two bicentennials would likely have been more similar. But, compared to the centennials, characterizations of Australia and the United States were more differentiated in the bicentennials. Important differences existed in other available ways of representing imagined community foundations; bicentennial organizers in the United States continued to appeal to shared political values and practices, while those in Australia emphasized the land instead.

Repertoires of national identity in the late twentieth century

International recognition, founding moments, general history, political culture, the land, diversity, and spectacle: these were the symbolic expressions of national identity in Australian and American bicentennials. These symbols stocked the cultural toolkit with which bicentennial organizers made events, organized programs, promoted their celebrations, challenged apathy, and appealed to critics. They could be thinly developed or elaborated in great detail, and they could be synthesized in different combinations, in different contexts or genres. Shared spectacle could make good grounds for claims about national identity in a lively press release, but not in appeals to doubtful critics; international recognition could be linked to talk of political values, or to talk of the land. Such repertoires of symbols provided fertile and robust grounds for imagined national community, despite difference and disinterest, in a wide variety of circumstances.

In both bicentennials, as in both centennials, talk of national identity involved two discursive dimensions: place in the world and shared community experience. Different symbols could express these dimensions, and they could be differentially salient in different circumstances, but all talk of national identity was formed within this discursive field. Otherwise, there seems no reason why American bicentennial organizers would have spoken of international recognition at all, or why Australian organizers made the vague references to national history they did. Place in the world and shared community experience provided the discursive framework within which particular symbols could make sense as symbols of national identity, rather than doing other sorts of symbolic work. The imagined community of the nation was constituted, in all these events, by the same discursive field.

Within this field, the particular symbols mobilized for meaning in the United States and Australia differed. Symbolic repertoires in the two countries differed more in the bicentennials than in the centennials. For American bicentennial organizers, the main symbolic grounds for claims about national identity were the founding moment, political values and practices, diversity, and spectacle. In 1976, these themes were most thickly elaborated and were mobilized in the widest range of discursive and organizational contexts, from promotional stories, to meetings with critics, to programs of bicentennial activities. By contrast, the main symbolic grounds for claims about national identity by Australian bicentennial organizers in 1988 were international recognition, general history, the land, diversity, and spectacle; these themes were most thickly elaborated and appeared in the widest range of contexts and formulations. Using these elements – the founding moment, political culture, diversity, and spectacle in the United States, and international recognition, general history, the land, diversity, and spectacle in Australia – a "foreigner" could speak fluently in each language of national identity, could make relevant claims, plausible rituals, feasible programs, and compelling images.

Many of these themes have rich histories in their own right, and they are largely consistent with influential twentieth-century social, economic, and political developments noted by historians of American and Australian *comparison* [handwritten marginal note]

national identities. But new questions and a fresh perspective emerge by setting them in a systematic comparative light, and noting similarities and differences both across time and between countries. In particular, the comparisons show that emergent differences in meanings attached to "the nation" were matters of connotation rather than denotation, plausibility and richness rather than truth or falsity. In each country, organizers might have appealed more often to symbols which were common in the other. American organizers might have appealed more often to international recognition, general history, and the land; Australian organizers might have appealed to founding moment history and political culture. This is shown by the rare use by organizers of "recessive" themes stronger in the other country, like the occasional Australian appeals to the founding moment – even though "it wasn't glorious" – or the existence of American talk of international recognition – like the "exhibit in the heart of Sao Paolo." Talk and activity outside cultural centers, like the frequent use of land symbols in American community activities, or the otherwise insignificant ceremony honoring Australia's "father and founder," also shows that similar themes were possible in each country. The centennials show the same thing. Reflection about place in the world or the flow of history was not always so foreign to promoters of American national community, and nor was reflection about the founding moment or political culture always so irrelevant to promoters of Australian national community as it became in the bicentennials.

Yet, although all were available, some symbolic formulations of imagined community were more resonant, and gained more currency, in each country. Comparing these similar cases challenges presuppositions about what might be naturally or properly labeled as shared national identity in each country. Why didn't Americans speak of how "the United States is more than qualified to play the role of hosting international events," or Australians speak of celebrating "a free nation governed by free people casting their free vote?" Why are these counterfactual possibilities, formed only by reversal, also counterintuitive? What accounts for the resonance and currency of the major symbols of national identity in each country, given the range of possibilities illustrated by the available comparisons?

Further questions are raised by the changes in national identities between nineteenth and twentieth centuries. Some symbols of national identity were the same in events a century apart; some were lost; and new formulations were introduced. Having examined the meanings associated with these nations in each centennial and bicentennial, we can now look at connections which have not been the focus to this point. Americans referred again in their bicentennial to their founding moment and political

values to express imagined community; but they no longer spoke much of
international recognition. Australians continued to find international
recognition appealing, but they no longer spoke much of their founding
moment or political values. Australians added the land to the range of
symbols which might plausibly express their nationality. In both countries,
talk of identification with powerful others, progress, and prosperity lost
any significance they had once held for promoters of national identity. In
both countries, too, talk of diversity and spectacle became newly plausible
ways of grounding national community. What made some old formulations more robust than others, and what made new formulations plausible?

   The centennials and the bicentennials in the United States and Australia
raise two sorts of questions: those about cultural difference and those about
cultural change. First, what accounts for differences between the two
countries in the symbols to which they appealed to express national identity
in their bicentennials? Second, what accounts for persistence and change in
the symbols which most commonly expressed national identity? In many
circumstances, such broad questions about cultural difference and cultural
change could invite only speculation. But the systematic comparison of
similar cases here allows more precise accounts of how particular symbolic
repertoires expressing national identity become meaningful. It also allows
comparative reflection about the implications of different ways of thinking
about "the nation." The implications of this comparative analysis of
changing symbolic repertoires are discussed in the following chapter.

5

Making nations meaningful in the United States and Australia

We have explored some of the many paths Americans and Australians have taken through the forest of symbols which they might have used to represent their nations. What does the aerial view look like? Where did they take the same paths, where did they diverge, and why?

The four events I have examined here were frameworks for expressions of national identity which were culturally dense and intended to be inclusive. They provide, in cross-sections, a broad overview of what Australians and Americans have been able to claim, with most plausibility, to share. With this sort of comparison we can move beyond the simple claim that nations are culturally constructed imagined communities to ask systematic and specific questions about exactly how they are imagined and constructed. And whereas historians have certainly told us a great deal about particular nationalist themes – about how Americans have thought of their political values, or Australians of their land, for instance – and about developments in the intervening century, looking at national identity in these events means that we can assess the comparative salience of different themes in different times and places. The approach here casts a new light on persistence, loss, and innovation in national representations.

In all four events, there were two core ways that meanings and values associated with the United States and Australia could make sense as expressions of national identity. Whatever the particular symbols invoked, they expressed either world position or internal integration or both. Americans and Australians answered for themselves the questions of where they stood in the world and what they shared as they expressed their national identities. The most widely invoked and intensely meaningful ways of expressing national identity could provide answers to both these questions simultaneously.

World position could become a meaningful part of national identity in two ways in the events I have examined here: through imagined recognition or through identification. First, the sense – or fantasy – of world recognition was evident in every event. World position strengthened national identity, paradoxically, by providing reassurance of status and commonality. In both centennials, and in the Australian bicentenary, imagined recognition in a world of nation-states was central to expressions of national identity. Talk of international recognition could also be found in the American bicentennial, although it was less frequent and it carried less weight. In contrast to many views of national identity which have focused on the part it has played in nationalist political conflict, these cross-sectional cases emphasize that relations with others may be figured positively as contributing to a sense of nationality.

In the late nineteenth century, most Australians and some Americans even expressed their patriotism in identification with powerful others, especially Britain, and this is the second way in which world position could be represented in these events. Drawing confirmation of national identity from identification with powerful others seems an unlikely formulation from a strictly nationalist point of view, but it was often very meaningful nonetheless. It lay at the center of Australian national identity in 1888 and was also evident among some elites even in the American centennial. It was no longer plausible in either country in 1976 or 1988.

The second core way of expressing national identity was in claims about what people shared across controversial internal divisions. Such claims could take several highly elaborated forms. Shared history was always important; so too were shared community foundations.

Shared history was seen as founding moment and progress in both "new nation" centennials: the founding moment was more important to Americans, and progress more important to Australians, but their visions of shared history took essentially the same form. By the time of the bicentennials, historical visions were more fragmented and differentiated. Progress was not mentioned in either country, and Australians no longer spoke of their founding moment, either, although they did make eclectic historical references. To Americans, talk of the founding moment of revolution remained a powerful way of expressing their national identity.

Shared community foundations express characteristic qualities of imagined community. In both centennials, political culture was a matter of national pride, and it remained so in the American bicentennial. Australians no longer identified with their political values in their bicentenary (which suggests the more general reminder that the link often made between political culture and national identity needs to be investigated empirically). In both centennials, talk of national prosperity was also an important way of expressing what members of the nation shared, but prosperity no longer seemed to make sense as a characterization of either nation in the bicentennials. Talk of the land was a minor theme in both centennials. A hundred years later, Australians had adopted geographic themes as a central part of their identity, but these themes remained largely peripheral in the United States. New themes of diversity and spectacle had entered the repertoire of possible claims about what members of the nation shared in both bicentennials.

In each event, many different people spoke about what characterized their nations with many different purposes and audiences in mind. Table 1 summarizes their sense of what was worth celebrating, and what made them who they were.

This overview of symbolic repertoires raises important new questions about national identity in each country, and about the ways available formulations of national identity have changed. Why were some themes robust to the changes of a century, while others lost their meaning, and why were new ways of representing national identity invented? I suggest here two sorts of reasons for shared developments and emergent differences in American and Australian national identity. First, changes in center/periphery relations in the production of talk about national identity account for shared developments in themes between the nineteenth and twentieth centuries, and for some differences between the countries. Second, the differing relevance of concerns about national integration and world position in each country has caused increasing differentiation in American and Australian identities. Taken together, comparative production context and the comparative salience of world position and integration explain developments, similarities, and differences in the meanings and values Americans and Australians have attached to their nations.

Center/periphery relations and national identity

Americans and Australians – or those in the process of adopting such identities – seemed to differ in some important ways at the time of their centennials. Most obviously, Americans were marking a century of formal sovereignty, whereas Australians were not yet independent or unified. But as I argued in chapter 2, and further illustrated in chapter 3, the centennials show that to take this commonsense criterion of national identity for granted would be a mistake. While political structure and cultural identity interact in many important ways, the political differences displayed at the time of the centennials only serve to illustrate that the global diffusion of

Table 1 *Symbolic repertoires expressing national identity*

	United States	Australia
Centennials	International recognition	International identification
	(International identification)	International recognition
	Founding moment	Progress
	Progress	Founding moment
	(Future)	Future
	Political culture	Prosperity
	Prosperity	Political culture
	(Land)	(Land)
Bicentennials	(International recognition)	International recognition
	Founding moment	General history
	(General history)	(Founding moment)
	Political culture	Land
	Diversity	Diversity
	Spectacle	Spectacle

Themes in parentheses were available but not widely salient.

the idea of the nation was just as important as independence – or even the desire for independence – in creating national identities in these cases. Australians and Americans spoke of what they shared, and how they stood in the world, in strikingly similar ways during their centennial celebrations.

But the centennials were not simply sudden and spontaneous enactments of growing popular realization of shared national communities. Common symbols had developed in the previous century; more immediately pertinent, the events were intensively organized by cultural centers, and invited the participation of cultural peripheries. Many projects and intentions motivated centennial participation. Many different sorts of group ties were symbolically associated with the nation in the course of centennial mobilization and critique. Whatever the particular projects and intentions, though, the attachment of a wide variety of goals and groups to the marking of events labeled as national centennials further strengthened the persuasiveness of the larger social grouping of the nation.

Understanding the organization of these widespread, diffuse, and transient events in terms of cultural centers and peripheries advances our understanding by providing a framework within which to grasp uninstitutionalized yet intense cultural production and to compare different cases. What made the four big events I have examined here comparable is the similar structure of their cultural production.

Some differences in center/periphery relations did distinguish Australian and American centennials: patterns of inclusion, critique, and exclusion differed in ways which mostly confirm what we know of each country and of the differences between them, as I have discussed in chapter 2 and further in chapter 4. In 1876, a cultural center coalesced around Eastern manufacturing and commercial elites, and the federal government was notable for its comparative lack of involvement in the representation of national identity. In Australia in 1888, on the other hand, the stronger, though multiple, colonial states formed the core at the cultural center of the celebration. In both countries, issues of regional integration dominated the agenda of celebration organizers at this time, but these issues were more problematic for Americans.

By the time of the bicentennials, federal governments were active at the center of national commemoration, and the central promotion of bicentennial events addressed a wider public sphere. In both countries, links between cultural centers and peripheries had tightened; more systematic links between official and vernacular experience were forged than had been possible a hundred years earlier. This meant that organizers and participants at the cultural centers of the bicentennial celebrations faced the need to address and encourage a wider public sphere in order to present a plausible expression of imagined community. While issues of regional integration had been largely superseded, bicentennial organizers found themselves focusing their efforts on eliciting widespread community participation, and attempting the symbolic inclusion of previously marginalized groups, especially racial and ethnic groups. Their major critics based their critique on the disadvantage and exclusion faced by marginalized groups in the nation.

While one might imagine that more sophisticated and systematic organizational and technological means for influencing cultural peripheries might lead to more intense indoctrination in central national symbols, the effect on national identity has ultimately been more paradoxical, though equally consequential. Tighter links between cultural centers and peripheries mean that those who make claims about shared national community must attempt to address and to include more different sorts of people, and to deal with a wider variety of threats to imagined integration. As the relevant public sphere has broadened, ideological ambiguity has been adopted as a central strategy of representation.

Thus, changes in center/periphery relations between the nineteenth and twentieth centuries suggest why some themes lost plausibility and some themes were invented for the representation of these nations in the course of the century. For instance, prosperity lost its meaning in talk of national identity between centennials and bicentennials. Analogously, visions of historical progress and the national future, evident among some groups in the American centennial and strong for most centennial Australians, no longer seemed to make sense as representations of the nation. And this was despite the fact that on any measure of economic development, and many available measures of social change, the twentieth century had been at least as important for prosperity and progress – as the nineteenth century conceived them – as the centuries celebrated in 1876 and 1888. The more extensive the periphery – or the broader the public sphere – to which claims about the nation were addressed, the less was self-congratulation about progress and prosperity on the part of elites broadly plausible.

On the other hand, vaguely postmodern experiences of diversity and spectacle were taken as foundations of shared community by organizers trying to make plausible claims in both bicentennials, and Australians also substituted for progress a vague and eclectic vision of shared history. Less substantive grounds for national identifications could make more sense, because they allowed greater integration of local and vernacular meanings, values, and practices, and they discouraged dissent which might threaten national celebration.

Was this cultural innovation itself "progress"? From the point of view of those who wished to strengthen and broaden the basis of attachment to the nation, ideological ambiguity could certainly allow the cultural incorporation of more differing groups in the nation, and defuse challenge to nationalist projects. But for nationalists there are also inherent limits to the language of shared diversity and spectacle. Promotions of the significance of the nation are more easily dismissed or ignored the more the pragmatic, local, and personal meaning of the syncretic events and practices supposedly absorbed in national celebration comes to dominate their national significance.

For marginalized groups, there are also both advances and limitations in the new languages of national diversity and spectacle. Talk of diversity and spectacle at the cultural center of the celebrations offered the possibility of claiming recognition for a wider range of vernacular experiences within the nation. But at the same time it weakened the common ground on which the problems of marginalized groups could be identified and addressed. When "prosperity" is taken to characterize the imagined community of the nation, those who are not prosperous have grounds for making their own problems national problems, and calling for change; when "diversity" or "spectacle" ground imagined national community, marginalized groups have no common language in which to make their own issues national issues, no widely persuasive reasons for appeals for change.

So significant changes in center/periphery relations lay behind some of the developments in languages of national identity in the course of the twentieth century, developments with paradoxical consequences which were evident in both countries. Some differences in center/periphery relations between the Australian and American centennials, and between bicentennials, also account for some differences in themes of national identity between countries. Most strikingly, American centennial organizers mobilized appeals to the founding moment of revolution as common ground they hoped would be plausible to those who were disaffected and alienated in the South in 1876. A "founding moment" view of history also dominated the American bicentennial a hundred years later. In both American events, important critics of the celebrations also used "founding moment" appeals to make their points. By contrast, although Australians, too, made much of their founding moment in their centennial celebration, this disreputable founding moment was more plausible as an object of than as a grounding for critique. At the time of the Australian centennial, a few peripheral critical voices were heard making a mockery of the reason for celebration; by the time of the bicentenary, the fear of widespread dissent from Aboriginal critics and their supporters led celebration organizers to drop their interest in the supposed occasion for their work almost entirely. While it is useful to remember that talk of the founding moment as a part of national identity was possible for Australians – as the centennial and some few peripheral bicentennial voices indicate – it was not a plausible grounding for national identity given the audiences faced by those who most wanted to speak of the nation. Even in the nineteenth century, Australian visions of history tended to emphasize progress a little more than the founding moment; by the time of the bicentenary, with neither founding moment nor progress plausible to peripheral groups, Australian visions of history were eclectic and vague. By contrast, the American founding moment was less vulnerable to criticism; it could make common ground with critics, and it was important to the critics themselves as they made their claims.

So relations between cultural centers and peripheries in celebration help to account for the persistent American focus on their founding moment as crucial to their identity, and the ultimate fading of this theme for Australians. More generally, changing center/periphery relations led to losses and innovations in themes of national identity used in both countries; prosperity, progress, and the future lost any viable currency as shared qualities they had once possessed, but diversity and spectacle were introduced as representations of the shared experience of imagined community.

But as the persistence of American attachment to the founding moment seems to suggest, symbols of "contentless consensus" are not always the most valuable ones for the expression of national identity. Another reason to believe that ideological ambiguity could not be the only way national identity is expressed, even where center/periphery relations make vagueness appealing, is the increasing differentiation in themes adopted to express national identity between centennials and bicentennials in the two countries. If both countries had tended to the limit of ideological ambiguity, they would have become more similar in their expressions of national identity.

But some important differences developed. In the late nineteenth century, Americans and Australians both made much of international recognition and political culture, and the land was a minor theme in the expression of national identity in each country. In the late twentieth century, Americans no longer placed much weight on international recognition, but Australians did; Australians did not identify with their political culture in expressing national identity, but Americans did; and the land had become a central theme of Australian national identity, while it remained minor and peripheral in the United States. In principle, all these themes were available for the expression of national identity in each country, and the centennials, along with bicentennial exceptions, show, for each theme, that it might have been possible to use them.

The production of expressions of national identity in the bicentennials in the dynamics of center/periphery relations cannot account for these emergent differences. There were no differences in cultural production which suggest why international recognition meant little to Americans, why political culture lost its national meaning to Australians, or why the land had come to carry such a freight of meaning for Australians when it meant little to American bicentennial organizers. In order to account for these emergent differences, I turn to a different sort of cultural explanation. I examine the comparative historical weight of the two core issues which give meaning to symbols of national identity, the representation of position in the world and the representation of internal integration.

Where do we stand in the world? What do we share?

In the late nineteenth century, nationalizing elites in both the United States and Australia talked quite a lot about their place in the world. They wanted other countries to notice them, and to recognize their successes and their potential. These issues of recognition still seemed compelling to Australian bicentennial organizers a hundred years later. But American bicentennial organizers, while they took it for granted that recognition from other countries was appropriate to the ritual expression of their national identity, were less excited and preoccupied about it.

What had changed that Americans lost much of their interest in international recognition, while Australians did not? Both remained well-off democracies, domestically secure nations of immigrants. What differentiated the two countries, by the late twentieth century, was their degree of global economic and geopolitical dependence. Australia continued to rely on world markets and friendly allies to remain, as it often thought of itself, "the lucky country." The United States, on the other hand, was much less dependent on world markets, and was more concerned about the management of major alliances than it was concerned about maintaining powerful allies. In the course of the century since the centennials, the United States had moved to the core of the world economy and to the status of world power, whereas Australia had remained solidly semi-peripheral.

So, in Australia, issues of international regard deriving from concerns about geopolitical and economic vulnerability still gave plausibility and meaning to themes of national identity. In the United States, by contrast, concerns about international recognition were not charged with implicit relevance to the security of imagined community.

At the same time, the comparative salience of concerns about internal integration also worked to reinforce the difference between the two countries. As I have underlined, American organizers of centennials and bicentennials faced more immediate challenges than Australians in making imagined community plausible across internal difference. Before 1876, the aftermath of the Civil War presented major problems, whereas Australian organizers, though they worked from different colonies, had no such critical or highly charged issues to deal with in 1888. Before 1976, the social movements of the 1960s created conflicts within presumptive national community which American bicentennial organizers experienced as significant threats to the legitimacy and success of their project. On the other hand, before 1988, though some similar movements had also enlivened Australian politics, their impact had faded or been absorbed. In both pairs of events, a hundred years apart, Americans making claims about the nation had much more to worry them about internal integration than Australians did.

Where do "we" stand in the world? What do "we" share? While both Americans and Australians were answering these questions for themselves as they found ways of representing their nations, the former question was more worrying for Australians, and the latter for Americans. By 1976, when Americans were quite secure at the core of the nation-state system, but facing new and highly conspicuous integration problems, they had little reason to place much weight on the theme of international recognition, or to elaborate the theme as the Australians would do twelve years later. For Australians, on the other hand, though they were now citizens of an independent nation-state and certainly drew stronger boundaries between themselves and powerful others than they had done in 1888, concern with the views of significant international others continued to charge symbols of Australian national identity with meaning.

So by placing in their comparative historical context the fundamental issues in the construction of national identities – issues of world position and issues of internal integration – we can better understand the differing presuppositions which led to the differing emphasis on international regard in American and Australian bicentennial imagined communities. But why did Australians no longer think of their political values, adopting instead their land as symbolic foundation of imagined community in their bicentenary in 1988, while political values remained much more meaningful than land in representing American national identity? The same presuppositional differences also account for differing use of themes of political culture and the land in the two bicentennials.

The centennials and bicentennials confirm that for Americans, political values are crucial to their identity. The symbolic weight Americans continue to attach to their democracy is attributable in this context to the way appeals to democratic values can represent what is shared across significant internal difference. Like the founding moment symbols discussed earlier, appeals to shared national political values are just as important a grounding for critical claims as they are for the claims of central nationalizing elites in national rituals. Since internal integration has often been a more difficult issue for Americans than Australians, the appeal to democratic values to ground American national identity gains force and currency from integrative concerns.

But American political values are even more charged with national meaning. For Americans, their political values are associated with their founding moment in revolution, and so expressing national identity in terms of political values serves to represent their unique place in world history. Democracy can figure as part of the answer to the question of "what is our place in the world?" Providing compelling answers to questions of world position as well as to questions of internal integration, political culture has been a persistently plausible theme of American national identity.

From an American point of view, talk of democracy was remarkably absent in Australian bicentennial rhetoric. Australians did not speak of their democratic political values as sacred, and do not now think of them when they think of their national identity. Rather, these values are part of the taken-for-granted infrastructure of their society. They may be quite well aware that part of what has given them the label of "the lucky country" has been their democracy, and domestic critics in Australia can appeal to democratic norms to ground their criticisms as well as Americans. Concerns about internal integration, though less immediate than they have been for Americans, would, one might imagine, encourage Australians to think a little of their democracy as they thought of their national identity during their bicentennial. They did not.

What differentiates Americans and Australians is not so much the way their political values can function as integrative symbols, but the way their political values have been associated with international distinctiveness. The strong emphasis that Australians have continued to give to their place in the world has meant that the talk of national identity in terms of political culture which was evident in the Australian centennial had faded almost completely by the time of the bicentennial. Australians took a lot of pride in their political values and institutions in the nineteenth century. But at that time, Australians' pride in their political values was closely linked to their identification with Britain. Though it took most of the next century, Australian identification with Britain had become largely peripheral by 1988; and since Australians no longer expressed much attachment to Britain, democracy itself lost significance in representations of national identity. Australian democracy did not seem so distinctive that it could be very compelling as an object of international regard. Without the additional charge given to political values by their earlier link to international identification, they no longer had much currency in the symbolizing of the Australian nation.

The Australian continent, on the other hand, was indeed taken to be globally distinctive – and could symbolize what Australians shared in comparison with the rest of the world. During the centennials, representations of the land as characteristic of the nation had been available in both countries, although not as frequently adopted as other symbols founding national unity. In the American bicentennial in 1976, surprisingly little talk of the land took place as Americans spoke of the nation, although there were several indications that this theme was more salient in local and regional contexts. But whereas in the American bicentennial discourse the land was, at most, a vernacular theme and not a central national symbol – the "Stars and Stripes" was taken to be much more relevant to the occasion than "America the Beautiful" – talk of the land was adopted as a central way of characterizing the Australian nation in 1988.

Although, in principle, Americans might talk more of their land when they talk of the nation, neither concerns about internal integration nor any issue of international regard make this a widely or intensely plausible symbol of imagined community. More densely settled than the Australian continent, and more politically subdivided, land in the United States has become a symbol characterizing region – and not primarily a symbol which can come to represent sharing across internal difference. For Australians, living mostly in a few big cities, the continent means less for regional differentiation, and can thus more plausibly be represented as something they all share. The very remoteness of the harsh continent from the lives of . most Australians allows it to become a symbol which can represent their integration. But more importantly, and unlike political values which might also ground shared community, the continent can be seen to encompass the nation, and its size, and ecological strangeness, can be imagined as worthy of international distinction. Long framed as alien from anything in the previous experience of its British invaders and settlers, and developing a mythological weight among those who thought about national identity from the late nineteenth century, by 1988 the land could make self-evident sense as a representation of the Australian nation. Again, the comparative relevance of international regard and internal integration, set in historical context, accounts for the way Americans and Australians diverged in the importance of appeals to the land to ground imagined national community.

Comparing these two similar countries, we have seen that it might have been possible for Americans to place more weight on international recognition, and to talk more of the land, during their bicentennial, and it might have been possible for Australians to place more weight on their political values in representing their nation in 1988. Conversely, Americans might have been more casual about their democracy, and Australians more casual about international recognition and the land. But the comparison of these similar cases also suggests why these alternative possibilities are counterfactual and counterintuitive. While the two countries had much in common, and might have been represented the same way, crucial differences in world position and internal integration led to emergent differences in what would make sense as a symbol of national identity. Comparative independence or dependence in the nation-state system, and relative amount of internal challenge to integration, worked together to make different symbols of national identity more plausible, or, as Levi-Strauss might have suggested, "good to think," in each country.

How deep did these presuppositions go? Were the differences in national identity we have seen in the bicentennials simply a matter of the rate of exchange, or the number of demonstrations, in the years of bicentennial planning? On the one hand, short-term influences seem powerful, especially when we see the complex, anxious cultural politics behind the breezy public statements of organizers. And short-term differences influencing framing presuppositions are certainly consistent with the explanatory logic of crucial differences suggested by similar-case comparison. Perhaps only the contemporary situation of the country, and not cumulative historical experience, influences the national identities emerging in the sorts of big patriotic rituals I have examined here. So, for instance, we might hypothesize that, if there were no critical social movements in the United States in the 2060s, American national symbols would be less tied to concerns about internal integration than they were in the bicentennial (assuming the conditions which would lead to an American tricentennial in the first place).

But looking at these cases in the longer term suggests that the different weight of geopolitical and integrative presuppositions in national identity formation did not simply emerge as organizers in ARBA and ABA offices sat down to look at the headline news stories and decide what the country needed to hear. Organizers did sometimes come close to acting this way (though their worlds were more unpredictable and contested than this social engineering vision would suggest). But presuppositions which made particular and different national symbols significant also had historical origins which went much deeper. These origins suggest that whatever the headline symptoms of disintegration or dependence in the United States or Australia, the different salience of integration concerns and world recognition in these two countries is not a feature of their nationalities which will alter every five or ten years. Though presuppositional worries about integration and world recognition may be muted or exaggerated by contemporary events, the cross-national differences are likely to persist. This is because the different times the two countries entered into the global process of nation-formation have meant that they have faced cumulatively different worlds in their institutional development.

As we saw in chapter 2, the United States achieved its sovereignty at a time when ideas and institutional forms for nations as political communities were shaky innovations. Paradoxically, this early American unification has made for a much more problematic and persistently contested national integration in the United States than in Australia. Major problems of institutional and cultural integration were unresolved up to the Civil War and even beyond; these problems were obvious in the organization of the centennial, and they can also be seen in the form ethnic politics took during waves of immigration, and in the form minority politics took during the civil rights movement of the middle of the twentieth century. This internal institutional fragmentation, however, has been little hindrance to economic expansion from semi-periphery to core of the world economy, and relative geopolitical security.

Whereas in their centennials and bicentennials, Americans were commemorating their Revolution and the subsequent achievement of a formally unified independent sovereignty, Australians were commemorating British invasion and the beginning of the first of six different colonies around the continent. But the nineteenth century, although it was only the first century after invasion and settlement in Australia, saw the global development of a vocabulary of nationalism, along with the spread of increasingly nationalized political institutions. Nineteenth-century political and institutional developments provided encouragement and resources for "national" conceptualizations of political community in Australia. Australians found integration in an imagined national identity less problematic because, in the course of the nineteenth century, the nation-state as an institution and nationalism as a language of politics had become common.

So, for instance, they found the institutional tools for the federation of different colonies readily to hand in the American and Canadian examples, whereas the very possibility of linking existing polities in a larger polity had been in question for the Americans. Perhaps even more importantly, and partly due to the experience of the American Revolution, British imperial policy-makers were early ready to concede self-government in the white settler colonies like Australia, and they encouraged Australian unification even before Australian colonial politicians were much interested. Unlike Americans – and partly because of the earlier American conflict – Australians did not fight a war of independence, and Australians' political experience of imperial administration was more positive than that of late colonial Americans. National models, federal institutions, and imperial politics all made the formation of an Australian nation-state more self-evident a process than it had been in the American case. Australian colonies at the end of the nineteenth century could take both the vocabulary and the institutions of the nation-state pretty much for granted. Further, the dominance of the British state in Australian exploration and development (again partly a consequence of the earlier American experience) encouraged sets of institutions and attitudes toward the role of central government which meant that the unification of Australian colonies was comparatively uncontested and the problems of integrating subnational governments, immigrants, and minorities which persistently faced American nationalizers were less common and, when faced, less persistently challenging to elites in Australia. Thus, Australian nationalizing elites have not, on the whole, faced integrative issues faced by their peers in the United States, and they have not done so because their political formation came later in the history of nation-formation. However, the later entry of Australia into the world economy, under the aegis of Britain, led to a more persistently uncertain economic and military dependence and a continuing reliance on powerful others. The timing of their formation in the global development of the nation-state system has meant that Australians have been faced with persistent, semi-peripheral, economic, and geopolitical dependence, but have found it simpler to develop and manage unified national institutions.

So while contemporary events and issues will certainly affect how influential the different presuppositions about national identity are in any given context, there is a lot of reason to think that those contemporary issues themselves are more likely to be problems of challenging internal difference in the United States, and are more likely to be problems of international status anxiety in Australia.

As we have seen, concerns about global position have influenced the presuppositions of cultural actors who made national identities in Australia more than these concerns have lately influenced their counterparts in the United States. On the other hand, more fragmented national institutions have influenced the presuppositions of cultural actors making national identities in the United States much more than their counterparts in Australia. Institutional constraints have influenced national identities through the presuppositions of cultural actors, creating differing patterns in what it made sense to stress as they spoke about national identity. We can view these differing patterns as emerging from short-term and contingent politics; but historical experience suggests that they are also, more profoundly, characteristic of the "nations" themselves.

Other nations, other questions, other identities

If we understand better the "elementary forms" of our national lives, what can we do with that understanding? It seems worth recapturing and reflecting on the long-forgotten buzz of national talk in the year-long ritual events I have examined here, and the huge range of people and groups who found something to say, if only because it sometimes seems curious that such massive efforts were made. But we can also use our understanding of these cases to three broader purposes. First, they tell us more about how to understand nation-formation. Second, they open unexamined territory in American and Australian national historiography. Third, they can give us options about how we choose to think of ourselves.

In the big picture of the global history of nation-formation, the United States and Australia usually attract little attention. But their experiences are worth examining, and precisely because they have been exceptional cases. In these settler countries, we can see more clearly the way nations become meaningful forms of social organization, and the conditions which make plausible symbolic repertoires expressing national identities. Even in places with more consequential nationalist movements or official nationalisms, the availability of compelling cultural representations of imagined national community is a crucial condition of nationalist mobilization. We can see better what makes representations of imagined community plausible, and what makes them vary, when we can view them apart from nationalist conflict. And examining these two similar nations, we also see more of the contingent cultural action in making nations meaningful, the complex patterns of persistence and change in national symbolizing.

If all nations are "imagined communities," we need to know more about the ways they can be imagined. What symbols are adopted and why? How do they change? Benedict Anderson's popular idea about what nations are is not as interesting for the way it names a sense of community in nationality as it is for what it suggests about looking at the different ways that community might be seen. Behind these different possibilities lies a cultural process of great complexity, contingency, and specificity. But as the analysis here has shown, the process is illuminated if we examine symbolic repertoires, cultural production in the dynamics of center/ periphery relations, and the relative salience of the two crucial dimensions of the discursive field within which national identities are formed. These three lenses on imagined community help to unpack and to understand the meanings associated with nations, the social relations within which those meanings are produced, and what makes them plausible. The value of the approach I have adopted here is not confined to understanding four big national rituals in two similar countries, but can also help develop explanations for what nations have meant in other, more contentious, and more disparate circumstances.

These cases also remind us that broad labels for types of national identities, like "liberal" or "ethnic," do not go very far in helping to understand the many ways communities can be imagined. In using such omnibus categories to label national identities, we can miss many ways nations are actually meaningful. Both the United States and Australia are said to have "liberal" national identities – though some would also say they are secure in that liberalism because of an "ethnic" British origin and core. Certainly, some nationalists we have heard speaking for the United States and Australia did not see their liberal and ethnic characterizations of their nations as mutually exclusive. Further, although "liberal" nations are sometimes thought to be less concerned with their status in the world than "ethnic" nations, world recognition has been important to Americans and Australians too often to ignore. Simply labeling both national identities "liberal" also misses the different ways they have envisioned their histories, and misses other symbols they have used to express what their nations meant – symbols which may also be used in more "ethnically" grounded nationalisms. For instance, using the experience of spectacle or imagined landscape to characterize national sharing and distinctiveness would not seem to be confined to these "liberal" nations. Perhaps most importantly, broad typologies of liberal and ethnic national identities cannot capture variation in the ways that political experience and values themselves have been represented in national identities. The cases examined here show that broad typologies provide too restricted an understanding of the ways nations are meaningful. National identities labeled "ethnic" seem just as unlikely to have restricted symbolic repertoires for national representation as these "liberal" national identities. Rather than making broad typologies of types of national identity, we should examine the full range of meanings associated with a nation by those who speak of it, building an analysis of symbolic repertoires which is no "restricted code" but captures the fluidity and variation in what that nation has meant.

National historians have paid more attention to the specific ways nations have been meaningful than have scholars concerned with the broader history of nation-formation. Many of the themes of national identity emerging in the centennials and bicentennials have long and important histories, histories which made them available for adoption as national identities were recreated for the events. But there is some truth to the observation of the centennial promoter in 1875 that "until we know other people we cannot know ourselves," and much of what we know of themes of American and Australian national identity focuses on what has been most obvious to Americans and Australians themselves. National historians have shown, for instance, many developments in common themes of national identity in the century intervening between centennials and bicentennials which are consistent with the more comparative assessment here. But without comparison we can have no good sense of what is truly distinctive, or what might have been emphasized, but was not. The value of this comparison of similar cases is that it shows themes of national identity which might have been used, but were instead ignored or abandoned. It points to "roads not traveled," and raises some important questions about national histories. For instance, when did Americans stop worrying about international regard, and under what circumstances? When did Australians stop talking about themselves as democratic, and under what circumstances? Questions like these ones raised in the course of this analysis are surely important and intriguing directions for furthering our historical understanding of national identity in each country.

Finally, understanding how we think about our nations gives us options for change. If we believe, echoing Marx, that people make their own histories, but not in circumstances of their own choosing, we should also notice the implicit rider in this idea, that we can make new histories only if we can envision alternative possibilities.

I have suggested the main circumstances which influence the sorts of things which can become meaningful as representations of our national identities. Meaningful symbols of national identity will have power and currency when they can represent place in the world, internal integration, or both; and large social contexts affect which issue will be more influential. But these historical circumstances create presuppositions of cultural action, not specific symbols; the process of meaning-making *within* the framework set by presuppositions about national identity is, as the stories of the centennials and bicentennials have also illustrated, highly contingent and creative.

So, within the discursive field which makes national identities meaningful, we have some options about specific ways we think about our nations, and these options can be consequential in public debate – as Americans reassess, for instance, what their geopolitical role should be, or as Australians debate republicanism. Americans might ask, for instance, about the advantages and limitations of their bicentennial inattention to world opinion. Australians might ask, similarly, about the advantages and limitations of their awareness of what the world might think of them. From these cases, too, we can see that unfamiliar ways of talking about what is important about our groups might be worthy of more elaboration and reflection. What would be the consequences if Americans put more symbolic weight on their land? What would be the consequences if Australians put more symbolic weight on their political values? Are there better ways to think of the past? Perhaps most important, yet neglected in recent visions of national identity, how should we think of our futures?

These questions and many others like them are suggested by the comparisons here of the ways the nation has been meaningful in American and Australian centennials and bicentennials. Answers to this sort of question can only emerge in the process of public discussion and debate, and not in further studies. But we do know that it is hard to open such debate without being aware, through comparison, of how we think about our nations and of alternative options. Exploring such questions can create the opportunity for significant innovations in the ways we think of what binds our groups together, in the ways we talk about the conflicts which emerge in those groups, and in the ways we see constraints and possibilities in our relations with others.

Notes

1 Comparing national identities

1 Max Farrand, ed., *The Records of the Federal Convention of 1787*, rev. edn., 4 vols. (New Haven and London: Yale University Press, 1966), vol. I, 552 (July 5); *Official Reports of the National Australian Convention Debates* (Adelaide: C. E. Bristow, Government Printer, 1897), 979.

2 Article 15 of the Universal Declaration of Human Rights, in B. G. Ramcharan, ed., *Human Rights: Thirty Years After the Universal Declaration* (The Hague, Boston, and London: Martinus Nijhoff, 1979), 266; Richard Rose, "National Pride in Cross-National Perspective," *International Social Science Journal* 37 (1) 1985, 85–96; Pierre Bourdieu, "Thinking About Limits," *Theory, Culture, and Society* 9 (1) February 1992, 39 (37–49); "St. Francis Won't Support Kiwis in Court," *San Francisco Chronicle*, January 31, 1990, D9; "Racist Group Challenges Government," *West Australian*, January 2, 1990, 13. Of Australians, 88 percent say they feel proud of their country, as do 96 percent of Americans (reported in Ian McAllister, "Patriotism Beats in Aussie Hearts," *Australian Society* 4 [10] October 1985, 25–26). The sense in which I am concerned to understand the meanings of nationality has recently received an important analysis in Michael Billig, *Banal Nationalism* (London and Thousand Oaks, CA: Sage, 1995).

3 George Santayana, *Soliloquies in England and Later Soliloquies* (London, Bombay, and Sydney: Constable and Company, 1922), 4.

4 Benedict Anderson, *Imagined Communities: Reflections on the Origin and Spread of Nationalism*, rev. edn. (London and New York: Verso, 1991), 6. Modal personality structures and cultural patterns are analytically distinct; see Alex Inkeles, "National Character Revisited," in Jesse R. Pitts and Roland Simon, eds., *Tocqueville Review* 12 (1990–91), 83–117. I am concerned here with cultural patterns, not the strength or nature of individual attachment to or expression of these widespread ways of thinking. The emotional dynamics of national identity are discussed in William Bloom, *Personal Identity, National*

155

Identity, and International Relations (Cambridge and New York: Cambridge University Press, 1990).

5 Max Weber, "Structures of Power: The Nation," in H. H. Gerth and C. Wright Mills, eds., *From Max Weber: Essays in Sociology* (New York: Oxford University Press, 1946), 172 (171–76). Similar questions to those introduced here, demanding better accounts of the ways nations are symbolized, guide the analysis in Karen A. Cerulo, *Identity Designs: The Sights and Sounds of a Nation*, ASA Rose Book Series (New Brunswick, NJ: Rutgers University Press, 1995).

6 Most of the few existing comparisons of the United States and Australia focus on political values and political culture. I examine national identity – however imagined – rather than what is more usually investigated as political culture, because of the variable degree to which political values may be incorporated in public cultures more broadly conceived. If national identity is taken to be equivalent to political culture, we can miss the variety in the ways national identities may be expressed, and assume what requires empirical investigation – whether there is any difference in national identities in liberal polities. As will become evident, though, comparisons of liberal political culture in the United States and other settler nations do cast important light on national identity, and have pioneered the sort of systematic comparison I pursue here. See Seymour M. Lipset, *The First New Nation: The United States in Comparative and Historical Perspective* (New York: W. W. Norton and Co. 1979 [1973]), and Lipset, *Continental Divide: The Values and Institutions of the United States and Canada* (New York: Routledge, 1990). The "Hartz thesis" has also generated some intriguing comparative debate about political culture in the settler societies: see, for example, Louis Hartz, *The Founding of New Societies* (New York: Harcourt, Brace, and World, 1964); Hugh Collins, "Political Ideology in Australia: The Distinctiveness of a Benthamite Society," *Daedalus* 114 (Winter 1985), 147–69; J. B. Hirst, "Keeping Colonial History Colonial: The Hartz Thesis Revisited," *Historical Studies* 21 (82) April 1984, 85–104; A. W. Martin, "Australia and the Hartz 'Fragment' Thesis," J. W. McCarty, "Australia as a Region of Recent Settlement in the Nineteenth Century," and G. C. Bolton, "Louis Hartz," *Australian Economic History Review* 13 (2) September 1973, 131–47, 148–67, and 168–76, respectively; and four articles (Louis Hartz, "Comments," 279–84; Harry V. Jaffa, "Conflicts Within the Idea of the Liberal Tradition," 274–78; Leonard Krieger, "A View from the Farther Shore," 269–73; and Marvin Myers, "Louis Hartz, *The Liberal Tradition in America*: An Appraisal," 261–68) in *Comparative Studies in Society and History* 5 (3) April 1963. See also Lyn Spillman, "'Neither the Same Nation Nor Different Nations': Constitutional Conventions in the United States and Australia," *Comparative Studies in Society and History* 38 (1) January 1996, 149–81.

7 For overviews of nationalism, see John Breuilly, *Nationalism and the State* (New York: St. Martin's Press, 1982); Anthony D. Smith, *Theories of Nationalism*, 2nd edn. (New York: Holmes and Meier, 1983); Smith, *The Ethnic Origins of*

Nations (Oxford and New York: Basil Blackwell, 1986); Ernest Gellner, *Nations and Nationalism* (Oxford and New York: Basil Blackwell, 1983); E. J. Hobsbawm, *Nations and Nationalism Since 1780* (Cambridge and New York: Cambridge University Press, 1990). For a useful theoretical synthesis and account of the continuing importance of nationalism, see Craig Calhoun, "Nationalism and Civil Society: Democracy, Diversity, and Self-Determination," in Craig Calhoun, ed., *Social Theory and the Politics of Identity* (Oxford and Cambridge, MA: Blackwell, 1994), 304–35.

8 On the development of the "world cultural frame" of the nation as a form of political community, see George M. Thomas, John W. Meyer, Francisco O. Ramirez, and John Boli, *Institutional Structure: Constituting State, Society, and the Individual* (Newbury Park, CA: Sage, 1987). Thomas *et al.* call for a "thick description" of how ideas like that of nationality came to be taken for granted; this study furthers that agenda. See also Liah Greenfeld, *Nationalism: Five Roads to Modernity* (Cambridge, MA, and London: Harvard University Press, 1992), and Anderson, *Imagined Communities*. Greenfeld and Anderson both argue, though on very different grounds, that the American case was an important step in this development.

9 One important recent explanation of national cultural difference which also uses the tools discussed below is provided in Michèle Lamont, *Money, Morals, and Manners: The Culture of the French and American Upper-Middle Class* (Chicago and London: University of Chicago Press, 1992), ch. 7.

10 On cultural repertoires, see Ann Swidler, "Culture in Action: Symbols and Strategies," *American Sociological Review* 51 (2) April 1986, 273–86.

11 E. Hobsbawm and T. Ranger, eds., *The Invention of Tradition* (Cambridge and New York: Cambridge University Press, 1984); George L. Mosse, "Caesarism, Circuses, and Monuments," *Journal of Contemporary History* 6 (2) 1971, 167–82; David Glassberg, *American Historical Pageantry: The Uses of Tradition in the Early Twentieth Century* (Chapel Hill and London: University of North Carolina Press, 1990); Emile Durkheim, *The Elementary Forms of Religious Life*, trans. and intro. by Karen Fields (New York: Free Press, 1995 [1912]); W. Lloyd Warner, "The Past Made Present and Perfect," in his *The Living and the Dead: A Study of the Symbolic Life of Americans* (Greenwich, CT: Greenwood Press, 1975 [1959]), 156–225; Robert Bellah, "Civil Religion in America," in W. G. McLoughlin and R. Bellah, eds., *Religion in America* (Boston: Beacon Press, 1968), 3–23; Steven Lukes, "Political Ritual and Social Integration," *Sociology* 9 (2) May 1975, 289–308; Lynn Hunt, *Politics, Culture, and Class in the French Revolution* (Berkeley: University of California Press, 1984); David Kertzer, *Ritual, Politics, and Power* (New Haven: Yale University Press, 1989); and John R. Gillis, ed., *Commemorations: The Politics of National Identity* (Princeton, NJ: Princeton University Press, 1994). For an assessment of the application of the notion of civil religion to Australia, see Richard Ely, "Secularisation and the Sacred in Australian History," *Historical Studies* 19 (77) October 1981, 553–66.

12 See Neil J. Smelser, *Comparative Methods in the Social Sciences* (Englewood Cliffs, NJ: Prentice-Hall, 1976), 202–05, on idiographic and nomothetic explanation.
13 On these three different types of cultural explanation, see Lyn Spillman, "Culture, Social Structure, and Discursive Fields," *Current Perspectives in Social Theory* 15 (1995), 129–54. A similar threefold approach to cultural accounts is developed in Robert Wuthnow, *Communities of Discourse: Ideology and Social Structure in the Reformation, the Enlightenment, and European Socialism* (Cambridge, MA: Harvard University Press, 1989).
14 See Richard A. Peterson, "Culture Studies Through the Production Perspective: Progress and Prospects," and for an overview of institutions generally relevant to the production of national cultures, Michael Schudson, "Culture and the Integration of National Societies," both in Diana Crane, ed., *The Sociology of Culture: Emerging Theoretical Perspectives* (Oxford and Cambridge, MA: Blackwell, 1994), 163–89 and 21–43, respectively.
15 On discursive fields, see Wuthnow, *Communities of Discourse*, 13; and Bourdieu, "Thinking About Limits." Jeffrey C. Alexander and Philip Smith, "The Discourse of American Civil Society: A New Proposal for Cultural Studies," *Theory and Society* 22 (2) April 1993, 151–207, provide an important argument for and exemplar of the analysis of discursive structure.

   Both dimensions of national identity have long been recognized in work on nationalism, although they have not been characterized in this way, and "international" and "integrative" aspects of national consciousness are stressed to different degrees depending on theoretical perspective and historical case. As Habermas summarizes,

> The nation is a (not yet adequately analyzed) structure of consciousness that . . . makes the formally egalitarian structures of bourgeois civil law (and later of political democracy) in internal relations subjectively compatible with the particularistic structures of self-assertion of sovereign states in external relations.

   See Jürgen Habermas, "Legitimation Problems in the Modern State," ch. 5 in *Communication and the Evolution of Society*, trans. by Thomas McCarthy (Boston: Beacon Press, 1976), 191.
16 Melvin L. Kohn, "Cross-National Research as an Analytic Strategy," *American Sociological Review* 52 (December 1987), 716 (713–31).
17 I also interviewed a number of Australian organizing officials and made some use of video evidence. I further discuss available documents and their possibilities and limits for inference more specifically in chapters 3 and 4. As I will note, documents available from bicentennials allowed more systematic sampling than documents available from centennials. However, for all events my conclusions are based on and supported by examining the broadest range of surviving documents feasible, so the more systematic sampling for bicentennials is intended to add to, rather than substitute for, the broader though less systematic grounding for the overall conclusions about both centennials and bicentennials.

In general, where I draw comparisons about the use of different themes across time or between countries, I am reporting from my analysis of the broadest range of available evidence my best assessment of how frequently they were used, while being conscious of avoiding any fallacy of misplaced precision.

18 Vernon K. Dibble, "Four Types of Inference from Documents to Events," *History and Theory* 2 (1963), 203–21.

19 Philip McMichael, "Incorporating Comparison Within a World-Historical Perspective: An Alternative Comparative Method," *American Sociological Review* 55 (June 1990), 392 (385–97); see also, for instance, Theda Skocpol, ed., *Vision and Method in Historical Sociology* (Cambridge and New York: Cambridge University Press, 1984).

20 Neil J. Smelser, "The Methodology of Comparative Analysis of Economic Activity," in his *Essays in Social Explanation* (Englewood Cliffs, NJ: Prentice-Hall, 1968), 72 (62–75).

21 Lipset, *First New Nation*, 248; Mattei Dogan and Dominique Pelassy, *How to Compare Nations: Strategies in Comparative Politics* (Chatham, NJ: Chatham House Publishers, 1984), 120. See also Smelser, *Comparative Methods*, 215–20.

2 "Every one admits that commemorations have their uses": producing national identities in celebration

1 Francisco O. Ramirez, "Institutional Analysis," in George M. Thomas, John W. Meyer, Francisco O. Ramirez, and John Boli, *Institutional Structure: Constituting State, Society, and the Individual* (Newbury Park, CA: Sage, 1987), 323 (316–28); *Sydney Morning Herald*, November 28, 1889, *Newspaper Cuttings*, vol. 140, 138–39, Mitchell Library, Sydney; [Executive Committee of the Women's Branch of the Centennial Association for Connecticut], *Spirit of 'Seventy-Six* 1 (June 1875), 3.

2 Russell Faeges, in "Why a Soviet Union?" (Department of Political Science, University of California at Berkeley, photocopy), suggests the "political triangle," of land, peoples, and political arrangements as theoretically prior to nations, a formulation I adopt here.

3 See, for example, John Breuilly, *Nationalism and the State* (New York: St. Martin's Press, 1982), 9; Anthony D. Smith, *Theories of Nationalism*, 2nd edn. (New York: Holmes and Meier, 1983), 84, 183; Ernest Gellner, *Nations and Nationalism* (Oxford and New York: Basil Blackwell, 1983), 108–09; and E. J. Hobsbawm, *Nations and Nationalism Since 1780* (Cambridge and New York: Cambridge University Press, 1990), 78; Smith, *The Ethnic Origins of Nations* (Oxford and New York: Basil Blackwell, 1986), 276. Benedict Anderson and Liah Greenfeld provide, in different ways, exceptions to this neglect: see n. 5 below. A parallel argument contrasting state-promoted development of public education with an earlier, more diffuse expansion of enrollments in the United States is made in John W. Meyer, David Tyack, Joane Nagel, and Audri Gordon, "Public Education as Nation-Building in America: Enrollments and

Bureaucratization in the American States, 1870–1930," *American Journal of Sociology* 85 (3) November 1979, 591–613. A similar theme about the distinctiveness of Australian "nationalism" is developed in W. G. McMinn, *Nationalism and Federalism in Australia* (Melbourne: Oxford University Press, 1994).

4 Forrest McDonald, *Novus Ordo Seclorum: The Intellectual Origins of the Constitution* (Lawrence, KS: University Press of Kansas, 1985), 7; Douglas Cole, "The Crimson Thread of Kinship: Ethnic Ideas in Australia, 1870–1914," *Historical Studies* 14 (April 1971), 511–25; Stephen P. Shortus, "'Colonial Nationalism': New South Welsh Identity in the Mid-1880s," *Journal of the Royal Australian Historical Society* 59 (March 1973), 31–51. See also chapter 3 in this volume.

5 Liah Greenfeld, *Nationalism: Five Roads to Modernity* (Cambridge, MA, and London: Harvard University Press, 1992), 10, 402; Benedict Anderson, *Imagined Communities: Reflections on the Origin and Spread of Nationalism*, rev. edn. (London and New York: Verso, 1991), 7. Similar and further important reflections on the core cultural logic of nationalism, with implications beyond the cases, are made in Bruce Kapferer, *Legends of People, Myths of State: Violence, Intolerance, and Political Culture in Sri Lanka and Australia* (Washington, DC, and London: Smithsonian Institution Press, 1988). Kapferer's work builds on that of Anderson in examining the cosmology and ontological implications of nationalist culture, while it is relevant to that of Greenfeld in its attention to the contrast between the "egalitarian individualism" of Australian nationalism and an encompassing and hierarchical unity of people and state in Sinhalese Buddhist nationalist culture.

Earlier forms of collective identity had been, in general, both more universalistic and more particularistic than national identity. In Europe, national identity superseded religious and dynastic forms of collective identity – and identification with particular places, lands, ruling families, heroes, saints, and miracles. On this early history, see the changing authority relations traced by Reinhard Bendix, especially in *Kings or People: Power and the Mandate to Rule* (Berkeley and Los Angeles: University of California Press, 1978), 247–72; the "prehistory" of national identity formation in Western Europe discussed in Orest Ranum, ed., *National Consciousness, History, and Political Culture in Early Modern Europe* (Baltimore and London: Johns Hopkins University Press, 1975); Charles Tilly, ed., *The Formation of National States in Western Europe* (Princeton, NJ: Princeton University Press, 1975); Anthony Giddens, *The Nation State and Violence* (Berkeley: University of California Press, 1985); Breuilly, *Nationalism and the State*, ch. 1; and Royal Institute for International Affairs, "The Rise of National Feeling in Western Europe," in *Nationalism* (London: Oxford University Press, 1939), 8–24.

6 Hobsbawm, *Nations and Nationalism*; Breuilly, *Nationalism and the State*; Greenfeld, *Five Roads*; Smith, *Ethnic Origins*; and Anderson, *Imagined Communities*. Still useful for its historical overview is Hans Kohn, *Nationalism: Its Meaning and History* (Princeton, NJ: D. Van Nostrand Co., 1955). For more

detail on the French and German "models" of nationalism, see Hans Kohn, *Prelude to Nation States* (Princeton, NJ: D. Van Nostrand Co., 1967). The extensive early literature on the development of a politics of nationalism from the late eighteenth century onwards is summarized well in Kenneth R. Minogue, *Nationalism* (New York: Basic Books, 1967).

Focusing on cultures of national identity rather than nationalist mobilization, Greenfeld, in *Five Roads*, develops Hans Kohn's distinction between "Eastern" and "Western," more ethnic and more liberal, groundings for national identity. In this analysis, both Australia and the United States had a core liberal identity early. Anthony D. Smith, in *Ethnic Origins*, also emphasizing the cultural ground of nation-formation, suggests briefly, in contrast to Greenfeld, that "a closer examination always reveals the ethnic core of civic nations . . . with their early pioneering and dominant (English or Spanish) culture in America, Australia, or Argentina, a culture that provided the myths and language of the would-be nation" (216). While both Greenfeld and Smith focus on culture rather than political mobilization, as I do here, they both find core characteristics for the United States – and also by implication Australia – which they would take to be in opposition. Since both the United States and Australia might be said to have had both a British "ethnic core" – Australia more than the United States – and also a liberal grounding to their national identities, these accounts do not go far enough in illuminating the way their national identities developed. Beyond the cultural core – however identified – lies a much richer and more fluid set of symbolic expressions of nationality. In this context, what I am focusing on here is probably better described as public culture than political culture. Bruce Kapferer, in *Legends of People*, would also move beyond "liberal/ethnic" distinctions, although his argument concerning Australia could be used to support its characterization as liberal, but his project should also be distinguished from the one here in its focus on putatively "core" rather than fluidly constructed expressions of nationality.

7 See George L. Mosse, "Caesarism, Circuses, and Monuments," *Journal of Contemporary History* 6 (2) 1971, 167–82; Mosse, "Mass Politics and the Political Liturgy of Nationalism," in Eugene Kamenka, ed., *Nationalism: The Nature and Evolution of an Idea* (New York: St. Martin's Press, 1973), 39–54; Eric Hobsbawm and Terence Ranger, eds., *The Invention of Tradition* (Cambridge and New York: Cambridge University Press, 1983); John R. Gillis, ed., *Commemorations: The Politics of National Identity* (Princeton, NJ: Princeton University Press, 1994).

8 John M. Murrin, "A Roof Without Walls: The Dilemma of American National Identity," in Richard Beeman, Stephen Botein, and Edward C. Carter II, eds., *Beyond Confederation: Origins of the Constitution and American National Identity* (Chapel Hill and London: University of North Carolina Press, published for the Institute of Early American History and Culture, Williamsburg, VA, 1987), 339 (333–48). Among those who note the absence of nationalist claims in the Revolution are Max Savelle, "Nationalism and Other

Loyalties in the American Revolution," *American Historical Review* 67 (July 1962), 901–23; and Carl Becker, *The Declaration of Independence: A Study in the History of Political Ideas* (New York: Alfred A. Knopf, 1960 [1922]), ch. 2. Bernard Bailyn stresses the importance of ideas of the British political opposition in revolutionary thinking: see *The Ideological Origins of the American Revolution* (Cambridge, MA, and London: Belknap Press of Harvard University Press, 1967), and *The Origins of American Politics* (New York: Alfred A. Knopf, 1970). On the British beginnings of the use of the collective term for the colonies, see Richard L. Merrett, *Symbols of American Community, 1735–1775* (New Haven and London: Yale University Press, 1966). To argue that American "national" identity was weak at the time of the Revolution is not to argue that "America" had accumulated no distinctive meaning or value. For a more nuanced account of pre-revolutionary identity than I can provide here, see also Jack P. Greene, "Search for Identity: An Interpretation of the Meaning of Selected Patterns of Social Response in Eighteenth-Century America," *Journal of Social History* 3 (1969–70), 189–220; Greene, *The Intellectual Construction of America: Exceptionalism and Identity from 1492 to 1800* (Chapel Hill and London: University of North Carolina Press, 1993); Michael Zuckerman, "Identity in British America: Unease in Eden," in Nicholas Canny and Anthony Pagden, eds., *Colonial Identity in the Atlantic World, 1500–1800* (Princeton, NJ: Princeton University Press, 1987), 115–57; and David G. Hackett, "The Social Origins of Nationalism: Albany, New York, 1754–1835," *Journal of Social History* 21 (1987–88), 659–81.

9 McDonald, *Novus Ordo Seclorum*, 166; Jack P. Greene, "A Fortuitous Convergence: Culture, Circumstance, and Contingency in the Emergence of the American Nation," in *Religion, Ideology, and Nationalism in Europe and America: Essays Presented in Honor of Yehoshua Arieli* (Jerusalem: Historical Society for Israel and the Zalman Shazar Center for Jewish History, 1986), 259 (243–61). See also John Shy, "The American Revolution: The Military Conflict Considered as a Revolutionary War," in Stephen G. Kurtz and James H. Hutson, eds., *Essays on the American Revolution* (Chapel Hill: University of North Carolina Press, 1973), 121–56; Heidi Tarver, "The Creation of American National Identity, 1774–1796," *Berkeley Journal of Sociology* 37 (1992), 91 (55–99); Jack P. Greene, *Peripheries and Center: Constitutional Development in the Extended Polities of the British Empire and the United States, 1607–1788* (Athens, GA, and London: University of Georgia Press, 1986), 162–63; Zuckerman, "Unease in Eden." For a useful survey of significant colonial and regional differences militating against unity, see Josephine F. Pacheco, "Introduction," in Pacheco, ed., *Antifederalism: The Legacy of George Mason* (Fairfax, VA: George Mason University Press, 1992), 1–23.

10 Paul C. Nagel, *One Nation Indivisible* (New York: Oxford University Press, 1964), 160, 279–80. Nagel provides a useful history of the idea of union in American thought. On the legal ambiguity of the American union, see Kenneth M. Stampp, "The Concept of Perpetual Union," *Journal of American History*

65 (June 1978), 5–33. Peter S. Onuf, *The Origins of the Federal Republic* (Philadelphia: University of Pennsylvania Press, 1983), ch. 8, discusses fear of disunion in the years of the Constitutional Convention. Tocqueville observed this problem of the limits of national sovereignty in the early nineteenth century: see Alexis de Tocqueville, *Democracy in America*, edited by J. P. Mayer and trans. by George Lawrence (Garden City, NY: Doubleday, 1969), 385–94. An analysis of the implications for sovereignty of the Articles of Confederation is provided in William P. Murphy, *The Triumph of Nationalism: Sovereignty, the Founding Fathers, and the Making of the Constitution* (Chicago: Quadrangle Books, 1967), 12–47. State jurisdictional disputes in this period are examined in Onuf, *Origins*. For further discussion of failures in national unity in this period, see Seymour Martin Lipset, *The First New Nation: The United States in Comparative and Historical Perspective* (New York: W. W. Norton and Co., 1979 [1973]), 34–35; Peter D. Hall, *The Organization of American Culture, 1780–1900: Private Institutions, Elites, and the Origins of American Nationality* (New York: New York University Press, 1982); and Yehoshua Arieli, *Individualism and Nationalism in American Ideology* (Cambridge, MA: Harvard University Press, 1964).

11 John Bodnar, *Remaking America: Public Memory, Commemoration, and Patriotism in the Twentieth Century* (Princeton, NJ: Princeton University Press, 1992), 23, 22–25; Gustav de Beaumont, quoted in Lipset, *First New Nation*, 19, 15–23. See also Barry Schwartz, *George Washington: The Making of an American Symbol* (Ithaca, NY, and London: Cornell University Press, 1987); Schwartz, "Social Change and Collective Memory: The Democratization of George Washington," *American Sociological Review* 56 (2) April 1991, 221–36; Wilbur Zelinsky, *Nation into State: The Shifting Symbolic Foundations of American Nationalism* (Chapel Hill and London: University of North Carolina Press, 1988), 30–35; Philip F. Detweiler, "The Changing Reputation of the Declaration of Independence: The First Fifty Years," *William and Mary Quarterly* 19 (October 1962), 557–74; Donald Raichle, "The Image of the Constitution in American History: A Study in Historical Writing from David Ramsay to John Fiske (1789–1888)" Ph.D. dissertation, Columbia University, 1956; Michael Kammen, *A Machine That Would Go of Itself: The Constitution in American Culture* (New York: Vintage Books, 1987), ch. 2. Barry Schwartz, in "The Social Context of Commemoration: A Study in Collective Memory," *Social Forces* 61 (December 1982), 372–402, argues that national representations before the Civil War focused on the Revolution in the face of other problems of unity, and that representations became more varied after the Civil War.

12 Michael Kammen, *Mystic Chords of Memory: The Transformation of Tradition in American Culture* (New York: Knopf, 1991), 49; Charles Warren, "Fourth of July Myths," *William and Mary Quarterly* 2 (1945), 237–72; Robert Pettis Hay, "Freedom's Jubilee: One Hundred Years of the Fourth of July, 1776–1876," Ph.D. dissertation, University of Kentucky, 1967; Diana Karter Appelbaum,

The Glorious Fourth: An American Holiday, An American History (New York and Oxford: Facts on File, 1989); Zelinsky, *Nation into State*, 70–73.

13 Kammen, *Mystic Chords*, 75; Bodnar, *Remaking America*, 26; Tocqueville, *Democracy in America*, 367. On regional orientation of historical organizations, see Kammen, *Mystic Chords*, 74–75; on more state-promoted "invention of tradition," see Hobsbawm and Ranger, *Invention of Tradition*; on the laissez-faire character of early American tradition, see Susan G. Davis, *Parades and Power: Street Theatre in Nineteenth-Century Philadelphia* (Philadelphia: Temple University Press, 1986), 9; on 1837, see Kammen, *Mystic Chords*, 49; on 1832, see Bodnar, *Remaking America*, 26. It should be clear in what follows, though, that celebration forms were often adapted from parades, marches, and so on which characterized local and partisan politics in the period. See Michael McGerr, *The Decline of Popular Politics: The American North, 1865–1928* (New York: Oxford University Press, 1986), 22–41; and Jean H. Baker, *Affairs of Party: The Political Culture of Northern Democrats in the Mid-Nineteenth Century* (Ithaca, NY: Cornell University Press, 1983).

14 Wallace E. Davies, *Patriotism on Parade: The Story of Veterans' and Hereditary Organizations in America, 1783–1900* (Cambridge, MA: Harvard University Press, 1955), 2; Morton Keller, *Affairs of State: Public Life in Late Nineteenth-Century America* (Cambridge, MA, and London: Belknap Press of Harvard University Press, 1977), 439–47. On the flag, see Merle Curti, *The Roots of American Loyalty* (New York: Russell and Russell, 1967), 190–91; on Uncle Sam, see Alton Ketchum, *Uncle Sam: The Man and the Legend* (New York: Hill and Wang, 1959); on Thanksgiving, see Janet Siskind, "The Invention of Thanksgiving: A Ritual of American Nationality," *Critique of Anthropology* 12 (2) 1992, 167–91; on Memorial Day, see Zelinsky, *Nation into State*, 74. Zelinsky provides the most extensive recent inventory of American patriotic symbols and practices: for his interpretation, see *Nation into State*, 215–22. He characterizes the shift he finds as one from spontaneous and liberal national feeling to "statism," but does not ask whether this might in fact be evidence that national identity became more salient, because he tends to assume in a teleological way that national identity must have been important after the Revolution. (On this sort of assumption, see David Hackett Fischer, *Historians' Fallacies: Toward a Logic of Historical Thought* [New York: Harper and Row, 1970], 236–40.) This is also true of Curti's work and of Hans Kohn, in *American Nationalism: An Interpretive Essay* (New York: MacMillan, 1957), but both present evidence of a substantial shift in the late nineteenth century. The fundamental point here about this late nineteenth-century innovation and institutionalization in American national identity is made with extensive supporting evidence in Kammen, *Mystic Chords*. On anxiety about nationality, see also Stephen Skowrenek, *Building a New American State: The Expansion of National Administrative Capacities, 1877–1920* (Cambridge: Cambridge University Press, 1982). On Progressive pageantry, see David Glassberg, *American Historical Pageantry: The Uses of Tradition in the Early Twentieth Century* (Chapel Hill and London:

University of North Carolina Press, 1990). Also useful on this topic are the essays in Merle Curti, *Probing Our Past* (Gloucester, MA: Peter Smith, 1962); and Kammen, *Constitution in American Culture*.

15 An entry into debates about the proper explanation of Australia's founding is provided in Ged Martin, ed., *The Founding of Australia: The Argument About Australia's Origins* (Sydney: Hale and Iremonger, 1978). The debates have continued: see G. J. Abbott, "The Botany Bay Decision," *Journal of Australian Studies* 16 (May 1985), 21–40; Alan Atkinson, "The First Plans for Governing New South Wales, 1786–1787," *Australian Historical Studies* 24 (94) April 1990, 22–40; Alan Frost, "Historians, Handling Documents, Transgressions, and Transportable Offences," *Australian Historical Studies* 25 (99) October 1993, 192–219.

16 On convicts and free settlers, see, for example, James Jupp, *Immigration* (Melbourne: Sydney University Press with Oxford University Press, 1991), 1–13. Robin Haines and Ralph Shlomowitz, in "Immigration from the United Kingdom to Colonial Australia: A Statistical Analysis," *Journal of Australian Studies* 34 (September 1992), 43–52, show that "about 47 percent of UK 'free' (that is, non-convict) immigrants were government assisted" (44), and that Victoria was unusual, compared to other colonies, in that most immigrants were unassisted (because of gold rushes there). On New South Wales and Van Diemen's Land (later Tasmania), see, for example, G. J. Abbott and N. B. Nairn, eds., *Economic Growth of Australia, 1788–1821* (Melbourne: Melbourne University Press, 1969); Alan Frost, "The Conditions of Early Settlement: New South Wales, 1788–1840," in John Carroll, ed., *Intruders in the Bush: The Australian Quest for Identity* (Melbourne: Oxford University Press, 1982), 69–81, criticizes historiographical overstatement about the experience of alienation and desperate struggle in the new land.

17 R. V. Jackson, *Australian Economic Development in the Nineteenth Century* (Canberra: Australian National University Press, 1977). On nineteenth-century Australian political economy, see Malcolm Alexander, "Australia: A Settler Society in a Changing World," in James Walter, ed., *Australian Studies: A Survey* (Melbourne: Oxford University Press, 1989), 51–60; and Philip McMichael, *Settlers and the Agrarian Question: Foundations of Capitalism in Colonial Australia* (Cambridge: Cambridge University Press, 1984).

18 Beverley Kingston, *1860–1900: Glad, Confident Morning*, vol. III, *The Oxford History of Australia* (Melbourne: Oxford University Press, 1988), 279. On the agricultural workforce compared to the United States, see Jackson, *Australian Economic Development*, 106; on the Australian workforce, see ibid., 20–22; see also Ken Buckley and Ted Wheelwright, *No Paradise for Workers: Capitalism and the Common People in Australia, 1788–1914* (Melbourne: Oxford University Press, 1988), 11. On urbanization, see Jackson, *Australian Economic Development*, 21, 92–111, especially, compared to the United States, 95–96; on average wealth per head see Kingston, *Glad, Confident Morning*, 41–42. Urbanization in Australia has received extensive scholarly attention; for an introduction to the

literature, see Gail Reekie, "Nineteenth-Century Urbanization," in Walter, *Australian Studies*, 84–96; and Sean Glynn, "Urbanisation in Australian History," in Gillian Whitlock and David Carter, eds., *Images of Australia* (St. Lucia, Queensland: University of Queensland Press, 1992), 229–39. A useful and detailed overview of many aspects of Australian economic development in the late nineteenth century is provided in Noel G. Butlin, "Colonial Socialism in Australia, 1860–1890," in Hugh G. J. Aitken, ed., *The State and Economic Growth* (New York: Social Science Research Council, 1959), 26–78. See also the classic study by N. G. Butlin, *Investment in Australian Economic Development, 1861–1900* (Cambridge: Cambridge University Press, 1964).

19 For a more nuanced historical and theoretical analysis of this dependence than is possible here, see McMichael, *Settlers and the Agrarian Question*. See also Philip McMichael, "State Formation and the Construction of the World Market," in Maurice Zeitlin, ed., *Political Power and Social Theory: A Research Annual* 6 (1987), 187–237; Butlin, "Colonial Socialism," and *Investment*; Jackson, *Australian Economic Development*; Michael Dunn, *Australia and the Empire: From 1788 to the Present* (Sydney: Fontana/Collins, 1984), 13–86; Peter Cochrane, *Industrialization and Dependence: Australia's Road to Economic Development, 1870–1939* (St. Lucia, Queensland: University of Queensland Press, 1980), 1–10. On geopolitical relations and concerns, see T. B. Millar, *Australia in Peace and War: External Relations, 1788–1977* (New York: St. Martin's Press, 1978), 55–65. A vivid sense of the taken-for-granted quality of imperial relations in mainstream Australian culture is provided by K. S. Inglis, "The Imperial Connection: Telegraphic Communication Between England and Australia, 1872–1902," in A. F. Madden and W. H. Morris-Jones, eds., *Australia and Britain: Studies in a Changing Relationship* (Sydney: Sydney University Press in association with the Institute of Commonwealth Studies, University of London, 1980), 21–38. Important background on imperial history and context is provided in P. J. Cain and A. G. Hopkins, *British Imperialism: Innovation and Expansion, 1688–1914* (New York: Longman, 1993).

20 W. G. McMinn, *A Constitutional History of Australia* (Melbourne: Oxford University Press, 1979), 90. I. D. McNaughton, "Colonial Liberalism, 1851–1892," in Gordon Greenwood, ed., *Australia: A Social and Political History* (North Ryde and London: Angus and Robertson, 1955), 98–114; Kingston, *Glad, Confident Morning*, 237, 295–96; A. G. L. Shaw, "London and the Governors: Relations in Eastern Australia, 1825–1845," in Madden and Morris-Jones, *Australia and Britain*, 1–20. On governors' wives, see Beverley Kingston, "The Lady and the Australian Girl: Some Thoughts on Nationalism and Class," in Norma Grieve and Ailsa Burns, eds., *Australian Women: New Feminist Perspectives* (Melbourne: Oxford University Press, 1986), 32 (27–41). For an important and sophisticated overview which traces the development of the Australian state to early colonial governance, see Alastair Davidson, *The Invisible State: The Formation of the Australian State, 1788–1901* (Cambridge: Cambridge University Press, 1991), esp. 19–64.

21 Kingston, *Glad, Confident Morning*, 237–58; McMinn, *Constitutional History*, 40–91; J. B. Hirst, *The Strange Birth of Colonial Democracy: New South Wales, 1848–1884* (Sydney: Allen and Unwin, 1988); McNaughton, "Colonial Liberalism"; J. M. Main, "Making Constitutions in New South Wales and Victoria, 1853–1854," in Margot Beever and F. B. Smith, *Historical Studies: Selected Articles*, 2nd edn. (Melbourne: Melbourne University Press, 1967), 51–74; J. A. Ryan, Geoffrey Bartlett, B. K. de Garis, and C. T. Stannage, "Colonial Politics in Australia: A Symposium," *Australian Economic History Review* 8 (1) March 1968, 37–61; R. D. Walshe, *Australia's Fight for Independence and Parliamentary Democracy* (Sydney: Current Books, 1956). For a useful overview of Australian politics in the late nineteenth century, and of Australian political culture, see Brian Head, "Political Dependency and the Institutional Framework," and "Political Ideologies and Political Parties," in Walter, *Australian Studies*, 275–80 and 284–94, respectively. On the limits of "responsible government," the Australian version of liberal political ideas, see Davidson, *Invisible State*. On later developments, see Patrick Weiler and Dean Jaensch, eds., *Responsible Government in Australia*, special edn. of *Politics* 15 (2) November 1980 (Richmond, Victoria: Drummond Publishing for the Australian Political Studies Association, 1980). On Australian political culture, see Don Aitken, "Australian Political Culture," *Australian Cultural History* 5 (1986), 5–11. Australia's liberalism is often characterized as "egalitarian": in the comparison with the United States this makes it, for Lipset, in *First New Nation*, 270, more collectivist, but in comparison with Sri Lanka, for Bruce Kapferer, in *Legends of People*, more individualistic.

22 On railway loans, see Jackson, *Australian Economic Development*, 68, and more generally on capital imports, 12–13, and chs. 3 and 8; Butlin, "Colonial Socialism" and *Investment*; Buckley and Wheelwright, *No Paradise*, 104–07. Brian Head, "The Role of State Intervention," in Walter, *Australian Studies*, 295–303, surveys Australian debates on late nineteenth-century state intervention. For a comparison of US state intervention in the same period, see Henry W. Broude, "The Role of the State in American Economic Development, 1820–1890," in Hugh Aitken, *The State and Economic Growth*, 4–25. Broude draws attention to American government contributions which are sometimes overlooked, but his argument, taken alongside that of Butlin in the same collection, only serves to stress that "colonial socialism" in Australia made much larger contributions to economic development. However, Lipset, in *First New Nation*, 54–55, points to the neglected influence of government investment – and capital imports – in the development of the American economy in the first half of the nineteenth century. On the transformation of this industrial governance, with a more nuanced analysis of state in economy than is possible here, see Frank Dobbin, *Forging Industrial Policy: The United States, Britain, and France in the Railway Age* (Cambridge: Cambridge University Press, 1994), 28–94. For a useful discussion of the ways state intervention affected Australian political culture, with comparisons with the

United States, see Don Aitken, "Australian Political Culture," and Brian Galligan, "The State in Australian Political Thought," *Politics* 19 (2) November 1984, 82–92.

23 Kingston, *Glad, Confident Morning*, 273; Geoffrey Serle quotes Royce in his more generally pertinent essay, "Victoria's Campaign for Federation," in A. W. Martin, ed., *Essays in Australian Federation* (Melbourne: Melbourne University Press, 1969), 53 (1–56). See also C. D. Allin, *A History of the Tariff Relations of the Australian Colonies*, University of Minnesota Studies in the Social Sciences, VII (Minneapolis, MN: Bulletin of the University of Minnesota, February 1918). On the issue of river waters, see G. D. Patterson, "The Murray River Border Customs Dispute, 1853–1880," *Business Archives and History* 2 (1962), 122–50. Issues of railways, tariffs, and waters are noted in most discussions of federation politics: see n. 25 below. Intercolonial disputes and rivalries encouraged pro-federation feeling in one important frontier mining town: see Brian Kennedy, "Regionalism and Nationalism: Broken Hill in the 1880s," *Australian Economic History Review* 20 (1) March 1980, 64–76.

24 Richard White, *Inventing Australia: Images and Identity, 1688–1980* (Sydney: George Allen and Unwin, 1981), 32, 52, 29–84; Lipset, *First New Nation*. A useful account of early political issues evoking an "Australian" identity is provided in Charles S. Blackton, "The Dawn of Australian National Feeling, 1850–1856," *Pacific Historical Review* 24 (2) May 1955, 121–38. Peter Hoffenberg, in "Colonial Innocents Abroad? Late Nineteenth-Century Australian Visitors to America and the Invention of New Nations" (paper presented at the 107th annual meeting of the American Historical Association, Washington, DC, 1992), suggests that Australian notables who visited Philadelphia in 1876 "negotiated Australia's national identity between [British and American] models and found much more in common with their fellow 'new' nation and society across the Pacific" (2). Both models were adopted freely by Australians, depending on context. See also chapter 3 of this volume.

25 McMinn, *Constitutional History*, 97; P. Lucien Buddivent, *The "CENTENNIAL," or Simple Rhymes of an "Idle Rhymster"* (Sydney: Wm MacLardy, Printer, 1888; held in Petherick Collection, National Library of Australia, Canberra). K. T. Livingston, in "Anticipating Federation: The Federalising of Telecommunications in Australia," *Australian Historical Studies* 26 (102) April 1994, 97–118, shows a neglected side of the slow process by which federation came to seem natural. For the full story, see the recent synthesis provided in McMinn, *Nationalism and Federalism*. See also C. D. Allin, *The Early Federation Movement of Australia* (Kingston, Ontario: Press of the British Whig Publishing Co., 1907); L. F. Crisp, *The Later Australian Federation Movement, 1883–1901: Outline and Bibliography* (Canberra: Australian National University Research School of Social Sciences, 1979), 1–8; J. A. La Nauze, *The Making of the Australian Constitution* (Melbourne: Melbourne University Press, 1972), chs. 1, 2, 6; B. K. de Garis, "The Colonial Office and the Commonwealth Constitution Bill," in A. W. Martin, *Essays in Australian Federation*, 94–121; Davidson,

Invisible State, ch. 8. Hoffenberg, "Colonial Innocents Abroad?," suggests that Australian visitors to the Philadelphia exhibition felt themselves to be and were treated as Australians, not members of different colonies.

26 On controversies about Colonial Office foreign policy, see, for example, McMinn, *Constitutional History*, 87–90; McNaughton, "Colonial Liberalism," 124; and Kingston, *Glad, Confident Morning*, 293. On the first Australian generation and a nationally oriented culture industry, see White, *Inventing Australia*, 85–96, and Leigh Astbury, "Cash Buyers Welcome: Australian Artists and Bohemianism in the 1890s," *Journal of Australian Studies* 20 (May 1987), 23–37. On the Australian Natives' Association, see White, *Inventing Australia*, 73; J. E. Menadue, *A Centenary History of the Australian Natives' Association* (Melbourne: Horticultural Press, n.d.); and Jan Pettman, "The Australian Natives' Association and Federation in South Australia," in A. W. Martin, *Essays in Australian Federation*, 122–36. On the imperial federation movement in relation to these developments, see Charles Blackton, "Australian Nationality and Nationalism: The Imperial Federationist Interlude, 1885–1901," *Historical Studies* 7 (1955), 1–16.

On republican nationalism, see Glenn A. Davies, "A Brief History of Australian Republicanism," in George Winterton, ed., *We, the People: Australian Republican Government* (Sydney: Allen and Unwin, 1994), 49–62. Davies concludes that "there has not existed in Australia a republican movement. Rather there has been a collection of republican episodes" (60). See also David Headon, James Warden, and Bill Gammage, eds., *Crown or Country: The Traditions of Australian Republicanism* (Sydney: Allen and Unwin, 1994); R. A. Gollan, "Nationalism, the Labour Movement, and the Commonwealth, 1880–1900," in Greenwood, *Social and Political History*, 145–95; Kingston, *Glad, Confident Morning*, 104–07; Ailsa Thompson, "The *Bulletin* and Australian Nationalism" (MA thesis, Canberra University College, 1953); and H. Anderson, ed., *Tocsin: Radical Comments Against Federation, 1897–1900* (Melbourne: Melbourne University Press, 1977). For American influences on one of Australia's better-known republicans of the late nineteenth century, see David Headon, "Preparing for the Grandest Experiment – Daniel Deniehy's New-World Vocabulary," *Journal of Australian Studies* 17 (November 1985), 59–68.

On the *Bulletin*, which has had an exceptionally large impact on Australian historiography, see David Carter with Gillian Whitlock, "Institutions of Australian Literature," in Walter, *Australian Studies*, 112–29; and Ailsa G. Zainu'ddin, "The Early History of the *Bulletin*" in Beever and Smith, *Historical Studies*, 199–216. An overview of the period touching on most important aspects relevant to developing Australian identity can be found in Stephen Alomes, *A Nation at Last? The Changing Character of Australian Nationalism, 1880–1988* (North Ryde and London: Angus and Robertson, 1988), 12–38.

27 White, *Inventing Australia*, 86, 96–109; on constitutional conventions and referendums in the 1890s, see n. 25 above, and Lyn Spillman, "'Neither the

Same Nation Nor Different Nations': Constitutional Conventions in the United States and Australia," *Comparative Studies in Society and History* 38 (1) January 1996, 149–81. On national mythology, see Russel Ward, *The Australian Legend*, 2nd edn. (Melbourne: Oxford University Press, 1966 [1958]); Ward, "The Australian Legend Re-visited," *Historical Studies* 18 (71) October 1978, 171–90; Graeme Davison, "Sydney and the Bush: An Urban Context for the Australian Legend," *Historical Studies* 18 (71) October 1978, 191–209; J. B. Hirst, "The Pioneer Legend," *Historical Studies* 18 (71) October 1978, 316–37; Alan Lawson, "Acknowledging Colonialism: Revisions of Australian Tradition," in Madden and Morris-Jones, *Australia and Britain*, 135–44; Marilyn Lake, "The Politics of Respectability: Identifying the Masculinist Context," *Historical Studies* 22 (86) April 1986, 116–31. See also responses to Lake's influential feminist re-interpretation by Chris McConville, "Rough Women, Respectable Men, and Social Reform: A Response to Lake's 'Masculinism,'" *Historical Studies* 22 (88) April 1987, 432–41, and Judith Allen, "'Mundane' Men: Historians, Masculinity, and Masculinism," *Historical Studies* 22 (89) October 1987, 717–28. Useful collections of many of the classic statements about Australian national images and character can be found in Whitlock and Carter, *Images of Australia*, and Carroll, *Intruders in the Bush*. On the slow attenuation of the constitutional and legislative dependence on Britain in Australia, see W. J. Hudson and M. P. Sharpe, *Australian Independence: Colony to Reluctant Kingdom* (Melbourne: Melbourne University Press, 1988). On economic dependence, see n. 20 above. Peter Spearritt, "Royal Progress: The Queen and Her Australian Subjects," in S. L. Goldberg and F. B. Smith, eds., *Australian Cultural History* (Cambridge: Cambridge University Press, 1988), 138–57, shows tellingly the continuing intensity of mainstream attachment to Britain in the 1950s; Jane Connors, "The 1954 Royal Tour of Australia," *Australian Historical Studies* 25 (100) April 1993, 371–82, provides further evidence that Australian identity and attachment to Britain have generally not been thought to be mutually exclusive. J. D. B. Miller, in "'An Empire That Don't Care What You Do . . . '" in Madden and Morris-Jones, *Australia and Britain*, 90–100, argues that mainstream conservative governments in Australia have taken their own line against Britain in a variety of policy areas; while this evidence does not invalidate more common arguments about Australian geopolitical, economic, and ideological dependence, it does establish in a different way that Australian and British identities were not mutually exclusive. See also Charles Grimshaw, "Australian Nationalism and the Imperial Connection, 1900–1914," *Australian Journal of Politics and History* 3 (2) May 1958, 161–82.

28 Ward, *Australian Legend*, 6. See also Cole, "Crimson Thread of Kinship," and Shortus, "'Colonial Nationalism,'" both of whom show different configurations of the same symbolic repertoire. Useful summaries of the centrifugal and centripetal forces at work in federation are provided in A. W. Martin, "Australian Federation and Nationalism: Historical Notes," in R. L. Mathews, ed., *Public Policies in Two Federal Countries: Canada and Australia* (Canberra:

Centre for Research on Federal Financial Relations, Australian National University, 1982), 28–30 (27–46); John Eddy, "Nationalism and Nation-making from Federation to Gallipoli," in John Eddy and Deryck Schreuder, eds., *The Rise of Colonial Nationalism* (Sydney: Allen and Unwin, 1988), 132–37.

29 Serle, "Victoria's Campaign for Federation," 35, 34. On the history of Australia Day, including more general discussion of variant practices and institutionalization throughout Australia's history, other Australian holidays, and some comparison to American holidays, see K. S. Inglis, "Australia Day," *Historical Studies* 13 (49) October 1967, 20–41. See also Kingston, *Glad, Confident Morning*, 184. For a summary of Parkes's somewhat inconsistent actions on federation, see McMinn, *Constitutional History*, 102.

30 Edward Shils, "Center and Periphery," in *Center and Periphery: Essays in Macrosociology* (Chicago and London: University of Chicago Press, 1975), 3 (3–16); Shils, "Center and Periphery: An Idea and Its Career, 1935–1987," in Liah Greenfeld and Michel Martin, eds., *Center: Ideas and Institutions* (Chicago and London: University of Chicago Press, 1988), 252, 251 (250–82). See also Michael Schudson, "Culture and the Integration of National Societies," in Diana Crane, ed., *The Sociology of Culture: Emerging Theoretical Perspectives* (Oxford and Cambridge, MA: Blackwell, 1994), 24–25 (21–43), for a similar use of Shils's framework. Center/periphery models have been used most commonly in analyses of political systems (see, for example, Seymour Martin Lipset, "The Social Requisites of Democracy Revisited," *American Sociological Review* 59 [1] February 1994, 14 [1–22]). The use of Shils's framework here should also be distinguished from the use of center/periphery terminology in world systems theory and in imperial history, although clearly there are important theoretical analogies which merit further development.

31 Shils, "Society and Societies: The Macrosociological View," in *Center and Periphery*, 39 (34–47).

32 David Kertzer, *Rituals, Politics, and Power* (New Haven: Yale University Press, 1989), 69. See also Ann Swidler, "Culture in Action: Symbols and Strategies," *American Sociological Review* 51 (2) April 1986, 273–86; Gene Burns, *The Frontiers of Catholicism: The Politics of Ideology in a Liberal World* (Berkeley and Los Angeles: University of California Press, 1992), 193–96; Peter Stromberg, "Consensus and Variation in the Interpretation of Religious Symbolism: A Swedish Example," *American Ethnologist* 8 (3) August 1981, 544–59.

33 Shils, "Idea and Career," 258; Steven Lukes, "Political Ritual and Social Integration," *Sociology* 9 (2) May 1975, 300 (289–308). The importance of ritual, and political culture more generally, for contesting and oppositional groups is stressed, for example, in Lynn Hunt, *Politics, Culture, and Class in the French Revolution* (Berkeley: University of California Press, 1984), and Kertzer, *Rituals, Politics, and Power*. The importance of recognizing peripheral apathy is stressed in Michael Mann, "The Social Cohesion of Liberal Democracy," *American Sociological Review* 35 (3) June 1970, 435 (423–39); Michel de Certeau, *The Practice of Everyday Life* (Berkeley and Los Angeles: University

of California Press, 1988), 31; Nicholas Abercrombie and Bryan Turner, "The Dominant Ideology Thesis," *British Journal of Sociology* 29 (2) June 1978, 151–63; and Nicholas Abercrombie, Stephen Hill, and Bryan Turner, *The Dominant Ideology Thesis* (London: George Allen and Unwin, 1980). Mabel Berezin extends our understanding of the ways ritual may be influential where its content does not express any central ideology by emphasizing the influence of formal properties. See "Cultural Form and Political Meaning: State-Subsidized Theater, Ideology, and the Language of Style in Fascist Italy," *American Journal of Sociology* 99 (March 1994), 1237–86.

34 On the Fourth of July orations, see Frederick Saunders, ed., *Our National Centennial Jubilee: Orations, Addresses, and Poems Delivered on the Fourth of July, 1876, in the Several States of the Union* (St. Clair Shores, MI: Scholarly Press, 1976 [1877]), 4. For centennial publications, see Benson J. Lossing, *The American Centenary: A History of the Progress of the Republic of the United States During the First One Hundred Years of Its Existence* (Philadelphia: Porter & Coates, 1876); Des Moines Public Schools, Third Ward, No. 10, *1876, a Centennial Offering* (Ames, IA: Iowa State University Press, 1977); Morse Brothers, Druggists and Pharmacists, *Ye Centennial Almanac* (Rutland, VT: Tuttle and Co., Printers, 1876; held in Library of Congress, Washington, DC). Appelbaum, *The Glorious Fourth*, 109, reports that the Fourth of July celebrations were the biggest in twenty years: she discusses the Canton, CT, Worcester, MA, and Logansport, IN, celebrations among others, 114–15. On Indianapolis, see Walter T. K. Nugent, "Seed Time of Modern Conflict: American Society at the Centennial," in Lillian B. Miller, Walter T. K. Nugent, and H. Wayne Morgan, *1876: The Centennial Year. Indiana Historical Society Lectures, 1972–1973* (Indianapolis: Indiana Historical Society, 1973), 32 (30–45). New Year's celebrations in St. Paul, Cincinnati, Cleveland, and New York, and Fourth of July celebrations in Denver and Raleigh, are noted in William Pierce Randel, *Centennial: American Life in 1876* (Philadelphia and New York: Chilton Book Co., 1969), 2–3, 116, 423. On Pottstown, PA, see L. H. Davis, "The Centennial Celebration at Pottstown, PA, July 4, 1876, and Historical Sketch Written . . . at the Request of the Centennial Committee" (Pottstown, PA: n.p., 1876; held in Library of Congress, Washington, DC). On Galena, IN, see Bodnar, *Remaking America*, 120; Bodnar also analyzes important local and regional differences in public memory of the period, providing a useful perspective on the more elite-oriented view presented here.

35 United States Centennial Commission (USCC), *The National Celebration of the Centennial Anniversary of the Independence of the United States by an International Universal Exhibition, to be held in Philadelphia in the Year 1876* (accompanied by a Classified Compilation of the Journal of the Proceedings of the Commission and other Papers), compiled and arranged by H. D. Pratt (Washington, DC: Government Printing Office, 1873), 37; Thomas J. Schlereth, "The 1876 Centennial: A Model for Comparative American Studies," in *Artifacts and the American Past* (Nashville, TN: American Association for State

and Local History, 1980), 133 (130–42), describes the exhibition as a cultural olympics (of course, the Olympics were not to be launched for another twenty years). On participation by states and foreign countries, see USCC, *International Exhibition 1876. Appendix to the Reports of the USCC and Centennial Board of Finance* (Philadelphia: J. B. Lippincott, 1879; held in Bancroft Library, University of California at Berkeley), Appendices D, G, H, and I. See also Robert Rydell, *All the World's a Fair: Visions of Empire at American International Expositions, 1876–1916* (Chicago and London: University of Chicago Press, 1984), 9–37; Merle Curti, "America at World Fairs, 1851–1893," in *Probing our Past*, 246–77. Curti also discusses the US part in Australian exhibitions, including in 1888. For the converse story, see Peter Hoffenberg and Marc Rothenberg, "Australia at the 1876 Exhibition in Philadelphia," *Historical Records of Australian Science* 8 (1990), 55–60. For important examinations of nineteenth-century exhibitions as signifiers of global relations, see Carol A. Breckinridge, "The Aesthetics and Politics of Colonial Collecting: India at World Fairs," and Timothy Mitchell, "The World as Exhibition," *Comparative Studies in Society and History* 31 (2) April 1984, 195–216 and 217–36, respectively. A useful overview of what exhibitions were like is provided in Burton Benedict, "The Anthropology of World's Fairs," in Benedict, ed., with Marjorie M. Dobkin, Gray Brechin, Elizabeth N. Armstrong, and George Starr, *The Anthropology of World's Fairs: San Francisco's Panama Pacific International Exposition of 1915* (London and Berkeley: Lowie Museum of Anthropology in association with Scolar Press, 1983), 1–65. One of the most extensive scholarly studies of exhibitions to date, providing context and analysis for many aspects only mentioned here, is Paul Greenhalgh, *Ephemeral Vistas: The Expositions Universelles, Great Exhibitions, and World's Fairs, 1851–1939* (Manchester: Manchester University Press, 1988).

36 David Bailey, *"Eastward Ho!" or Leaves from the Diary of a Centennial Pilgrim: Being a Truthful Account of a Trip to the Centennial City . . .* (Highland County, OH: published by the author, 1877), 33. On the passenger railway, see William Pepper, medical director, Bureau of Medical Service, report submitted to Alfred Goshorn, director-general of the USCC, 1877 (advance proofsheets held in Toner Collection, Rare Books and Special Collections Division, Library of Congress, Washington, DC), 16. On the Idaho woman receiving exhibition pictures, see Randel, *Centennial*, 75. For overviews of the exhibition, see, along with the official reports and unofficial commentary cited below, Rydell, *All The World's a Fair*, 11–17; Randel, *Centennial*, 284–306; James W. Campbell, in *America in Her Centennial Year, 1876* (Washington, DC: University Press of America, 1980), 5–21; Dee Brown, *The Year of the Century: 1876* (New York: Charles Scribner's Sons, 1966), 112–37; John Hicks, "The United States Centennial Exhibition of 1876," Ph.D. dissertation, University of Georgia, 1972; Lillian B. Miller, "Engines, Marbles, and Canvases: The Centennial Exposition of 1876," in Lillian B. Miller, Nugent, and Morgan, *Centennial Year*, 3–29. On art in international exhibitions, see Elizabeth Gilmore Holt, ed.,

Universal Expositions and State-Sponsored Fine Arts Exhibitions, vol. I, *The Expanding World of Art, 1874–1902* (New Haven and London: Yale University Press, 1988).

37 William D. Kelley, "National Centennial Celebration and Exposition," speech delivered in the House of Representatives, January 10, 1871 (Washington, DC: F. J. Rives and Geo. A. Bailey, Reporters and Printers of the Debates of Congress, 1871), 2; [American Association of School Administrators], *Education at the Centennial. Extracts from the Proceedings of the Department of Superintendance of the National Education Association, Washington, January 27 & 28, 1875* (Washington, DC: Government Printing Office, 1875), 12. On the mobilizing work, see, for example, Appendix B, "Circulars, Announcements, etc.," in USCC, *International Exhibition 1876*. For some biographical background of official organizers, see S. Edgar Trout, *The Story of the Centennial of 1876: Golden Anniversary* (Lancaster, PA: n.p., 1929), 12–14, 191–201. Most observers of the exhibition have discussed the organizing elite; see Rydell, *All the World's a Fair*, 17–19; Curti, "America at World's Fairs"; John Cawelti, "America on Display, 1876, 1893, 1933," in Frederic C. Jaher, ed., *America in the Age of Industrialism* (New York: Free Press, 1968), 317–63; Bodnar, *Remaking America*, 29; and Randel, *Centennial*, 285. The International Exhibition in Chicago in 1893 has received more scholarly attention than the 1876 exhibition; in addition to the works cited above, see Alan Trachtenberg, *The Incorporation of America: Culture and Society in the Gilded Age* (New York: Hill and Wang, 1982), ch. 7.

38 D. L. Love, *Love's Southerner's Illustrated Guide to the Centennial Exposition. "Multum in Parvo." All About the Centennial, How to Go: Where to Stop, What to See, How to See It &c &c* (New York: Wheat and Cornell, Printers, 1876), 28; Rydell, *All the World's a Fair*, 17. Rydell stresses the hegemonic function of American international exhibitions, which "propagated the ideas and values of the country's political, financial, corporate, and intellectual leaders and offered these ideas as the proper interpretation of social and political reality" (3). On business failures, workforce, manufacturing index, railroad mileage, GNP, and balance of payments, in that order, see US Department of Commerce, *Historical Statistics of the United States, Colonial Times to 1970* (Washington, DC: Government Printing Office, 1975), 913, 138, 667, 731, 225, 867–68; Randel, *Centennial*, 115, 163–65. See also Mira Wilkins, *The History of Foreign Investment in the United States to 1914* (Cambridge, MA, and London: Harvard University Press, 1989); Trachtenberg, *Incorporation of America*, 38, 41, 70–86; Peter Gourevitch, *Politics in Hard Times: Comparative Responses to International Economic Crises* (Ithaca, NY, and London: Cornell University Press, 1986), 105–11; and Dobbin, *Forging Industrial Policy*, 28–94.

39 Bailey, *"Eastward Ho!"*, 33; Randel, *Centennial*, ch. 5; Campbell, *America in Her Centennial Year*, chs. 2 and 8; Brown, *Year of the Century*, ch. 4, ch. 10, ch. 12.

40 Daisy Shortcut [pseud.] and 'Arry O'Pagus [David Solis Cohen], *Our Show; a*

Humorous Account of the International Exposition in Honor of the Centennial Anniversary of American Independence, . . . etc., illustrated by A. B. Frost (Philadelphia: Claxton, Remson, and Haffelfinger, 1876; held in Rare Books and Special Collections Division, Library of Congress, Washington, DC), 10. More serious accounts of the series of difficulties in obtaining congressional "countenance" and funding are given in USCC, *The National Centennial: The International Exhibition of 1876. Message of the President of the United States to Congress Transmitting the Third Report of the USCC on the Progress of the Work . . . Embracing the Report on the Vienna Exhibition of 1873* (Washington, DC: Government Printing Office, 1874), 3–12; Francis A. Walker, *The World's Fair. Philadelphia 1876. A Critical Account* (New York: A. S. Barnes & Co., 1877), 5–28; Edward C. Bruce, *The Century: Its Fruits and Its Festival. Being a History and Description of the Centennial Exhibition, with a Preliminary Outline of Modern Progress. With Numerous Illustrations* (Philadelphia: J. B. Lippincott, 1877), 61–64; Lossing, *American Centenary*, 582–87. On the US government exhibits, see *Report of the Board on Behalf of the United States Executive Departments at the International Exhibition, Held at Philadelphia, PA, 1876, Under Acts of Congress of March 3, 1875, and May 1, 1876,* 2 vols. (Washington, DC: Government Printing Office, 1884); H. Craig Miner, "The United States Government Building at the Centennial Exhibition, 1874–1877," *Prologue* 4 (1972), 203–18; Randel, *Centennial*, 296. On the American state in this period, Skowrenek, *Building a New American State*, 19–35; Keller, *Affairs of State*, 439–47; Randel, *Centennial*, 190, 246, 260–79, 284.

Rydell, in *All the World's a Fair*, examines the influence and organization of Smithsonian contributions to the exhibition. While these were highly significant for the development and influence of racist classifications, as Rydell argues, they should not be taken as dominant aspects of the exhibition as it appeared to contemporaries. In focusing on implications for racial categories, Rydell gives an impression of greater federal government influence in 1876 than is apparent in the contemporary documents I have examined.

41 On "state days," see James D. McCabe, *The Illustrated History of the Centennial Exhibition, Held in Commemoration of the One Hundredth Anniversary of American Independence . . .* (Philadelphia: National Publishing Co., 1876), 783; on the Southern club, see *Guide to the Centennial Exposition and Fairmount Park* (Philadelphia: J. H. Smythe, c1876), 16; on state boards, see USCC, *International Exhibition 1876*, Appendix G on State Boards; on state buildings and the Southern Tournament, see McCabe, *Illustrated History*, 668, 815; and Randel, *Centennial*, 302.

42 International Order of Oddfellows, Sovereign General Lodge, *Centennial Celebration in Honor of the Anniversary of American Independence . . . September, 1876* (Philadelphia: Burk and Caldwell, Printers, 1876); Elbridge G. Spaulding, "Address at the Bank Officers and Bankers Building, Centennial Grounds, Fairmount Park, Philadelphia, on the Occasion of the Formal Opening, May 30, 1876" (Philadelphia: Richard Magee and Son, Printers,

1876); the Grangers' Hotel, among many other centennial actions, is mentioned in Floyd Rinhart and Marion Rinhart, *America's Centennial Celebration (Philadelphia – 1876)* (Winter Haven, FL: Manta Books, 1976), 49; B'nai B'rith (given as B'nai Berith) and ground-breaking ceremonies appear in Centennial Board of Finance (CBF), *Celebration of the Ninety-Ninth Anniversary of American Independence in Fairmount Park, Philadelphia, July 5th, 1875* (Philadelphia: King and Baird, Printers, 1875); National Liberal League, *Equal Rights in Religion: Report of the Centennial Congress of Liberals and Organization of the National Liberal League, at Philadelphia, on the Fourth of July, 1876* (Boston: National Liberal League, 1876); on the fire departments, see J. S. Ingram, *The Centennial Exposition, Described and Illustrated, Being a Concise and Graphic Description of this Grand Enterprise, Commemorative of the First Centenary of American Independence . . .* (Philadelphia: Hubbard Bros., 1876), 558; on the Social Science Association, see McCabe, *Illustrated History*, 831, and more generally, 830–37, for a fascinating miscellany of recorded events; on meetings of police, doctors, and writers, see Bruce, *Fruits and Festival*, 107–08; on the chess congress, see W. Henry Sayen, ed., *The Grand International Centennial Chess Congress, held in Philadelphia in August, 1876, During the Celebration of the American Centennial*, annotated by Jacob Elson, B. M. Neil, and W. H. Sayen (Philadelphia: Claxton, Remsen, and Haffelfinger, 1876); on the regatta, see McCabe, *Illustrated History*, 753–59. For reports on the events of the exhibition, see McCabe, *Illustrated History*, ch. 26; Ingram, *Centennial Exposition*, ch. 25; and the histories cited in n. 36 above.

43 William Dean Howells, "A Sennight at the Centennial," *Atlantic Monthly* 38 (July 1876), 93–107, quoted in Randel, *Centennial*, 104; Randel, *Centennial*, 115–16, 93, 87–156; US Department of Commerce, *Historical Statistics*, 22.

44 On the Western vote, see Trout, *Golden Anniversary*, 25–26; Randel, *Centennial*, 111–56. On the West in American culture in this period, see Trachtenberg, *Incorporation of America*, 11–25.

45 John W. Forney, *A Centennial Commissioner in Europe, 1874–1876* (Philadelphia: J. B. Lippincott, 1876), 385; US Department of Commerce, *Historical Statistics*, 22; Randel, *Centennial*, 43, 93–94, 104, 227–36, 240–59.

46 Women's Centennial Executive Committee, *Second Annual Report* (Philadelphia: Thomas S. Dando, Steam-Power Printer, 1875), 7, 14, 24–41; see also their *First Annual Report (February 16, 1874)* (Philadelphia: J. B. Lippincott, 1874), 1–3; and their "Women's Department. International Exhibition, Fairmount Park, Philadelphia," *Third Annual Report, March 31st, 1876* (Philadelphia: Press of Henry B. Ashmead, 1876), 5–6, 9; USCC, *National Centennial*, 70; Ladies' Centennial Committee of Rhode Island, *Herald of the Centennial* 1 (November 1875), 77; [Executive Committee of the Women's Branch of the Centennial Association for Connecticut], *Spirit of 'Seventy-Six* 1 (June 1875), 32; 1 (December 75), 59; 1 (February 1876), 76; 1 (December 1876), 130; Brown, *Year of the Century*, 138–66; Randel, *Centennial*, 314–15; for descriptions of the

Women's Pavilion, see McCabe, *Illustrated History*, 654–58; Bruce, *Fruits and Festival*, 76–78. See also William D. Andres, "Women and the Fairs of 1876 and 1893," *Hayes Historical Journal* 1 (1976–77), 173–83; Greenhalgh, *Ephemeral Vistas*, 174–78.

47 On the July 3 parade, see Trout, *Golden Anniversary*, 139–40; on the appeal to "mechanics and artisans," see [?USCC], *Additional Notes on the International Exhibition and the Centennial* (N.p.: n.p., ?1874; held in the Library of Congress, Washington, DC), 6; internal evidence suggests that this pamphlet was printed to promote the exhibition in 1874 at the height of a funding debate. On national pride and diligent labor, see USCC, *Journal of the Proceedings of the United States Centennial Commission, at Philadelphia, 1872* (Philadelphia: E. C. Markley and Son, Printers, 1872), Appendices, 47; on workers' excursions, see [New Jersey State Centennial Board], *Report of the New Jersey Commissioners on the Centennial Exhibition* (Trenton, NJ: Naar, Day, and Naar, Printers, 1877; held in Doe Library, University of California at Berkeley), 91. Rydell, *All the World's a Fair*, 32–33, summarizes further contemporary evidence of discussion and programs concerned with providing opportunities to workers to see the exhibition. On the Knights of Labor, see Kim Voss, *The Making of American Exceptionalism: The Knights of Labor and Class Formation in the Nineteenth Century* (Ithaca, NY, and London: Cornell University Press, 1993), 72–79; on the Knights of Labor, coal miners, and mainstream discourse on workers, see Randel, *Centennial*, 193 n. 1, 194, 191–93; on the mill and railway strikes, see Brown, *Year of the Century*, 346, 348. On the history of workers' collective representation in parades such as the Philadelphia parade, see Susan Davis, *Parades and Power*. See also Trachtenberg, *Incorporation of America*, 86–100.

48 On the Liberty hand, see Brown, *Year of the Century*, 128; for immigration statistics, see US Department of Commerce, *Historical Statistics*, 117. On foreigners' reunions, see Randel, *Centennial*, 302; on the Catholic fountain and Italian statue, see USCC, *International Exhibition 1876*, Appendix A; *Guide to the Centennial Exposition and Fairmount Park*, 18, 29; Ingram, *Centennial Exposition*, 588, 618; and McCabe, *Illustrated History*, 802. For a comparative overview of American immigration in this period, see Walter Nugent, *Crossings: The Great Transatlantic Migrations, 1870–1914* (Bloomington, IN: Indiana University Press, 1992); for comparison of American and Australian immigration, see n. 59 below.

49 Randel, *Centennial*, 76, 134, 71; Ladies' Centennial Committee of Rhode Island, *Herald of the Centennial* 1 (July 1875), 44–45; Rydell, *All the World's a Fair*, 25; and Bruce, *Fruits and Festival*, 105. On the Smithsonian exhibit, see Robert A. Trennert, "A Grand Failure: The Centennial Indian Exhibition of 1876," *Prologue* 6 (Summer 1974), 118–29, and Rydell, *All the World's a Fair*, 23–27. On Native American population, see US Department of Commerce, *Historical Statistics*, 14. See also Michael Rogin, "Liberal Society and the

Indian Question," in *"Ronald Reagan," the Movie and Other Episodes in Political Demonology* (Berkeley and Los Angeles: University of California Press, 1987), 134–68; Trachtenberg, *Incorporation of America*, 25–37.

50 US Department of Commerce, *Historical Statistics*, 14, 8; David W. Blight, "'For Something Beyond the Battlefield': Frederick Douglass and the Struggle for the Memory of the Civil War," in David Thelen, ed., *Memory and American History* (Bloomington and Indianapolis, IN: Indiana University Press, 1990), 27–39. On Douglass at the Fourth of July ceremony, see Philip S. Foner, "Black Participation in the Centennial of 1876," *Negro History Bulletin* 39 (February 1976), 533 (532–38), and Brown, *Year of the Century*, 120; on the Tallahassee jubilee, see [Executive Committee of the Women's Branch of the Centennial Association for Connecticut], *Spirit of 'Seventy-Six* 1 (March 1876), 96; on the snub of black women in Philadelphia, see Foner, "Black Participation," 534. Foner provides a very useful general overview of attempted black participation. On the colored schools, see McCabe, *Illustrated History*, 351–52; on the black band, see *Guide to the Centennial Exposition and Fairmount Park*, 16; on the tobacco firm exhibit, see [*New York Tribune*], *New York Tribune Extra No. 35: Letters About the Exhibition*, 38; on the Hamburgh Massacre, see "A Centennial Fourth of July Democratic Celebration: The Massacre of Six Colored Citizens of the United States at Hamburgh, SC, on July 4, 1876," in *Pamphlets on US History and Politics* (N.p., n.d.; held in Doe Library, University of California at Berkeley) – this is the record of a debate in the House of Representatives on July 15 and 16, 1876; and Brown, *Year of the Century*, 267–74. See also Rydell, *All the World's a Fair*, 27–29, for further evidence of discrimination against African American participation; and Leon E. Litwak, "Trouble in Mind: The Bicentennial and the Afro-American Experience," *Journal of American History* 74 (2) September 1989, 315–37, on the centennial of the Constitution in 1887 and the contradictions between black experience and national ceremonial representations.

51 The most comprehensive contemporary overview of the Sydney events, with details of the politics of their planning, attendances, and even banquet guests, is J. Sheridan Moore, *Memorials of the Celebration of the Australasian Centenary in New South Wales, 1888* (Sydney: Charles Potter, Government Printer, 1888; held in Mitchell Library, Sydney). Many other ephemeral records like programs and invitations are also held in the Mitchell Library. An intriguing example is *Official Programme, New South Wales Centennial Regatta*, which carries an illustration including the flags of all six colonies on the cover. The best, and perhaps only, modern overview is given in [Graeme Davison], "Centennial Celebrations," ch. 1 in Graeme Davison, J. W. McCarty, and Ailsa McLeary, eds., *Australians 1888* (Sydney: Fairfax, Syme, and Weldon, 1988), 1–29. On Centennial Park politics, see Paul Ashton and Kate Blackmore, *Centennial Park: A History* (Kensington, New South Wales: New South Wales University Press, 1988).

52 *Hutchinson's Australian Almanac 1889* (Melbourne: M. L. Hutchinson, 1889;

held in Mitchell Library, Sydney), 106. Some outline of the story of the Australian problems can be found in Moore, *Memorials*, 19–23; [Centennial International Exhibition Commission], *Official Record . . . Melbourne, 1888–1889, Containing a Sketch of the Industrial and Economic Progress of the Australasian Colonies During the First Century of Their Existence: and of the Exhibition Held in Melbourne, Victoria, to Commemorate the Close of That Period . . .* published by the authority of the Executive Commissioners (Melbourne: Sands and McDougall Limited, Printers, 1890), 128–31; and Oscar Comettant, *In the Land of Kangaroos and Gold Mines*, trans. by Judith Armstrong (Adelaide: Rigby, 1980 [1899]), 230. For criticism of Victoria's appropriation of the centennial exhibition, see *Brisbane Courier*, August 2, 1888, 4; and *Sydney Morning Herald*, July 26, 1888, 7; August 2, 1888, 7. See also [Davison], "Centennial Celebrations," 3. For the history of exhibitions from an Australian point of view, see Graeme Davison, "Festivals of Nationhood: The International Exhibitions," in Goldberg and Smith, *Australian Cultural History*, 158–77; Kingston, *Glad, Confident Morning*, 57–58, 227. For an interesting contemporary overview of the history of exhibitions, see also *Notes on Exhibits and Exhibitors, Centennial International Exhibition, Melbourne 1888* (?Melbourne: McLean Brothers and Prigg Limited, Publishers, 1888; held in Mitchell Library, Sydney).

53 [CIE Commission], *The Official Catalogue of the Exhibits, with Introductory Notices of the Countries Exhibiting*, 2 vols. (Melbourne: published by M. L. Hutchinson, printed by Mason, Firth, and McCutcheon, 1888); bound with CIE Melbourne 1888, *Commission. List of Commissioners, Rules, and Regulations*, and *Official Guide to the Picture Galleries and Catalogue of Fine Arts*, compiled and edited for the commissioners by J. Lake, superintendent of Fine Arts, 4th edn., 1889 (all bound together and held in Mitchell Library, Sydney). See also [CIE Commission], *Official Daily Programme* (programs from August 14 and December 7–21 are in Mitchell Library, Sydney). The packages from Queensland are reported in *Brisbane Courier*, July 28, 1888, 3. Orchestral concerts are mentioned in Kingston, *Glad, Confident Morning*, 228.

54 For the comparative assessment of attendance, see Davison, "Festivals of Nationhood," 170–72.

55 Buddivent, *"CENTENNIAL," or Simple Rhymes of an "Idle Rhymster"; Celebration in Commemoration of the Centennial of Australia and the Jubilee Year of the Foundation of the Sisters of Charity in Australia, St. Vincent's Convent, 23rd January 1988* (Sydney: J. G. O'Connor, Nation Office, 1888; held in National Library of Australia); [?Savory Appleton] *The Exhibition Historical and Descriptive Geography of the Australian Colonies, by Mrs Savory Appleton* (Melbourne: n.p., 1888; held in Dixson Library, Sydney). Unofficial centennial celebrations around Sydney in January are noted in Moore, *Memorials*, 45. On celebrations of January 26 around Australia, press commentary, provincial attendance, and the "exodus to Melbourne," see [Davison], "Centennial Celebrations," 19–21, 26–29; on histories written on the occasion of the

Australian centennial, see Brian H. Fletcher, "The 1888 Celebrations," in *Australian History in New South Wales, 1888–1938* (Kensington: New South Wales University Press, 1993), 1–19.

56 Harold Stephen, quoted in Moore, *Memorials*, 19; [CIE Commission], *Official Record*, 207; *Brisbane Courier*, August 2, 1888, 4. Centennial rhetoric and the exhibitions genre covered up some important economic differences between the countries. Annual growth rates in Australia at the time were close to high growth rates in the United States but a "long boom" (1860–90) was drawing to a close. As in the United States, manufacture was increasing in Australia, to around 11 percent of economic product, but it was relatively inefficient and the small domestic market did not generate the same sort of domestic demand or industrialization process as in the United States: "there was no prospect of anything like the self-sustaining, domestically oriented growth that emerged after the Civil War in the United States" (Jackson, *Australian Economic Development*, 11). Most consumer and capital goods were imported. High capital imports, not increasing exports or sizable domestic markets, were sustaining Australia's growth in the 1880s; indeed, capital imports were probably higher than basic economic growth could sustain. The Australian economy was internationally vulnerable both to export and financial markets, and would pay a high price for this vulnerability soon after the centennial, in the severe depression in the 1890s. Whereas the American centennial would be in part a cultural mediation of growing industrialization and a coming economic boom, the Australian centennial was more a projection of past economic trends. See Jackson, *Australian Economic Development*, 14–15, 115–19; W. D. Rubinstein, "Men of Wealth," in Goldberg and Smith, *Australian Cultural History*, 110 (109–22); Kingston, *Glad, Confident Morning*, 34–38; Cochrane, *Industrialization and Dependence*.

57 Sydney Morning Herald, January 27, 1888, 2; January 24, 1888, 11. At the procession before the opening of the Melbourne exhibition, "the spectacular portion of the procession was mostly contributed by the Trade Societies," when fifty-four groups of different tradesmen joined firemen, friendly societies, military, and official dignitaries: [CIE Commission], *Official Record*, 200–01. On intercolonial trades union conferences, see Gollan, "Nationalism, the Labour Movement and the Commonwealth"; on the Socialist League, see Kingston, *Glad, Confident Morning*, 99–100; on employers' organizations, see T. V. Matthews, "Business Associations and the State, 1850–1976," in Brian Head, ed., *State and Economy in Australia* (Melbourne: Oxford University Press, 1983), 118 (115–49); on Australian labor politics in the period, see, for example, Buckley and Wheelwright, *No Paradise*, 164–84; Ray Markey, "Populism and the Formation of a Labor Party in New South Wales, 1890–1900," *Journal of Australian Studies* 20 (May 1987), 38–48; and Verity Burgmann, "Racism, Socialism, and the Labour Movement, 1887–1917," *Labour History* 47 (November 1984), 39–54.

58 [CIE Commission], *Official Catalogue*, vol. I, 43; *Tribune and News of the Week*, January 20, 1888, 7; Kingston, *Glad, Confident Morning*, 103. On the work of

suffrage activists, see Audrey Oldfield, *Woman Suffrage in Australia: A Gift or a Struggle?* (Cambridge: Cambridge University Press, 1992). Oldfield provides a long-needed account of women's suffrage work in the Australian states in the period, rebutting assumptions that women's suffrage in Australia was a gift. But explaining "why politicians in Australia were more susceptible to pressure [than in Britain and the United States]" (213) she points to "the strength of radical Liberalism . . .; the happy coincidence of Australia's federation movement in the period of most intense suffrage activity; the desire of Australians to show the world, and especially Britain, that Australia was a progressive society; and the perception that the woman's vote would be a tool which the politicians could use to impose order and morality on the emerging nation" (217). Marian Quartly, "Mothers and Fathers and Brothers and Sisters: The AWA and the ANA and Gendered Citizenship," in Renate Howe, ed., *Women and the State*, special edn. of *Journal of Australian Studies* (Bundoora, Victoria: La Trobe University Press, 1993), 22–30, shows that middle-class federation organizations were receptive to women's suffrage claims. But although suffrage, problematic for the strong women's movement in the United States, came early to Australian women, national identity was constructed much more resolutely as masculine. See, for example, Susan Baggett Barham, "Conceptualizations of Women Within Australian Egalitarian Thought," *Comparative Studies in Society and History* 30 (3) July 1980, 483–510; Desley Deacon, "Political Arithmetic: The Nineteenth-Century Australian Census and the Construction of the Dependent Woman," *Signs* 11 (1) 1985, 27–47; Lake, "Politics of Respectability"; Kay Schaffer, *Women and the Bush: Forces of Desire in the Australian Cultural Tradition* (Cambridge and Melbourne: Cambridge University Press, 1988); Susan Magarey, Sue Rowley, and Susan Sheridan, eds., *Debutante Nation: Feminism Contests the 1890s* (Sydney: Allen and Unwin, 1993); Jill Roe, "Chivalry and Social Policy in the Antipodes," *Historical Studies* 22 (88) April 1987, 395–410; Patricia Grimshaw, "'Man's Own Country': Women in Colonial Australian History," in Grieve and Burns, *Australian Women*, 182–209; S. Sheridan, "Louisa Lawson, Miles Franklin, and Feminist Writing, 1888–1901," *Australian Feminist Studies* 7–8 (Summer 1988), 29–48; Miriam Dixson, "Gender, Class, and the Women's Movements in Australia, 1890, 1980" in Grieve and Burns, *Australian Women*, 17–21 (14–26); Kingston, "Lady and the Australian Girl." Useful reviews are provided by Judith Allen, "From Women's History to a History of the Sexes," in Walter, *Australian Studies*, 220–41; and Gail Reekie, "Contesting Australia: Feminism and Histories of the Nation," in Whitlock and Carter, *Images of Australia*, 145–55.

59 R. V. Jackson, *The Population History of Australia* (Melbourne: McPhee Gribble/Penguin, 1988), 5–6, 39; Jupp, *Immigration*, 14–26; [Davison], "Centennial Celebrations," 29. See also Haines and Shlomowitz, "Immigration from the United Kingdom." The *Bulletin* noted pointedly that "no Australian native spoke at the centennial banquet" (February 11, 1888, 9). For a comparative overview of immigration to the United States and Australia, though mostly

focusing on the twentieth century, see Gary P. Freeman and James Jupp, eds., *Nations of Immigrants: Australia, the United States, and International Migration* (Melbourne: Oxford University Press, 1992). John Higham, James Jupp, Peter Rose, and Glenn Withers all contribute essays on immigration with the Australia/United States comparison in mind in Glenn Withers, ed., *Commonality and Difference: Australia and the United States*, vol. I, *Australian Fulbright Papers* (Sydney: Allen and Unwin in association with the Australian–American Educational Foundation, 1991).

60 See Jupp, *Immigration*, 27–53, on Celtic and non-European migration in the nineteenth century. Somewhat dated but useful for its discussion of Irish immigration in a comparative perspective is Andrew Parkin, "Ethnic Politics: A Comparative Study of Two Immigrant Societies, Australia and the United States," *Journal of Commonwealth and Comparative Politics* 15 (1) March 1977, 22–38. Useful on imperial politics concerning Chinese immigration, and on Irish immigrants, is Charles Price, "Immigration," in J. D. B. Miller, ed., *Australians and British: Social and Political Connections* (Sydney: Methuen, 1987), 17–20, 25–26 (13–44). Irish Catholic issues may have been lying behind a controversy at the opening of the exhibition in Melbourne over whether the Anglican bishop should read the opening prayer at the exhibition; the contest was simply resolved when the president of the centennial commission read the prayer instead. The story about the reading of the prayer is mentioned in *Brisbane Courier*, August 1, 1888, 5; see also Davison, "Festivals of Nationhood," 164; Kingston, *Glad, Confident Morning*, 271–72. On Chinese immigration, see also A. T. Yarwood and M. J. Knowling, *Race Relations in Australia: A History* (Sydney: Methuen, 1982), 228–31; and Kathryn Cronin, "The Yellow Agony," in Raymond Evans, Kay Saunders, and Kathryn Cronin, *Exclusion, Exploitation, and Extermination: Race Relations in Colonial Queensland* (Sydney: ANZ Book Co., 1975), 235–340. Although precise comparative assessments are difficult to construct, it is important to note that racist discourse seemed to be much more central to Australian public discourse than to American public discourse; it was taken for granted in the late nineteenth century and is a commonplace of Australian historiography. For a valuable if polemical reminder of racism in Australian history, see Humphrey McQueen, *A New Britannia: An Argument Concerning the Social Origins of Australian Radicalism and Nationalism*, rev. edn. (Ringwood, Victoria: Penguin, 1986 [1970]), ch. 2.

61 On Australian imported labor, see, for example, Jupp, *Immigration*, 44, 47, 49; Kay Saunders, "The Black Scourge," Evans *et al.*, *Exclusion, Exploitation, and Extermination*, 147–234; Marie de Lepervanche, "Nineteenth-Century Experiments with Cheap Coloured Labour," in *Indians in a White Australia: An Account of Race, Class, and Indian Immigration to Eastern Australia* (Sydney: George Allen and Unwin, 1984), 36–55; Kay Saunders, "'The Middle Passage?' Conditions on Labour Vessels from Queensland to Melanesia, 1863–1907," *Journal of Australian Studies* 5 (November 1979), 38–49; and Barry York,

"Sugar Labour: Queensland's Maltese Experiment, 1881–1884," *Journal of Australian Studies* 25 (November 1989), 43–56.

62 Robert Herbert, *Australian Centennial Ode, 1888* (Sydney: n.p., 1892; held in Mitchell Library, Sydney), 4; [CIE Commission], *Official Record,* 61; *Sydney Morning Herald,* January 27, 1888, 2; January 30, 1888, 10; [CIE Commission], *Official Catalogue,* vol. I, 99–101. On the background to this period, see, for example, Henry Reynolds, "Racial Thought in Early Colonial Australia," *Australian Journal of Politics and History* 20 (1) April 1974, 45–55; Raymond Evans, "'The Nigger Shall Disappear . . .': Aborigines and Europeans in Colonial Queensland," in Evans, *et al., Exclusion, Exploitation, and Extermination,* 25–146; Davidson, *Invisible State,* 77–89. For an introduction to the long-denied place of Aborigines in Australian history, see, for example, Yarwood and Knowling, *Race Relations;* Henry Reynolds, *Frontier: Aborigines, Settlers, and Land* (Sydney: George Allen and Unwin, 1987); Bain Attwood, *The Making of the Aborigines* (Sydney: Allen and Unwin, 1989); Henry Reynolds, *The Other Side of the Frontier: An Interpretation of the Aboriginal Response to the Invasion and Settlement of Australia* (Ringwood, Victoria: Penguin, 1982); Bain Attwood and John Arnold, eds., *Power, Knowledge, and Aborigines,* special edn. of *Journal of Australian Studies* (Melbourne: La Trobe University Press with the National Centre for Australian Studies, Monash University, 1992). For an intriguing if isolated comparison, see Diane Kirkby, "Frontier Violence: Ethnohistory and Aboriginal Resistance in California and New South Wales, 1770–1840," *Journal of Australian Studies* 6 (June 1980), 36–48.

63 Richard Peterson, "Revitalizing the Culture Concept," *Annual Review of Sociology* 5 (1979), 153 (137–66). See also Richard Peterson, "Cultural Studies Through the Production Perspective: Progress and Prospects," in Crane, *Sociology of Culture,* 163–89. Examining cultural production sometimes shifts focus from meanings and values produced to organizational context. Here, I suggest that Shils's framework helps understand the production context for these large national rituals, and go on in the following chapters to focus on sets of meanings and values themselves, against this background.

3 "Our country by the world received": centennial celebrations in 1876 and 1888

1 J. Sheridan Moore, *Memorials of the Celebration of the Australasian Centenary in New South Wales, 1888* (Sydney: Charles Potter, Government Printer, 1888; held in Mitchell Library, Sydney), 38; International Order of Oddfellows, Sovereign General Lodge, *Centennial Celebration in Honor of the Anniversary of American Independence . . . September, 1876* (Philadelphia: Burk & Caldwell, Printers, 1876), 38.

2 An analysis of national identity based on these documents can hardly do justice to their richness, and they deserve more attention with other questions in mind.

For my comparative purposes, documents available were of very similar genres. The Australian material was perhaps more concentrated in official reports, souvenir publications, and the press than the American material, although I have also included some evidence from Australian ephemera such as unofficial poetry and guidebooks. The difference in the extent to which I rely on different sorts of sources in the two countries is not great, and reflects the stronger Australian cultural center rather than greater selectivity.

As I will note in the next chapter, there was less opportunity to support the comparative thematic analysis of national identities with systematic sampling from the centennial documents than there was with the bicentennial documents. However, I aimed for exhaustive coverage and detailed analysis of the "universe" of centennial documents, and to the extent this was possible it rendered the issue of systematic sampling less relevant. In the following assessments of the comparative importance of different centennial themes I give my best judgment on the basis of a detailed analysis of the documents, articulating comparative assessments of frequency without imposing greater precision than the evidence warrants.

3 Benedict Anderson, *Imagined Communities: Reflections on the Origin and Spread of Nationalism*, rev. edn. (London and New York: Verso, 1991), 17 (emphasis in original); Liah Greenfeld, *Nationalism: Five Roads to Modernity* (Cambridge, MA, and London: Harvard University Press, 1992), 15. Greenfeld is following Reinhard Bendix, who early stressed the importance of extra-national politics for early nation-formation in Europe: see *Kings or People: Power and the Mandate to Rule* (Berkeley and Los Angeles: University of California Press, 1978), 266, 273. For an extended argument for the importance of the world polity in generating the authority of the nation-state, see George M. Thomas, John W. Meyer, Francisco O. Ramirez, and John Boli, *Institutional Structure: Constituting State, Society, and the Individual* (Newbury Park, CA: Sage, 1987). Greenfeld believes that the core of national identity is a liberal vision of political community, and since this core was established from the beginning in the United States, there was no basis for *ressentiment*. My analysis here suggests that while it is important to see the "liberal" settler countries as distinctive in a larger comparative context, beginning with less ideological commitment to the political relevance of status orders, it cannot be assumed that international comparisons are irrelevant to them. Further, although perhaps modeling "more often than not" suggested inferiority, it did not do so in every case, and even where it did, perceptions of kinship could be an antidote to *ressentiment*. See also Lyn Spillman, "'Neither the Same Nation Nor Different Nations': Constitutional Conventions in the United States and Australia," *Comparative Studies in Society and History* 38 (1) January 1996, 149–81.

4 USCC, *The National Centennial: The International Exhibition of 1876. Message of the President of the United States to Congress Transmitting the Third Report of the USCC on the Progress of the Work . . . Embracing Reports on the Vienna Exhibition of 1873* (Washington, DC: Government Printing Office, 1874), 2; for

one among several examples of the stress on international participation in organizers' talk, see [USCC], *1776–1876. The United States International Exhibition... Origin, Rise & Progress of the Work, Description of the Buildings, etc. . . .* (Philadelphia: n.p., 1873), 10–17; USCC, *Meeting of the Executive Committee, Philadelphia, August 1872* (Philadelphia: n.p., 1872), 5; John Welsh, Speech at the Opening Ceremony, in J. S. Ingram, *The Centennial Exposition, Described and Illustrated, Being a Concise and Graphic Description of This Grand Enterprise, Commemorative of the First Centenary of American Independence...* (Philadelphia: Hubbard Bros., 1876), 78.

5 Bayard Taylor, "Aspects of the Fair," in *[New York Tribune], New York Tribune Extra No. 35: Letters about the Exhibition,* 1876, 5; Women's Centennial Executive Committee, *Second Annual Report* (Philadelphia: Thomas S. Dando, Steam-Power Printer, 1875), 13; S. Edgar Trout, *The Story of the Centennial of 1876: Golden Anniversary* (Lancaster, PA: n.p., 1929), 34–35, 201.

6 On the certificate see Trout, *Golden Anniversary,* 21; on the centennial vase, see James D. McCabe, *The Illustrated History of the Centennial Exhibition, Held in Commemoration of the One Hundredth Anniversary of American Independence.. .* (Philadelphia: National Publishing Co., 1876), 373; records of the B'nai B'rith (given as B'nai Berith) ceremony appear in Centennial Board of Finance, *Celebration of the Ninety-Ninth Anniversary of American Independence in Fairmount Park, Philadelphia, July 5th, 1875* (Philadelphia: King and Baird, Printers, 1875), 37.

7 Moore, *Memorials,* 21; [CIE Commission], *Official Record . . . Melbourne, 1888–1889, Containing a Sketch of the Industrial and Economic Progress of the Australasian Colonies During the First Century of Their Existence: and of the Exhibition Held in Melbourne, Victoria, to Commemorate the Close of That Period...* published by authority of the Executive Commissioners (Melbourne: Sands and McDougall Limited, Printers, 1890), 61, 146; *[Argus], The Centennial International Exhibition, Melbourne, 1888, Inaugural Ceremony,* Souvenir Extract and Reprint from *Argus,* August 2, 1888, 3; [CIE Commission], *Official Record,* 207. See also Graeme Davison, "Festivals of Nationhood: The International Exhibitions," in S. L. Goldberg and F. B. Smith, *Australian Cultural History* (Cambridge: Cambridge University Press, 1988), 167 (158–77).

8 Moore, *Memorials,* 38, 29, 40.

9 James Jefferis, "Australia's Mission and Opportunity," *Centennial Magazine* 1 (1888–89), 104 (101–04); *West Australian,* August 4, 1888 (editorial); *Celebration in Commemoration of the Centennial of Australia and the Jubilee Year of the Foundation of the Order of the Sisters of Charity in Australia, St. Vincent's Convent, 23rd January 1888* (Sydney: J. G. O'Connor, Nation Office, 1888; held in National Library of Australia, Canberra), 8.

10 W. Frederick Morrison, *Aldine Centennial History of New South Wales,* 2 vols. (Sydney: n.p., 1888), vol. I, 224; [CIE Commission], *Official Record,* 291.

11 W. Allen, "Centennial Cantata," music by H. J. King, Jr., in [CIE Commission], *Official Record,* 195; Samuel Harper, *Australia and Mnason: A Centennial Poem,*

Being a Poetical History of the Colony of New South Wales (Sydney: F. Cunningham & Co, Steam Machine Printers, 1885), 13; David G. Ferguson, "The Future of the Australian Colonies," in *Centennial Magazine* 1 (1888–89), 769 (763–69).

12 E. Handel Jones, *The Centennial of Australasia: An Address Delivered . . . at a United Thanksgiving Service Held in St. George's Presbyterian Church, East St. Kilda, January 26, 1888, Commemorative of British Settlement in Australasia* (Melbourne: Crabb and Yelland, Printers, ?1888), 3; Moore, *Memorials*, 34. See also, for example, Morrison, *Centennial History*, vol. I, 224; and Moore, *Memorials*, 29.

13 [CIE Commission], *Official Record*, 59; [CIE Commission], *The Official Catalogue of the Exhibits, with Introductory Notices of the Countries Exhibiting*, 2 vols. (Melbourne: published by M. L. Hutchinson, printed by Mason, Firth, and McCutcheon, 1888), vol. II, 130–31; bound with CIE Melbourne 1888, *Commission. List of Commissioners, Rules, and Regulations*, and *Official Guide to the Picture Galleries and Catalogue of Fine Arts*, compiled and edited for the commissioners by J. Lake, superintendent of Fine Arts, 4th ed., 1889 (held in Mitchell Library, Sydney).

14 Jefferis, "Mission and Opportunity," 102; *Sydney Morning Herald*, November 28, 1889, in *Newspaper Cuttings*, vol. 140, 139, Mitchell Library, Sydney. Examples of similar identifications with the United States were common: see for example Robert Herbert, *Australian Centennial Ode, 1888* (Sydney: n.p., 1892; held in Mitchell Library, Sydney), 6; *Centennial Almanac '88: Facts About Ourselves and the Land We Live In: Guide to Sorrento*, Pamphlet Collection, vol. 270, National Library of Australia, Canberra; Ferguson, "Future of the Australasian Colonies," 765; Jones, *Centennial Address*, 3. A similar picture of the Revolution is given in American statements made within the Anglo-Saxon framework described below. See also Richard White, "Another America," in *Inventing Australia: Images and Identity, 1688–1980* (Sydney and Boston: George Allen and Unwin, 1981), 47–62.

15 Francis A. Walker, *The World's Fair. Philadelphia 1876. A Critical Account* (New York: A. S. Barnes & Co., 1877), 28; John L. Campbell, "The Centennial Celebration and International Exhibition of 1876," in USCC, *National Centennial*, 334; John W. Forney, *A Centennial Commissioner in Europe, 1874–1876* (Philadelphia: J. B. Lippincott, 1876), 87; Taylor, "Aspects of the Fair," 5; Ladies' Centennial Committee of Rhode Island, *Herald of the Centennial* 1 (June 1875), 39; [Executive Committee of the Women's Branch of the Centennial Association for Connecticut], *Spirit of 'Seventy-Six* 12 (March 1877), 141; "Noah Webster, 'The Schoolmaster of the Republic.' . . . United States Centennial," poster (Springfield, MA: Clark W. Bryan and Company, Printers, 1876; held in Broadside Collection, Rare Books and Special Collections Division, Library of Congress, Washington, DC); *The Centennial Eagle. In Twelve Numbers, July–September. An Illustrated Descriptive History of the Centennial Exhibition* (Philadelphia: Centennial Eagle Company, 1876), 101.

Much earlier, as pointed out for instance by Seymour Martin Lipset in *The First New Nation: The United States in Comparative and Historical Perspective* (New York: W. W. Norton, 1979 [1973]), ambivalence about the "mother country" was evident in American identity, so despite the Revolution, Britain was "emulated and admired as the representative of a superior civilization" (62). By the time of the centennial, apparently, the ambivalence could be reconfigured so as to buttress claims about American achievements. A similar story is central to Australian identity too, of course, but it plays out differently.

16 Zavarr Wilmshurst, *Liberty's Centennial, A Poem of 1876* (New York: Stephen English, 1876), 17.

17 Walker, *Critical Account*, 34; see also 28, 45, 49, 67, and 15–16; William Pepper, medical director, Bureau of Medical Service, report submitted to Alfred Goshorn, director-general of the USCC, 1877 (advance proofsheets held in Toner Collection, Rare Books and Special Collections Division, Library of Congress, Washington, DC), 6, 10. Pepper's reports indicate that fifty-five of his patients were British but only thirty-two Japanese; however, he did not include totals on which relative proportions of patients to visitors could be judged. See also Neil Harris, "All the World a Melting Pot? Japan at American Fairs, 1876–1904," in Akira Iriye, ed., *Mutual Images: Essays in American–Japanese Relations* (Cambridge, MA: Harvard University Press, 1975), 24–54, which also details more positive and curious reactions to Japanese presence; and Robert Rydell, *All the World's a Fair: Visions of Empire at the American International Expositions, 1876–1916* (Chicago and London: University of Chicago Press, 1984), 29–31.

18 Daisy Shortcut [pseud.] and 'Arry O'Pagus [David Solis Cohen], *Our Show; a Humorous Account of the International Exposition in Honor of the Centennial Anniversary of American Independence, . . . etc.*, illustrated by A. B. Frost (Philadelphia, Claxton, Remson, and Haffelfinger, 1876; held in Rare Books and Special Collections Division, Library of Congress, Washington, DC), 74.

19 USCC, *The National Celebration of the Centennial Anniversary of the Independence of the United States by an International Universal Exhibition, to be held in Philadelphia in the Year 1876* (accompanied by a Classified Compilation of the Journal of the Proceedings of the Commission and other Papers), compiled and arranged by H. D. Pratt (Washington, DC: Government Printing Office, 1873), 24: On the Revolution in American national identity, see Lipset, *First New Nation*, 74–98; Michael Kammen, *A Season of Youth: The American Revolution and the Historical Imagination* (New York: Oxford University Press, 1978).

20 William M. Evarts, "Oration, July 4th 1876, Philadelphia," reprinted in *His Royal Highness Prince Oscar at the National Celebration of the Centennial Anniversary of American Independence Held in Philadelphia, USA, July 4, 1876* (Boston: Printed at the Riverside Press for Private Distribution, 1876), 90; Trout, *Golden Anniversary*, 144; Shortcut and O'Pagus, *Humorous Account*, 46.

21 David Bailey, *"Eastward Ho!" or Leaves from the Diary of a Centennial Pilgrim: Being a Truthful Account of a Trip to the Centennial City . . .* (Highland County,

OH: published by the author, 1877), 76; Morse Brothers, Druggists and Pharmacists, *Ye Centennial Almanac* (Rutland, VT: Tuttle and Co., Printers, 1876; held in Library of Congress, Washington, DC), 3.

22 CBF, *Ninety-Ninth Anniversary*, 98; Elbridge G. Spaulding, "Address at the Bank Officers and Bankers Building, Centennial Grounds, Fairmount Park, Philadelphia, on the Occasion of the Formal Opening, May 30, 1876" (Philadelphia: Richard Magee and Son, Printers, 1876), 7; Kate Harrington [Rebecca Smith Pollard], *Centennial and Other Poems* (Philadelphia: J. B. Lippincott, 1876), 11. A similar use of claims about Catholic participation in the Revolution is found in William J. Clarke, S. J., "Centennial Discourse, Delivered July 4, 1876, in St. Joseph's Church, Philadelphia" (Philadelphia: P. F. Cunningham and Son, 1876).

23 USCC, *National Celebration*, 62; [?USCC], *Additional Notes on the International Exhibition and the Centennial* (N.p.: n.p., ?1874; held in the Library of Congress, Washington, DC), 9. Internal evidence suggests that this pamphlet was printed to promote the exhibition in 1874 at the height of a funding debate.

24 Thomas M. Norwood, "Centennial Exposition: Speech in the Senate of the United States, February 10, 1876" (Washington, DC: Government Printing Office, 1876), 9; Virginius [Dr Geo. M. Brown], "Centennial Dirge: A Song of Wrong," (?Continsville, VA: n.p., 1877), 3.

25 National Liberal League, *Equal Rights in Religion: Report of the Centennial Congress of Liberals and Organization of the National Liberal League, at Philadelphia, on the Fourth of July, 1876* (Boston: National Liberal League, 1876), 371; Women's Centennial Executive Committee, *Second Annual Report*, 14.

26 On omissions in Australian historical visions more generally, see Tom Griffiths, "Past Silences: Aborigines and Convicts in Our History-Making," *Australian Cultural History* 6 (1987), 18–32.

27 John Plummer, "Choral Parts of the Centennial Ode," music by Hugo Alpen (Sydney: John Sands, General Printer, 1887), 3; W. Allen, "Centennial Cantata," 195.

28 Morrison, *Centennial History*, vol. II, frontispiece; Agricultural Society, Invitation, Luncheon, January 25, 1888 (held in Ephemera 1888, Petherick Collection, National Library of Australia, Canberra); [CIE Commission], *Official Record*, 213; *Brisbane Courier*, January 25, 1888, 5.

29 Morrison, *Centennial History*, vol. I, 220, 221, 225, 214.

30 [CIE Commission], *Official Record*, 59, 62.

31 Bulletin, January 21, 1888, 10; August 4, 1888, 5.

32 Kenneth Bock, "Theories of Progress, Development, Evolution," in Tom Bottomore and Robert Nisbet, eds., *A History of Sociological Analysis* (New York: Basic Books, 1978), 59 (39–79); [*New York Tribune*], *New York Tribune, Extra No. 35*, 30.

33 *Official Programme, New South Wales Centennial Regatta* (held in Miscellaneous Publications File, Centennial Celebrations Box 2, Mitchell Library,

Sydney); for an example of this sort of cartoon showing progress, see *Tribune and News of the Week*, January 20, 1888, 3; for an example of this sort of verse structure, see *Celebration of the Sisters of Charity*.

34 Morrison, *Centennial History*, vol. I, 218; *Sydney Morning Herald*, December 2, 1889, in *Newspaper Cuttings*, vol. 140, 150, Mitchell Library, Sydney.

35 [CIE Commission], *Official Record*, 59–123; [CIE Commission], *Official Catalogue*, vol. I, iv; [CIE Commission], *Official Daily Programme*, no. 12, August 14, 1888 (held in Mitchell Library, Sydney); Moore, *Memorials*, 12. See also Davison, "Festivals of Nationhood," 166–69.

36 USCC, *National Centennial*, 326; USCC, *Meeting of the Executive Committee*. See also, for example, USCC, *Journal of the Proceedings of the United States Centennial Commission, at Philadelphia, 1872* (Philadelphia: E. C. Markley and Son, Printers, 1872), 7–8; John L. Campbell, "The Centennial Celebration and the International Exhibition of 1876," in USCC, *National Centennial*, 333; and John C. Bullitt, "Address . . . delivered at the banquet given by the citizens of Philadelphia, to the President, Supreme Court, and Senate and House of Representatives of the United States, at Horticultural Hall, upon their Visit to the Centennial International Exhibition Grounds, Saturday, Dec. 18, 1875" (Philadelphia: King and Baird, Printers, 1875). On the theme of progress in American identity before this period, see Michael Kammen, *Mystic Chords of Memory: The Transformation of Tradition in American Culture* (New York: Knopf, 1991), 44–48.

37 Trout, *Golden Anniversary*, 46–47; McCabe, *Illustrated History*, 372–73; "Key to the Star Monument" (held in Broadside Collection, Rare Books and Special Collections, Library of Congress, Washington, DC).

38 Benson J. Lossing, *The American Centenary: A History of the Progress of the Republic of the United States During the First One Hundred Years of Its Existence* (Philadelphia: Porter & Coates, 1876), v–vi; on the parade, see comment reprinted in Trout, *Golden Anniversary*, 148. See also Isaac T. Coates, "1776 Centennial 1876, Fourth of July Oration Delivered at Chester, Penna. . . ." (Philadelphia: J. B. Lippincott, 1876), 9; Edward C. Bruce, *The Century: Its Fruits and Its Festival. Being a History and Description of the Centennial Exhibition with a Preliminary Outline of Modern Progress. With Numerous Illustrations* (Philadelphia: J. B. Lippincott, 1877), chs. 1–2; A. A. Livermore, *The Centennial International Exhibition of 1876: A Lecture Delivered in the Court House, Meadville, PA, Before the City Library Association, December 8, 1874* (Meadville, PA: n.p., 1875), 7–9. See also Rydell, *All the World's a Fair*, ch. 3. But William Brotherhead's *Centennial Book of the Signers of the Declaration of Independence* (Philadelphia: J. M. Stoddart, ?1872), 18, which includes a historical essay, so strongly romanticizes the founding moment and Anglo-Saxonism that there is very little on the theme of progress, and if anything, a sense of nostalgia pervades the treatment of the century. In the United States, by contrast to Australia, the founding moment could take priority over progress.

39 Forney, *Centennial Commissioner*, 333–34; D. J. Morrell, USCC commissioner

of Pennsylvania, to John F. Hartranft, governor of Pennsylvania, February 4, 1873, printed in USCC, *National Celebration*, 174. Wilbur Zelinsky, in *Nation into State: The Shifting Symbolic Foundations of American Nationalism* (Chapel Hill and London: University of North Carolina Press, 1988), 86–87, emphasizes future orientation in the centennial. While commercial elites spoke of the future in the context of technological progress, the future of the nation was not an important theme in the broader range of contemporary documents I examine here.

40 Francis E. Abbott, president of the National Liberal League, in National Liberal League, *Equal Rights in Religion*, 60; Women's Centennial Executive Committee, "Women's Department. International Exhibition, Fairmount Park, Philadelphia," *Third Annual Report, March 31, 1876* (Philadelphia: Press of Henry B. Ashmead, 1876), 5.

41 Quote from *Harper's Weekly* in Ladies' Centennial Committee of Rhode Island, *Herald of the Centennial* 1 (May 1875), 31; Jacob Bailey Moore, comp., *New Hampshire at the Centennial. The Address of Governor Cheney, The Oration of Professor E. D. Sanborn, of Dartmouth College* . . . (Manchester, NH: Published by John B. Clarke, 1876), 45. The configuration of national identity in founding moment, progress, and the future deserves further attention with Sacvan Bercovitch's *The American Jeremiad* (Madison, WI: University of Wisconsin Press, 1978) in mind. Echoes of the "jeremiad" formula, with the affirmation through lament Bercovitch analyzes (157), are evident in centennial discourse, but they seem to have been in the process of fading. The founding moment of the Revolution was central, both in affirmation and critique, in the jeremiad as in the centennial vision of history. It is more difficult to draw conclusive parallels in the talk of progress and the future, but the unusual talk of future by centennial critics does seem to conform to the jeremiad tradition.

42 Morrison, *Centennial History*, vol. I, 222; Plummer, "Choral Parts of the Centennial Ode," 3, 3; Herbert, *Centennial Ode*, 6 (emphasis in original). Herbert is paraphrasing George Berkeley on America: see Horst Priessnitz, "Dreams in Austerica: A Preliminary Comparison of the Australian and the American Dream," *Westerly* 3 (Spring 1994), 45–64.

43 Morrison, *Centennial History*, vol. I, 221; Harper, *Australia and Mnason*, 5.

44 Ferguson, "Future of the Australasian Colonies," 767; [CIE Commission], *Official Catalogue*, vol. I, v; *Sydney Morning Herald*, November 28, 1889, in *Newspaper Cuttings*, vol. 140, 140, Mitchell Library, Sydney.

45 On the importance of claims about prosperity in new nations, and the link between claims about liberty and prosperity in the United States, see Lipset, *First New Nation*, 45–60.

46 *Centennial Eagle*, 224.

47 USCC, "Address . . . To the People of the United States," Appendix 1 in *Journal 1872*, 24; *Centennial Eagle*, 41. See also Michael Kammen, *Spheres of Liberty: Changing Perceptions of Liberty in American Culture* (Madison, WI: University of Wisconsin Press, 1986).

48 USCC, *Journal 1872*, 44; USCC, *National Centennial*, 1; USCC, *International Exhibition 1876, Appendix to the Reports of the USCC and the Centennial Board of Finance* (Philadelphia: J. B. Lippincott, 1879; held in Bancroft Library, University of California at Berkeley), 113; Bailey, *"Eastward Ho!"*, 30.

49 Trout, *Golden Anniversary*, frontispiece; Ingram, *Centennial Exposition*, cover engraving; Committee on the National Centennial Commemoration, *Proceedings on the One Hundredth Anniversary of the Introduction and Adoption of the "Resolutions Respecting Independency," Held in Philadelphia* . . . (Philadelphia: Printed for the Committee, 1876), title page; USCC, *National Celebration*, 139; [USCC], . . . *The United States International Exhibition* . . . *The Organization, The Work Proposed, The Work Already Done* (Philadelphia: n.p., 1875), 77; Trout, *Golden Anniversary*, 24; USCC, Complimentary Pass (held in Broadside Collection, Rare Books and Special Collections, Library of Congress, Washington, DC); CBF, *Ninety-Ninth Anniversary*, 46.

50 "Order of Musical Exercises on the Occasion of the Ushering In of the Centennial Anniversary of American Independence . . . ." (held in Broadside Coll., Rare Books and Special Collections, Library of Congress, Washington, DC); Wilmshurst, *Liberty's Centennial*, 7. See also, for example, George J. Johnson, *The Roll Call and Other Poems* (Philadelphia: J. B. Lippincott, 1876), 9–15.

51 Celinda A. B. Lilley, *Centenary Tract. The Coming Centennial, A.D. 1876* (East Calais, VT: published by the author, 1873), 1, 5.

52 Moore, *Memorials*, 25; [CIE Commission], *Official Record*, 60; Moore, *Memorials*, 12; Jones, *Centennial Address*, 2, 3; Herbert, *Centennial Ode*, 5. On characterizing the nation with political values, see also Spillman, "'Neither the Same Nation Nor Different Nations.'"

53 [CIE Commission], *Official Record*, 60; Jones, *Centennial Address*, 3. Lipset has pointed out that "new nations" tend to celebrate holidays marking political events and creeds which are thus also important in national identities, and contrasts this with "nations whose authority stems from traditional legitimacy," which "tend to celebrate holidays linked with a religious tradition or a national military tradition, not with political doctrine as such" (*First New Nation*, 75). The Australian centennial exemplifies a curious hybrid here.

54 Jefferis, "Mission and Opportunity," 104. The author used a common theme about the "excessive invasion of Asiatic races" along with an unusual view of different races having different strengths – the Chinese, for example, were granted "unswerving steadiness." He even went so far as to claim that the British empire was great because of the "mingling of races." Combining these themes created structural problems in the text; *political* national identity allowed him to gloss these contradictions.

Racist claims were much more available at the center of Australian political discourse of the time than at the center of the American discourse. But agitation against Asian immigration was similar to Australia in California, further away from the American cultural center. For example, one of the women's centennial magazines printed a contribution from California which, with vivid and virulently racist images, discussed Chinese immigration there: "the question of Mongolian emigration is the great social problem of the Pacific coast. It involves points which Eastern statesmen can but dimly appreciate . . . they are animals in the strict sense of the term": [Executive Committee of the Women's Branch of the Centennial Association for Connecticut], *Spirit of 'Seventy-Six* 1 (December 1876), 130.

55 Bulletin, January 21, 1888, 12–13. Priessnitz, in "Dreams in Austerica," 56–57, also points to a pervasive utopian characterization of Australia as (ideally) free and just, especially by contrast with the old world, in the literature of the period.

56 Memorial Certificate (held in Broadside Collection, Rare Books and Special Collections, Library of Congress, Washington, DC); Forney, *Centennial Commissioner*, 194; [USCC], *The Organization, The Work Proposed*, preface; John L. Campbell, "The Centennial Celebration and International Exhibition," in USCC, *National Centennial*, 333.

57 Ingram, *Centennial Exposition*, 3; Charles H. Kidder, ed., *Burley's United States Centennial Gazetteer and Guide, 1876* (Philadelphia: S. W. Burley, Proprietor and Publisher, 1876), 202.

58 *Centennial Almanac '88 . . . Guide to Sorrento*, 45; Ferguson, "Future of the Australian Colonies," 763. See also, for example, Jones, *Centennial Address*, 3; [CIE Commission], *Official Record*, 60.

59 [CIE Commission], *Official Record*, iii; Morrison, *Centennial History*, vol. I, 223.

60 Jones, *Centennial Address*, 1; Plummer, "Choral Parts of the Centennial Ode," 4, 9, 12; Herbert, *Centennial Ode*, 4.

61 Morrison, *Centennial History*, vol. I; Moore, *Memorials*, 14; *Bulletin*, August 18, 1888, 8. An example of the frequent praise of explorer heroes in poetry can be found in Harper, *Australia and Mnason*, 29.

62 W. G. De Saussure, "Congratulatory and Welcome Address," in International Order of Oddfellows, *Centennial Celebration*, 24; Harrington, *Centennial and Other Poems*, 9; Nathan Porter, "Address," in International Order of Oddfellows, *Centennial Celebration*, 60. Curiously, the "frontier" provided much more of a "myth of development" in Australia than in the United States in centennial discourse, where it did not seem to be integrated into the version of national identity produced by central organizers. See Richard Slotkin, *The Fatal Environment: The Myth of the Frontier in the Age of Industrialization, 1800–1890* (New York: Atheneum, 1985), ch. 4.

4 "To remind ourselves that we are a united nation": bicentennial celebrations in 1976 and 1988

1 American Revolution Bicentennial Commission (ARBC), *Bicentennial Era* 2 (1971), 1. Probably the most serious omission generated by the focus on centennials and bicentennials is Australia's Anzac tradition, which has accumu-

lated dense national meaning with both vernacular and official dimensions. It is central to the account in Bruce Kapferer, *Legends of People, Myths of State: Violence, Intolerance, and Political Culture in Sri Lanka and Australia* (Washington, DC, and London: Smithsonian Institution Press, 1988), among many others. See also, for instance, K. S. Inglis, "The Anzac Tradition," *Meanjin* 24 (1) 1965, 25–44; Geoffrey Serle, "The Digger Tradition and Australian Nationalism," *Meanjin* 24 (2) 1965, 148–58; Mary Wilson, "The Making of Melbourne's Anzac Day," *Australian Journal of Politics and History* 20 (2) August 1974, 197–209; and Chris Flaherty and Michael Roberts, "The Reproduction of Anzac Symbolism," *Journal of Australian Studies* 24 (May 1989), 52–69. This important tradition was not stressed by Australian bicentennial organizers. Both its original power and its absence in 1988 discourse can be explained within the framework developed here. To some extent, it was subject to the critiques of masculine, Anglo-Saxon exclusiveness to which, as the story below will show, organizers were highly sensitive. I would also argue that part of what had sustained the tradition was the way it symbolized the earning of a place "in the world" for the new nation after the First World War, but that this ay of representing international status lost plausibility along with connections to Britain. Thus, neither concerns about international position nor concerns about internal integration were well assuaged by focusing on this tradition in the overall construction of the nation in 1988.

2 Australian Bicentennial Authority (ABA), *Bicentenary '88* 8 (1): 5 (cited later as *B '88*).

3 Australian organizers visited and reported on a variety of other similar events overseas, and took account of the American bicentennial among them. According to one senior ABA official, "reams of people" made overseas trips, including at least four senior ABA officials (Wendy McCarthy, interview with author, Sydney, January 6, 1989). For example, Desmond Kennard, director of the Australian Bicentennial Exhibition (ABE), mentioned influences and ideas from the Bangkok Bicentenary, an Expo in Japan in 1985, an invited visit to Sweden to their permanent traveling exhibition in 1985, Tennessee and Indianapolis visits, and some knowledge of the Smithsonian Institution Traveling Exhibition Service (SITES), which was similar but much smaller than the ABE for which he was responsible (Desmond Kennard, interview with author, Sydney, January 17, 1989).

The influence of these overseas models was eclectic and not always direct. However, a "tall ships" spectacular and a communities program were among the ideas probably influenced by the American celebration: the Bicentennial Communities Program was organized "along the lines of the American plan," and "people had seen and liked" the Tall Ships Spectacular in the United States; this partly influenced the Australian event (Wendy McCarthy, interview with author, January 6, 1989). Australian officials generally spoke of American influences pragmatically and influences from other countries as equivalent to the American influence. As the ABA described the process:

Authority officers took account of major overseas celebrations, particularly the Canadian Centennial in 1967 and the United States Bicentennial in 1976.

Ideas and examples were drawn from these celebrations, but it was recognised that Australia's Bicentenary would have to reflect the history and texture of Australian society, have a distinctively Australian character and be relevant to the nation's contemporary concerns.

(ABA, *Second Annual Report on Activities to 30 June 1982* [Sydney: ABA, 1982], 5)

For a comparative overview of the two bicentennials, along with the Canadian Centenary (1967), see John Hutchinson, "State Festivals, Foundation Myths, and Cultural Politics in Immigrant Nations," in Tony Bennett, Pat Buckridge, David Carter, and Colin Mercer, eds., *Celebrating the Nation: A Critical Study of Australia's Bicentenary* (Sydney: Allen and Unwin, 1992), 3–25. Hutchinson discusses some of the most important similarities in organization and political consequences of these events: my analysis of the comparative importance of common themes in American and Australian bicentennials suggests that he overstates the importance of international regard in the American case.

4 See John Bodnar, *Remaking America: Public Memory, Commemoration, and Patriotism in the Twentieth Century* (Princeton, NJ: Princeton University Press, 1992), 226–44, for an overview of the celebration of the American bicentennial. Thomas J. Schlereth, "The 1876 Centennial: A Model for Comparative American Studies," in *Artifacts and the American Past* (Nashville, TN: American Association for State and Local History, 1980), 140–41 (130–42), briefly compares the American bicentennial with the centennial; so too does Wilbur Zelinsky, in *Nation into State: The Shifting Symbolic Foundations of American Nationalism* (Chapel Hill and London: University of North Carolina Press, 1988), 83–84. On the Australian bicentenary, see John Warhurst, "The Politics and Management of Australia's Bicentenary Year," *Politics* 22 (1) May 1987, 8–18; Susan Janson and Stuart MacIntyre, eds., *Making the Bicentenary*, special edn. of *Australian Historical Studies* 23 (91) 1988 (Melbourne: Australian Historical Studies, 1988); Tony Bennett, *et al.*, *Celebrating the Nation*.

5 American Revolution Bicentennial Administration (ARBA), *Final Report to the People*, 5 vols. (Washington, DC: Government Printing Office, 1977), vol. I, 240–53; Hawkens and Associates, *Bicentennial Sourcebook* (Washington, DC: n.p., c1973) I-1–13; American Revolution Bicentennial Commission (ARBC), *Annual Report, 1972*, reprinted in Hawkens and Associates, *Sourcebook*, A-25–59; ARBA, *First Report to the Congress*, 2 vols. (Washington, DC: Government Printing Office, 1974–75); and ARBA, *Second Report to the Congress*, 3 vols. (Washington, DC: Government Printing Office, 1975–76). For some discussion of the dissent, see ARBA, *Final Report*, vol. I, 246; Hawkens and Associates, *Sourcebook*, I-2; ARBA, *Second Report*, vol. I, Foreword; M. Kenneth Brody, "Sociological Theories of Symbolic Activity: A Case Study Application to the Bicentennial Observance" (Ph.D. dissertation, University of Iowa, 1977), 97. See also Bodnar, *Remaking America*, 229–34. Some idea of the crisis in the ARBC in the early 1970s, and the general perceptions of its

ineptitude, corruption, and weakness, is well conveyed in the discussion and
reprints in *Congressional Record*, 92nd Cong., 2nd sess., 1972, 118, pt. 14:
17618; pt. 22: 28530–49; pt. 23: 30793–99. See also *Congressional Record*, 93rd
Cong., 2nd sess., 1974, 120, pt. 20: 26446, for a claim that replacing ARBC by
ARBA had improved the situation.

6　ARBA, *Final Report*, vol. II, 274, 214. On federal government activities, see
ARBA, *Final Report*, vol. II, 268–91; on state and territory organization, see for
example ARBA, *Final Report*, vol. I, 58, 240, and ARBC, *Bicentennial Era*, 1
(1970), 1. On the public relations efforts, see ARBA, *Final Report*, vol. I, 224–35.
On the national entertainment events, see Brody, "Bicentennial Observance,"
97–98.

7　ABA, *First Annual Report on Activities to 30 June 1981* (Sydney: ABA, 1981), 3;
on the process of formation, see Australia, Department of Prime Minister and
Cabinet, *Annual Report, 1984–1985* (Canberra: Government Printing Office,
1985), 39–40; on states' activities, see for example ABA, *Second Annual Report*,
9–13; on programs for schools, youth, ethnic, union, older Australians, the
disabled, and church groups, see for example ABA, *Sixth Annual Report on
Activities to 30 June 1986*, edited by Kate Richardson (Sydney: ABA, 1986),
18–22; and *Seventh Annual Report on Activities to 30 June 1987*, edited by Kate
Richardson (Sydney: ABA, 1987), 21–28; on corporate sponsorship, see ABA,
Fifth Annual Report on Activities to 30 June 1985, edited by Robert Campbell
(Sydney: ABA, 1985), 37. See also Warhurst, "Politics and Management."

8　United States, General Accounting Office, *Planning for America's Bicentennial
Celebration – A Progress Report, June 6, 1975* (Washington, DC: Government
Printing Office, 1975), 18. On the failure of plans for an exposition and a system
of bicentennial parks in the American bicentennial, see Bodnar, *Remaking
America*, 230–31; ARBA, *Final Report*, vol. I, 240–53; Hawkens and Associates,
Sourcebook, I-1–13; ARBC, *Annual Report, 1972*; ARBA, *First Report*; and
ARBA, *Second Report*. The Philadelphia exhibition plans and their prob-
lems and ultimate failure are discussed in *Congressional Record*, 91st Cong.,
2nd sess., 1970, 116, pt. 109: 25394; 92nd Cong., 2nd sess., 1972, 118, pt. 15:
19497–99.

International exhibitions were no longer a major form for national celebration. Major exhibitions had been held in the United States in the interwar
period, and Robert Rydell argues that these both continued and altered
ideological and political trends evident in Victorian exhibitions: see his
important *World of Fairs: The Century of Progress Exhibitions* (Chicago and
London: University of Chicago Press, 1993). See also Paul Greenhalgh,
*Ephemeral Vistas: The Expositions Universelles, Great Exhibitions, and World's
Fairs, 1851–1939* (Manchester: Manchester University Press, 1988). On changes
in exhibitions, see also Tony Bennett, "The Shaping of Things to Come: Expo
'88," in Tony Bennett *et al.*, *Celebrating the Nation*, 127–29 (123–41). There is
no full account of the decline of exhibitions as representations of the nation
since the Second World War. In the planning for both American and Australian

bicentennials, international exhibitions were considered but rejected as vehicles of bicentennial celebration: costs and overcentralization of the celebration were reasons in both cases. On the politics behind the Australian decision, see Jennifer Craik, "Expo '88: Fashions of Sight and Politics of Site," in Tony Bennett *et al.*, *Celebrating the Nation*, 143–45 (142–59).

Despite the decline of exhibitions as central forms for national celebration, they did not disappear entirely. A "1974 World's Fair in Spokane, Washington" was "officially recognized" by ARBA and adopted an ecological theme: it was reported to have attracted five million visitors from May to November. See ARBA, *Bicentennial Times: Commemorative Reprints* (Washington, DC: Government Printing Office, 1977), 9, 134 (cited later as *BT*). A widely reported and locally well-attended exhibition was held in Australia in 1988, in Brisbane, but this was not funded as a central event by the ABA and it was only reluctantly supported by other Australian states. Most observers argue that this was "an intensely local affair" (Tony Bennett, "Shaping of Things To Come," 126), which was intended to represent the "modernisation of Brisbane" (135) and "serve as an instrument in [its] cosmopolitanisation" (140). Representing modernity had become the concern of peripheral regions rather than the nation-state. See Graeme Davison, "Festivals of Nationhood: The International Exhibitions," in S. L. Goldberg and F. B. Smith, eds., *Australian Cultural History* (Cambridge: Cambridge University Press, 1988), 173 (158–77). But Craik, in "Fashions of Sight," makes a strong case that local "growth-machine" politics account for exhibitions better than their role as "signs of modernity," if these explanations are mutually exclusive; she also provides extensive background on the Brisbane exhibition.

9 Hawkens and Associates, *Sourcebook*, I-27–28.

10 ARBA, *Final Report*, vol. III, i; Hawkens and Associates, *Sourcebook*, I-28. Among the many publications aiming to mobilize communities were Hawkens and Associates, *Sourcebook*; Robert G. Hartje, *Bicentennial USA: Pathways to Celebration* (Nashville, TN: American Association for State and Local History, 1973); and ARBA, *Call for Achievement* (Washington, DC: Government Printing Office, c1976).

11 ARBA, *Second Report*, vol. I, 23. Listings of community activities were independent of the registration of bicentennial communities.

Despite an early, carefully worded suggestion from organizers that community registration might "possibly enhance favorable consideration for requests for assistance" (Hawkens and Associates, *Sourcebook*, I-28), the Communities Program involved relatively little direct funding; as ARBA ultimately described it, there were "few tangible benefits from ARBC/ARBA official recognition – a certificate of recognition, a presentation ceremony, a Bicentennial flag and permission to display that flag and use that symbol" (ARBA, *Final Report*, vol. I, 82). The Binet database of community activities and events is contained in ARBA, *Final Report*, vols. III–V.

Indeed, bicentennial registration does not seem to have been driven primarily by funding considerations. A small random sample from the ARBA database of registered community activities and events showed that only 6 percent were beneficiaries of ARBA grants. Even purely symbolic attachment to the cultural center of the bicentennial enactment of national identity generated significant participation. At the least, it motivated local-level organizations to complete a number of fairly complicated forms for registration voluntarily. (This database does not represent only the "Bicentennial Communities," however, and funding may have been obtained through state organizations.) Local government, and state, federal, and military organizations operating in local communities accounted for about a quarter of sponsoring organizations, and schools and colleges for another 15 percent; state and local "bicentennial committees" sponsored another third of the events. See also n. 25 below.

12 ABA, *Third Annual Report on Activities to 30 June 1983* (Sydney: ABA, 1983), 3; ABA, *Second Annual Report*, 6. For other information in this paragraph, see ABA, *Ninth Annual Report 1989*, edited by Bruce Pollock, 2 vols. (Sydney: ABA, 1989), vol. II, 178; ABA, *Sixth Annual Report*, 1; ABA, *Third Annual Report*, 3; ABA, *Ninth Annual Report*, vol. II, 214.

13 Several recent studies of American collective memory show organizational precedents to the bicentennial; see Michael Kammen, *Mystic Chords of Memory: The Transformation of Tradition in American Culture* (New York: Knopf, 1991), esp. ch. 17; and Bodnar, *Remaking America*, ch. 8. Kammen argues that American collective memory has generally been more private than elsewhere, but shows that "decentralization by design" has characterized celebrations since 1960. An example of closer links between official and community celebration can be seen in the story of the "Freedom Train" events held during the bicentennial (see Kammen, *Mystic Chords*, 572, 579). Bodnar describes in most detail the ways in which vernacular celebration has remained independent and influential; while my concern is primarily with official celebration, his discussion provides crucial additional insights on the relation between vernacular and official in the bicentennial and in other American celebrations. See also Zelinsky, *Nation into State*, for further detailed discussion of American patriotic symbols and rituals, their history, and an argument that state involvement in their promotion and formulation has increased in the twentieth century.

There are inherent tensions in the role of "official" ritual specialists. In her useful study of Soviet ritual, Christel Lane suggested three tensions faced by official ritual planners: tensions between framing action as directed or spontaneous, tensions between orientations to individual or to collective goals and experience, and tensions between voluntarism and constraint. (See Christel Lane, *The Rites of Rulers: Ritual in Industrial Society – The Soviet Case* [Cambridge: Cambridge University Press, 1981], 55–64.) The first two of these three tensions could also be seen in the language of bicentennial organizers (the tension between voluntarism and constraint was less relevant to this case). For example, considered in this light, American newsletter stories turned out to be striking in two ways. Only a few framed action as spontaneous – mostly the actions were by various organizing groups *for* a populace. Second, a collective rather than an individual orientation predominated: actions were generally framed as by and for groups, organizations, or mass aggregates in the population. Both of these orientations could have been different, as a few counterexamples show. Overall, they give the sense of a rather anxious social distance between national organizers and the nation.

14 Bodnar, *Remaking America*, 206, 238–43. The sample of registered bicentennial activities seems to show evidence of this syncretism and pragmatism. At least a third of the activities and events registered as "bicentennial" would have occurred without the bicentennial or the encouragement of ARBA. For example, a Californian mayor invited to suggest bicentennial activities responded that "the City holds an annual Fiesta De Oro Negro each June and it may be possible to incorporate the Bicentennial Celebration with this annual event." As Brody also noted, many local activities "tended to reflect characteristics of the community in which they took place, rather than any revolutionary era or more contemporary national identity" (Stephen Wright, administrative assistant, City of Signal Hill, CA, to Charles Conrad, chairman, ARBC of California, January 19, 1970; bound with California ARBC, *The California Plan, Submitted to the National ARBC, April 1970* (held in Doe Library, University of California at Berkeley); Brody, "Bicentennial Observance," 96).

15 ABA, *Fifth Annual Report*, 4; ARBA, *Final Report*, vol. II, 78; ARBA, *First Report*, vol. I, 9. See Gene Burns, "The Sociology of Ideology: Social Structure, Autonomy, and Ambiguity," paper presented at the annual meeting of the American Sociological Association, San Francisco, August 1989; and Gene Burns, *The Frontiers of Catholicism: The Politics of Ideology in a Liberal World* (Berkeley and Los Angeles: University of California Press, 1992), 194–95. See also Bodnar, *Remaking America*, 232–33. The general trend to inclusive ambiguity was most explicit in one of the ABA's major projects, the traveling Australian Bicentennial Exhibition. The story of this exhibition makes an intriguing illustration of the possibilities and limits of postmodern representation. See Peter Cochrane and David Goodman, "The Great Australian Journey: Cultural Logic and Nationalism in the Postmodern Era," in Janson and MacIntyre, *Making the Bicentenary*, 21–44. See also n. 78 below.

16 ARBA, *Final Report*, vol. II, 78. For a useful overview of the developments which challenged and altered established frameworks of cultural authority and political legitimacy, see David Farber, ed., *The Sixties: From Memory to History* (Chapel Hill and London: University of North Carolina Press, 1994).

17 ARBA, *Final Report*, vol. I, 7. See also Bodnar, *Remaking America*, 228, 230. On the broader shifts in political context in this period, see, for example, J. Craig Jenkins, "Interpreting the Stormy 1960s: Three Theories in Search of a Political Age," *Research in Political Sociology* 3 (1987), 269–303. The history of the organization of the bicentennial supports arguments which consider shifting political opportunities due to shifting elite political alignments as one factor in

the explanation of the rise and decline of the contention of the time. Another side of this story is analyzed in Jeffrey C. Alexander, "Culture and Political Crisis: 'Watergate' and Durkheimian Sociology," in Jeffrey C. Alexander, ed., *Durkheimian Sociology: Cultural Studies* (Cambridge and New York: Cambridge University Press, 1988), 187–224.

18 ARBA, *First Report*, vol. I, 12; ARBA, *Final Report*, vol. I, 197. See also ARBA, *National Bicentennial Ethnic and Racial Council Conference Report, Washington, DC, January 20–22, 1975* (Washington, DC: Government Printing Office, 1975), cited later as *BERC*; Bodnar, *Remaking America*, 232, 237. On youth activists' claims and their influence on bicentennial organizers, see below, pp. 206–07, in the discussion of critical claims based on the founding moment. A somewhat similar process occurred to pre-empt challenges by feminists. Again on the initiative of the central organization, a task force of representatives of women's organizations met in 1972, and "urged the ARBC to assure the preparation of national documentation of women's contribution to the cultural, ethnic, social, economic, and political development of the United States, 1776–1976" (Hawkens and Associates, *Sourcebook*, A-40). A later meeting made specific recommendations to increase women's representation in the organization (ARBA, *Final Report*, vol. I, 204). Women's concerns continued to be raised occasionally at the board level, unlike those of the young activists:

> Mrs. [Congresswoman] Schroeder expressed strong views about the funding of Bicentennial programs devoted to the status of women in our society . . . For the most part there were grants to do projects such as the archaeological excavation of Andrew Jackson's home or the DAR putting plaques on historical homes. These obviously are not women's projects dealing with the role of women.
> (ARBA, "Minutes, 1975": 4, bound with ARBA, *Second Report*)

Once again, a pre-emptive concern was followed by an expansion of formal inclusion and the fading of more radical challenges. Compared to 1876, there seem to have been few national-level bicentennial events produced directly by feminists.

19 Brody, "Bicentennial Observance," 134; ARBA, *Final Report*, vol. I, 106, 116, 47. See also ARBA, *BERC*; Jeremy Rifkin, *Commonsense II: The Case Against Corporate Tyranny* (Boston: People's Bicentennial Commission, 1975); Heritage Foundation, *The Great Bicentennial Debate: History as a Political Weapon* (record of a debate between Jeremy Rifkin, director, People's Bicentennial Commission, and Jeffrey St. John, author and historian, held at St. Olaf's College, Minnesota, 1976; held in Doe Library, University of California at Berkeley); US Senate Judiciary Committee, Subcommittee to Investigate the Administration of the Internal Security Act and Other Internal Security Laws, *The Attempt to Steal the Bicentennial*, 1976; People's Bicentennial Commission, *America's Birthday: A Planning and Activity Guide for Citizens' Participation During the Bicentennial Years* (New York: Simon and Schuster, 1974); *Congres-*

sional Record, 94th Cong., 2nd sess., 1976, 122, pt. 11: 13561; pt. 17: 21778–79.
A "July 4th Coalition" of critical leftist groups also organized protest activities
in Philadelphia and elsewhere on Independence Day 1976: for one overview of
participation and activities, see *Congressional Record*, 94th Cong., 2nd sess.,
1976, 122, pt. 10: 11980; pt. 12: 14349, 14363–65; pt. 18: 22941–42. On the
PBC and other bicentennial criticism, see also Bodnar, *Remaking America*,
234–37.

20 ABA, *Third Annual Report*, 7; *Ninth Annual Report*, vol. II, 185; see also for
example, *Ninth Annual Report*, vol. I, 59–62. For a general overview of
Australian bicentennial politics, see Warhurst, "Politics and Management."
Some sense of the social movements of the 1960s in Australia, compared to
elsewhere, is provided in Richard Gordon, ed., *The Australian New Left: Critical
Essays and Strategy* (Melbourne: William Heinemann, 1970); see especially
Richard Gordon and Warren Osmond, "An Overview of the Australian New
Left," 3–39, and Peter O'Brien, "Some Overseas Comparisons," 219–34. See
also Dennis Altman, "The Creation of Sexual Politics in Australia," *Journal of
Australian Studies* 20 (May 1987), 76–82; and the review of more recent work on
the Australian experience of Vietnam in Rob Watts, "'Bringing Them Home':
Vietnam and the Sixties Revisited," *Journal of Australian Studies* 34 (September
1992), 82–86. On feminism, see, for example, Miriam Dixson, "Gender, Class,
and the Women's Movements in Australia, 1890, 1980," in Norma Grieve and
Ailsa Burns, *Australian Women: New Feminist Perspectives* (Melbourne: Oxford
University Press, 1986), 14–26; comparisons with American feminism are drawn
in Hester Eisenstein, *Gender Shock: Practising Feminism on Two Continents*
(Sydney: Allen and Unwin, 1991), and Marian Sawer, "Reclaiming Social
Liberalism: The Women's Movement and the State," in Renate Howe, ed.,
Women and the State, special edn. of *Journal of Australian Studies* (Bundoora,
Victoria: La Trobe University Press, 1993), 1–21. For a review and critique of the
treatment of gender in bicentennial publications, see Jill Julius Matthews, "'A
Female of All Things': Women and the Bicentenary," in Janson and MacIntyre,
Making the Bicentenary, 90–102.

21 *Australia, 1788–1988: Historical Newsletter* 3 (May 1980), 1, held in Mitchell
Library, Sydney; ABA, *First Annual Report*, 6; ABA, *Third Annual Report*, 3;
Peter Spearritt, "Celebration of a Nation: The Triumph of Spectacle," in
Janson and MacIntyre, *Making the Bicentenary*, 5–7, 13–14 (3–20); ABA, *Fifth
Annual Report*, 14; ABA, *Eighth Annual Report 1988: On Activities to 30 June
1988*, edited by Kate Richardson (Sydney: ABA, 1988), 40–42; ABA, *Ninth
Annual Report*, vol. I, 39–45; Hutchinson, "State Festivals, Foundation Myths,
and Cultural Politics," 17–18, 21–22. See also Treaty '88 Campaign, "Aborig-
inal Sovereignty – Never Ceded," in Janson and MacIntyre, *Making the
Bicentenary*, 1–2, and other essays in that volume; Robin Trotter, "Pioneering
the Past: A Study of the Stockman's Hall of Fame," in Tony Bennett *et al.*,
Celebrating the Nation, 163–64 (160–74); Jan Pettman, "Learning About Power
and Powerlessness: Aborigines and White Australia's Bicentenary," *Race and*

Class 29 (3) 1988, 69–85; and Tony Bennett, "Shaping of Things to Come," 47–48. Most studies of the Australian bicentenary make some mention of Aboriginal bicentennial politics. For a useful overview of Aborigines in conventional Australian politics, see Scott Bennett, *Aborigines and Political Power* (Sydney: Allen and Unwin, 1989). Scott Bennett discusses the possibility of a treaty, 155–56. See also Julian Thomas, "1938: Past and Present in an Elaborate Anniversary," in Janson and MacIntyre, *Making the Bicentenary*, 77–89, on organized Aboriginal resistance (and some proto-feminist interpretations) during the 1938 Sesquicentenary.

According to one ABA official, the earliest critic of the ABA plans for a bicentennial theme was the Uniting Church, which feared that Aborigines were being left out. And another official, reflecting on the legacies of the celebration, spoke of consciousness-raising about Aboriginal issues as one of those legacies (Denis O'Brien, Wendy McCarthy, interviews with author, January 6, 1989).

The issues for Australian organizers in 1988 are perhaps more comparable to issues faced during the Columbus Quincentenary in the United States in 1992, and account for the greater public profile of Aboriginal issues in 1988 than issues of Native Americans in 1976 (see n. 50 below). However, it is worth noting that ARBA, too, was early concerned with the reactions of Native Americans to the 1976 bicentennial. One of their earliest newsletters makes a "call for Indian participation," recognizing "the effects of discrimination, ignorance, and poor health," and describes "discussions . . . aimed at finding ways of involving the first Americans in planning for a better life in 1976" (ARBC, *Bicentennial Era* 1 [6] June 1970, 1). There are numerous reports in official ARBA documents of extensive outreach programs, and meetings between top officials and tribal leaders. John Warner, the ARBA leader, himself visited 111 tribes (thirty-eight eventually became "Bicentennial Communities"). Native American communities seem to have received more concrete, federally funded benefits – like jobs programs and public health facilities – as bicentennial communities than did other communities.

22 In addition to the criticism faced by central organizers from the groups discussed here, both ARBA and the ABA faced internal crises and reorganization a few years prior to the bicentennial years: American organizers in 1973 (when the ARBC was replaced by ARBA), and Australian organizers in 1985. Australian critics tended to come from the right, and American critics from the left, of the existing organizations. Notably, much American criticism concerned excessive commercialization of the national event, whereas criticism of early Australian plans as unrepresentative led to a new program of corporate sponsorship from 1985, and, as one official described it, the ABA became from 1985 "a pragmatic organization" and "deadlines became imperative" (Wendy McCarthy, interview with author, Sydney, January 6, 1989). The Australian critics continued to attack what in the American context would have been called the "liberal" themes of the ABA.

From the point of view of ritual organizers these crises were very memorable

and highly emotive. One worker recalled vividly the period of ABA's organizational crisis in 1985: she spoke of being "hounded by the press . . . all the people
you meet attacking you at dinner parties . . . well it was like that for me, I can't
imagine what it was like for higher ups . . . arriving at work . . . [and being]
tracked by cameras through the building . . . spiriting people down fire escapes"
(Dorothy Capoletto, interview with author, Sydney, January 17, 1989). An
ABA official spoke of 1985 as a "year of turbulence" and of the "aggravation,
anxiety, and mistakes in the whole process." This official spoke of ABA's
problems in 1985 as "the mirror image of the problems in the United States" in
1973 when "the corporate body fell apart." In his view, such problems were
typical in national ritual organization because "people attracted far in advance
are not people who can actually get things done," and there was a tension
between bureaucratic and entrepreneurial directions (Denis O'Brien, interview
with author, January 6, 1989). It certainly seems empirically likely that some
structural tension will lead to a crisis in national ritual organization of events
like the bicentennials: for example, there was a similar process of developing
tensions and crisis in the Civil War centennial (Kammen, *Mystic Chords*,
590–610).

More generally, issues of national representation were often displaced to
procedural and organizational battles and financial criticism, and not only
during the crises: competing political visions of the nation were expressed even
as different bicentennial slogans and colors were decided and replaced and
re-instituted. A full account of bicentennial politics would examine these battles
in more depth. For some of the Australian politics, see Spearritt, "Triumph of
Spectacle," Hutchinson, "State Festivals, Foundation Myths, and Cultural
Politics," 13–17, and Warhurst, "Politics and Management." For some of the
American politics, see n. 5 above.

23 Some regional jealousies and differential participation also characterized
bicentennial organization. See Hutchinson, "State Festivals, Foundation
Myths, and Cultural Politics," 14–15, for a comparative summary of major
regional disputes provoked in the course of bicentennial organization. See also
John Eddy, "What Are the Origins of Australia's National Identity?," in F. G.
Castles, ed., *Australia Compared: People, Policies and Politics* (Sydney: Allen
and Unwin, 1991), 25–27 (17–37). On declining but remaining regional
differences in the United States, see Kammen, *Mystic Chords*, 548.

Australian organizers spoke privately of differences in enthusiasm and minor
jealousies between states in the bicentennial celebration. In one assessment,
New South Wales and Queensland were "fully operative," Western Australia
was "responsive" but late, Victorian, South Australian, and Western Australian
celebrations were complicated by similar events like sesquicentennials in the
preceding years, and the bicentennial organization in Victoria complicated by
ongoing rivalry and jealousy of New South Wales's central role (Wendy
McCarthy, interview with author, January 6, 1989). Several ABA officials
observed that from their organizational point of view, "people tend to think of

themselves in terms of state ideas," whereas "our aim was to encourage people to think of themselves as Australian" (Desmond Kennard, interview with author, January 17, 1989). They also spoke of state/federal organizational conflicts as typical. Compared to the centennial, though, regional identifications were much less pronounced in both countries, and the problems of ritual organization they created were characteristic of any federal political initiative. Regional integration was occasionally mentioned but did not become a central theme of public national rhetoric (see n. 71 below).

24 ARBA, *BT* i; ABA, *Second Annual Report*, 7; ABA, *Third Annual Report*, 10; ABA, *Eighth Annual Report*, 79.

25 The more systematic mobilization and documentation of local community celebrations also changed the range of available formulations of national identity in the bicentennials by comparison with the centennials. Although I do not exploit the huge compilations of community activities to the full, I draw on the database of community celebrations in assessing the extent to which themes promoted by bicentennial organizers were shared in communities, especially in discussion of the American bicentennial. In particular, I refer to a small random sample of registered activities – including projects and events – listed and briefly described in ARBA's "Binet" database. These listings were symbolically much thinner than the newsletter stories but provided evidence of major themes, symbols, sorts of activities, and groups involved in the marking of the bicentennial at a more popular level. Since Binet was a collection made and published by ARBA, it was not technically an independent representation of community themes. However, there is no reason to think that there was any systematic bias in ARBA's listings; there were no set criteria for inclusion and the only activities which would be missing would be those not registered by the communities or participants themselves. See also n. 11 above.

26 ABA, *B '88* 8 (3): 12; ARBA, *BT* 423.

27 On the changing role of exhibitions, see n. 8 above.

28 ARBA, *BT* 354–55, 244; ABA, *B '88* 8 (3): 17; 8 (4): 20; ARBA, *BT* 400; ABA, *B '88* 8 (4): 21; 8 (1): 10; ARBA, *BT* 301. On ceremonial self-presentation in national ritual, see Daniel Dayan and Elihu Katz, "Television Ceremonial Events," in Arthur Asa Berger, ed., *Television in Society* (New Brunswick, NJ: Transaction Books, 1987), 41–55, and more generally *Media Events: The Live Broadcasting of History* (Cambridge, MA, and London: Harvard University Press, 1992).

29 ABA, *Ninth Annual Report*, vol. I, 96; Canberra College of Advanced Education, "The 29th International Mathematical Olympiad July 9–21, 1988, Canberra, Australia," 1985 (brochure held by author); ABA, *B '88* 8 (3): 34.

30 ARBA, *BT* 401, 418; ARBA, *Final Report*, vol. IV, 503. In the sample of ARBA community listings, only 3 percent of themes represented were "international" and most of those were minor references and not a central focus of activity. An interesting but rare argument that community service organizations could play an important role in forming international links, and more general claims that

the bicentennial had an important international dimension, can be seen in *Congressional Record*, 93rd Cong., 2nd sess., 1974, 120, pt. 27: 35804–06. An argument that foreign policy should be reversed to support movements of liberation on the occasion of the bicentennial was made in *Congressional Record*, 93rd Cong., 2nd sess., 1974, 120, pt. 27: 35753–55.

31 ABA, *Third Annual Report*, 6; ABA, *Ninth Annual Report*, vol. I, 71; ABA, *B '88* 8 (1): 24; 8 (3): 41. On sport, international orientations, and Australian nationalism, see, for example, W. F. Mandle, "Pommy Bastards and Damn' Yankees: Sport and Australian Nationalism," in *Going It Alone: Australia's National Identity in the Twentieth Century* (Ringwood, Victoria: Allen Lane, 1978), 24–46; Mandle, "Cricket and Australian Nationalism in the Nineteenth Century," *Journal of the Royal Australian Historical Society* 57 (4) December 1973, 225–46; Mandle, "Sport," in J. D. B. Miller, ed., *Australians and British: Social and Political Connections* (Sydney: Methuen, 1987), 140–57; Wray Vamplew, "Australians and Sport," in Wray Vamplew and Brian Stoddart, eds., *Sport in Australia: A Social History* (Cambridge: Cambridge University Press, 1994), 1–18; and Brian Stoddart, "Sport, Cultural Imperialism, and Colonial Response in the British Empire," *Comparative Studies in Society and History* 30 (1988), 649–73. For an interesting study of the interplay between international, national, and "ethnic" themes in the bicentenary, see Toby Miller, "The Unmarking of Soccer: Making a Brand New Subject," in Tony Bennett *et al.*, *Celebrating the Nation*, 104–20. On the overall importance of sport in Australia, including the importance of imagined international recognition, see T. D. Jacques and G. R. Pavia, *Sport in Australia: Selected Readings in Physical Activity* (Sydney: McGraw Hill, 1976); and Stephen Alomes, *A Nation at Last? The Changing Character of Australian Nationalism, 1880–1988* (North Ryde and London: Angus and Robertson, 1988), 3–8, 16–17, 157–59. On the masculinism of the link between sport and national identity in Australia, see for example Susanne Davies, "Diggers and Sportsmen," *Arena* 97 (1991), 30–36; and Sabine Erika, "Nationalism and Women," *Politics* 21 (1) May 1986, 82–88.

32 ARBA, *BT* 302. ARBA's system of "alliances" included a sporting alliance but activities of this group received little attention in bicentennial records. There was a statistically significant difference in the number of "sports" themes in sampled Australian and American newsletter stories.

33 On the prohibitions against commercial use of American bicentennial symbols, see Brody, "Bicentennial Observance," 97. Commercialism was an important critical issue when the bicentennial organization was under attack in 1972–73, and the "Buy-centennial" tag was remembered even in 1976: see ARBA, *Final Report*, vol. I, 246. John Wilson, in *Playing by the Rules: Sport, Society, and the State* (Detroit: Wayne State University Press, 1994), presents a well-grounded argument that state and sport are increasingly intertwined in the United States: he also argues, though, that "American culture discourages public goals for sport" (389), and that the belief that "sport should be the outcome of free contracts in civil society, not a public issue or a matter for the

state" (390) is normative. His overall analysis suggests that a further comparison of the contextual differences in relations between civil society, market,
and the state in struggles over outcomes in sporting policy would explain the
fact that sport became a vehicle for the expression of national identity in the
Australian bicentennial but not in the American bicentennial. My purpose
here, though, is not to account for this fact but to point out the distinctive
"international display" interpretation given to sports events by Australian
organizers.

34 ABA, *B '88* 8 (3): 37; 8 (2): 10; 8 (3): 19; Manning Clark, in ABA, *Australia Live!
The Celebration of a Nation*, produced by Peter Faiman for the Australian
Bicentennial Authority, 1988, video cassette, author's notes from video cassette
lent by ABA.

35 Lipset notes extensive discussion of differences between the countries in
Canadian literature, but not in American literature; see Seymour M. Lipset,
Continental Divide: The Values and Institutions of the United States and Canada
(New York: Routledge, 1990), 58. See also, for instance, Lucien W. Pye, "The
Politicians' Search for Identity," in *Politics, Personality, and Nation Building:
Burma's Search for Identity* (New Haven: Yale University Press, 1962), 244–66;
Edward LiPuma and Sarah Keene Meltzoff, "Ceremonies of Independence and
Public Culture in the Solomon Islands," *Public Culture* 3 (1990), 77–92. My
analysis here contrasts with that of Hutchinson, in "State Festivals, Foundation
Myths, and Cultural Politics," 8–9, 19, who suggests that international
recognition was also important in the American bicentennial; while I agree that
international recognition is a necessary dimension of the discursive field within
which any national identity is constructed, I argue that there were significant
differences in the importance of international regard in American and Australian bicentennials.

The talk of international recognition in the bicentennials seems to suggest, as
did the equivalent talk in the centennials, that symbolic expressions of the place
of the nation in the world are not necessarily framed invidiously. The wide range
of symbolic resources available to express a nation's place in the world could
connote satisfaction, display, pride, competition to cooperate, or participatory
hopes and ambitions, as well as resentment, humiliation, competition, and
aggrandizement. See Liah Greenfeld, *Nationalism: Five Roads to Modernity*
(Cambridge, MA, and London: Harvard University Press, 1992).

36 ARBA, *BT* 270; ABA, *B '88* 8 (1): 20; ARBA, *BT* 419; ABA, *B '88* 8 (2): 7.

37 Kammen, *Mystic Chords*, 137, suggests that the theme of progress lost
resonance in American collective memory from the 1930s onwards.

38 ARBA, *BT* 346, 400. See also Michael Kammen, *A Season of Youth: The
American Revolution and the Historical Imagination* (New York: Oxford
University Press, 1978), 233–42.

39 In the sample of newsletter stories, the difference between countries in
percentage of themes stressing "founding moment" history was statistically
significant at the 0.5 level (Fisher Exact Test). Although John Murphy has

indicated an emphasis on the "founding moment" in the official Australian bicentenary, this was negligible in the broader context of this comparison. However, his more general reflections on the "hesitation and implausibility" (54) in official history are important for their assessment of the disjuncture between official and vernacular history. See John Murphy, "Conscripting the Past: The Bicentenary and Everyday Life," in Janson and MacIntyre, *Making the Bicentenary*, 45–54.

40 Anxiety about how the convict past would affect the national image created controversy in the late 1920s, for example, when the young Australian film industry adapted to the screen Marcus Clarke's novel about convict life, *For the Term of His Natural Life*. See Michael Roe, "Vandiemenism Debated: The Filming of 'His Natural Life,' 1926–1927," *Journal of Australian Studies* 24 (May 1989), 35–51; and more generally Tom Griffiths, "Past Silences: Aborigines and Convicts in Our History-Making," *Australian Cultural History* 6 (1987), 18–32.

41 Julian Thomas, "1938." The quotation from "Governor Phillip's" speech in the 1938 re-enactment appears on 83–84.

42 ABA, *Australia Live! The Celebration of a Nation*. This marathon New Year bicentenary broadcast was apparently quoting writing for the occasion by Colleen McCullough. For an example of the immigration waves formulation, see ABA, *Eighth Annual Report*, 23. On the politics of founding moment avoidance, see also Hutchinson, "State Festivals, Foundation Myths, and Cultural Politics," 15–18.

43 "Captain Arthur Phillip R. N. 250th Anniversary Programme, 1988," Miscellaneous Publications File: Commonwealth Celebrations 2, Mitchell Library, Sydney.

44 ARBC, *Bicentennial Era* 2 (6) 1971, 7. John Rockefeller initiated the meeting of twenty-two young activists; some of them later presented reports to the national organization. The organizers responded by expanding its board to include eight young, minority, and female members in early 1972, and initiating a "Youth Awareness Campaign." The commission's youth taskforce soon abandoned, with protests, their role in the official organization: see *Congressional Record*, 92nd Cong., 2nd sess., 1972, 118, pt. 22: 28534–35. This incident provides, incidentally, a good example of the interpretive doubt through which ARBA's official descriptions of the bicentennial should be read. In ARBA's final report, the critique is noted, more radical input is then elided, and the story moves on to tell of projects like recognition of the activities of Scouts. It then concludes, "there is every indication of widespread participation in the Bicentennial by the nation's youth" (see ARBA, *Final Report*, vol. I, 200, 203; Hawkens and Associates, *Sourcebook*, I-25).

45 California ARBC, *Minutes*, December 14, 1968, 3; December 13, 1969, 2; March 21, 1970, appendix, 1.

46 Jeremy Rifkin, quoted in ARBA, *BERC*, 34; Brody, "Bicentennial Observance," 134; PBC, *America's Birthday*, 181. See also Rifkin, *Commonsense II*,

and Heritage Foundation, *Great Bicentennial Debate*. The Afro-American Bicentennial Corporation also appealed to founding moment and political values in testimony about the ARBA in 1973: see *Congressional Record*, 93rd Cong., 1st sess., 1973, 119, pt. 11: 13352–54.

47 ABA, *B '88* 8 (3): 20; 8 (2): 19; 8 (2): 19; 8 (4): 4.

48 ARBA, *BT* 245, 394, 368; Bodnar, *Remaking America*, 234. David Glassberg, in *American Historical Pageantry: The Uses of Tradition in the Early Twentieth Century* (Chapel Hill and London: University of North Carolina Press, 1990), identifies a shift in American historical visions in the 1920s from a vision linking extended past to present, to a vision of history as distant and separate from the present. The evidence here suggests that distant history was chosen as unifying by American bicentennial organizers in the same way.

49 Kammen, *Mystic Chords*, 629, 679–85; Bodnar, *Remaking America*, 238–43. On the "Paul Revere Ride," see ARBA, *Final Report*, vol. III, 111. The comparison of historical themes in ARBA newsletters and community activities is based on the samples described earlier.

50 Chilla Bulbeck, "Australian History Set in Concrete? The Influence of the New Histories on Australian Memorial Construction," *Journal of Australian Studies* 28 (March 1991), 6 (3–16). For a useful summary of quincentenary critique, see Matthew Dennis, "America (Re)Invents Itself: Centenary Celebrations of Columbus's Voyage of 'Discovery,' 1792–1992" (paper presented at the 107th annual meeting of the American Historical Association, Washington, DC, 1992), 35–47; Sam Dillon, "Schools Growing Harsher in Scrutiny of Columbus," *New York Times*, October 12, 1992, A1, B5; Dillon, "He's the Explorer/ Exploiter You Just Have to Love/Hate," *New York Times*, 12 October 1992, B5. But see also n. 21 above on ARBA's work to pre-empt Native American criticism in 1976. More generally, see Michel-Rolph Trouillot, "Good Day Columbus: Silences, Power, and Public History (1492–1892)," *Public Culture* 3 (1) Fall 1990, 1–24.

51 See, for example, Barry Schwartz, "The Reconstruction of Abraham Lincoln," in David Middleton and Derek Edwards, eds., *Collective Remembering* (London and Newbury Park, CA: Sage, 1990), 81–107, and other essays in that volume; Schwartz, "The Social Context of Commemoration: A Study in Collective Memory," *Social Forces* 61 (December 1982), 372–402; Schwartz, *George Washington: The Making of an American Symbol* (Ithaca, NY, and London: Cornell University Press, 1987); and Schwartz, "Social Change and Collective Memory: The Democratization of George Washington," *American Sociological Review* 56 (2) April 1991, 221–36; Michael Schudson, "The Present in the Past Versus the Past in the Present," *Communication* 11 (1989), 105–13; Schudson, *Watergate in American Memory: How We Remember, Forget, and Reconstruct the Past* (New York: Basic, 1992), 51–66, 205–21; John R. Gillis, ed., *Commemorations: The Politics of National Identity* (Princeton, NJ: Princeton University Press, 1994); and Jeffrey K. Olick and Daniel Levy, "Mechanisms of Cultural Constraint: Holocaust Myth and Rationality in

German Politics" (Department of Sociology, Columbia University, photo-copy). See also Kammen, *Season of Youth*, on interpretation of the American Revolution; and Kate Darian-Smith and Paula Hamilton, eds., *Memory and History in Twentieth-Century Australia* (Melbourne: Oxford University Press, 1994), for a range of cases generating reflection on aspects of collective memory in Australia.

52 Greenfeld, *Five Roads*, 10; Louis Hartz, *The Founding of New Societies* (New York: Harcourt, Brace, and World, 1964); Seymour Martin Lipset, *The First New Nation: The United States in Comparative and Historical Perspective* (New York: W. W. Norton and Co., 1979 [1973]). For Australian critique and development of the Hartz thesis, see A. W. Martin, "Australia and the Hartz 'Fragment' Thesis," J. W. McCarty, "Australia as a Region of Recent Settlement in the Nineteenth Century," and G. C. Bolton, "Louis Hartz," *Australian Economic History Review* 13 (2) September 1973, 131–47, 148–67, and 168–76, respectively; J. B. Hirst, "Keeping Colonial History Colonial: The Hartz Thesis Revisited," *Historical Studies* 21 (82) April 1984, 85–104; see also chapter 1, n. 6, in this volume. On Australian political culture, see Hugh Collins, "Political Ideology in Australia: The Distinctiveness of a Benthamite Society," *Daedalus* 114 (Winter 1985), 147–69; Don Aitken, "Australian Political Culture," *Australian Cultural History* 5 (1986), 5–11; Clive Bean, "Orthodox Political Participation in Australia," *Australian and New Zealand Journal of Sociology* 25 (3) November 1989, 451–79; Krzysztof Zagorski, "Australian 'Left' and 'Right': (Social Composition and Ideological Integrity)," *Politics* 23 (1) May 1988, 90–100; and Tim Rowse, *Australian Liberalism and National Character* (Melbourne: Kibble Books, 1978).

53 ARBA, *BT* 232, 268, 419, 296, 296, 322. See, more generally, Michael Kammen, *Spheres of Liberty: Changing Perceptions of Liberty in American Culture* (Madison, WI: University of Wisconsin Press, 1986), ch. 3.

54 California ARBC, *Minutes*, December 13, 1969, 9; March 21, 1970, 2, 4–5; PBC, *America's Birthday*, 33.

55 In the random sample from community listings, there were no activities labeled with political themes, whereas this was an important theme of the sample of newsletter stories. Brody found a similar emphasis on political values in the rhetoric of organizers (at both national and state levels), and he reports the findings from bicentennial essays by schoolchildren in "Bicentennial Observance," 116–17.

56 In one of the rare Australian appeals to political values, Prime Minister Bob Hawke, in his Australia Day speech, referred to "the Australian cause, the cause of freedom, fairness, justice, and peace"; but only after appealing to symbols of "a nation of immigrants," the "vast continent," and "diversity" (Australian Broadcasting Commission, *Australia's Day*, produced by ABC Bicentennial Unit, 1988, 92 min., video cassette). The framing seemed so bland, and the connection to multiculturalism so direct, that it is perhaps over-interpretation to see this as a claim about national political values. On the opening of the new

Parliament House, see Spearritt, "Triumph of Spectacle," 19; ABA, *Eighth Annual Report*, 36.

57 ABA, *B '88* 8 (2): 7. An important tradition in Australian historiography and cultural criticism examines the way perceptions of "the bush," or "the outback," have been influential in forming Australian identity. For cultural analysis of variants closest to those evident in the bicentenary, see Ann McGrath, "Travels to a Distant Past: The Mythology of the Outback," *Australian Cultural Studies* 10 (1991), 113–24; E. R. Hills, "The Imaginary Life: Landscape and Culture in Australia," *Journal of Australian Studies* 29 (June 1991), 12–27; and David Day, "Aliens in a Hostile Land: A Re-appraisal of Australian History," *Journal of Australian Studies* 23 (November 1988), 3–15.

There has been an extended debate on the influence of the rural worker in national identity formation: see Russel Ward, *The Australian Legend*, 2nd edn. (Melbourne: Oxford University Press, 1966 [1958]); John Barrett, "Melbourne and the Bush: Russel Ward's Thesis and a La Trobe Survey," *Meanjin* 31 (1972), 462–70; Russel Ward, "The Australian Legend Re-visited," *Historical Studies* 18 (71) October 1978, 171–90; Graeme Davison, "Sydney and the Bush: An Urban Context for the Australian Legend," *Historical Studies* 18 (71) October 1978, 191–209. The current significance of this rural legend is addressed in Judith L. Kapferer, "Rural Myths and Urban Ideologies," *Australian and New Zealand Journal of Sociology* 26 (1) March 1990, 87–106. Some insight on the function of myths of the land in denying pastoral invasion is provided in Patrick Wolfe, "On Being Woken Up: The Dreamtime in Anthropology and in Australian Settler Culture," *Comparative Studies in Society and History* 33 (2) April 1991, 210–11 (197–224). More generally on symbolic geography in Australian national identity, see, for example, Richard White, *Inventing Australia: Images and Identity, 1688–1980* (Sydney: George Allen and Unwin, 1981), 104–09; Oskar Spate, "Geography and National Identity in Australia," in David Hoosen, ed., *Geography and National Identity* (Oxford and Cambridge, MA: Blackwell, 1994), 277–82; and Paul Foss, ed., *Island in the Stream: Myths of Place in Australian Culture* (Sydney: Pluto Press, 1988).

Even brief acquaintance with the literature on Australian symbolic geography will show more differences than similarities with the American myth of the frontier: an extended comparison would be fruitful. Some useful points are made in Fred Alexander, *Moving Frontiers: An American Theme and Its Application to Australian History* (Port Washington, NY: Kennikat Press, 1969 [1946]), 26–39; Ward, *Australian Legend*, 238–61; and Horst Priessnitz, "Dreams in Austerica: A Preliminary Comparison of the Australian and the American Dream," *Westerly* 3 (Spring 1994), 45–64. Most important here is the point that symbolic geography became central in the Australian bicentenary but was little discussed in the American event.

58 ABA, *B '88* 8 (1): 5; 8 (4): 20.

59 ABA, *B '88* 8 (4): 4; ABA, *Eighth Annual Report*, 9–13, 33; ABA, *Ninth Annual Report*, vol. I, 13–17. In the first half of the twentieth century, as Donald Horne

points out, many celebrations adopted the form of "landings" on the continent; see *Ideas for a Nation* (Sydney: Pan Books, 1989), 21–25. Horne also provides intriguing reflections on Australian national identity more generally.

60 "Linking the Nation: Bicentennial Birthday Beacons, 18 June 1988" (pamphlet held in Mitchell Library, Sydney). The Birthday Beacons event was the idea of a sociology professor: the idea was said to be "similar in concept" to the Hands Across America project (ABA, *B '88* 8 (3): 12). This too was suggested and organized independently of the central organization in the American bicentennial year; but it was not the success which Australia's event became. On the concept and origins of "Hands Across the Nation," see *Congressional Record*, 93rd Cong., 2nd sess., 1974, 120, pt. 19: 24493–94; 94th Cong., 1st sess., 1975, 121, pt. 27: 35576. The originators stressed diversity themes much more than the land themes of the more successful Australian appropriation of the concept.

61 ARBA, *BT* 394. Twelve percent of sampled Australian newsletter stories had a geographic theme; only 5 percent of sampled American bicentennial newsletter stories made reference to the land. This difference was statistically significant at the 0.5 level.

62 In the random sample from American community listings, 11 percent of community activities and events referred to symbolic geography, compared to only 5 percent in the sample of ARBA newsletter stories. See also Bodnar, *Remaking America*, e.g., 118, 121, 123–35, 144–45.

63 ABA, *Ninth Annual Report*, vol. I, 8; ARBC, *Bicentennial Era* 1 (5) May 1970, 2–3.

64 This slippage between demographic and historic experience of diversity, on the one hand, and cultural forms asserting diversity, on the other, is an important reminder that cultural forms cannot be assumed to reflect directly underlying demographic realities, and must be analyzed independently. There is no question that American immigration has been much more demographically diverse over a much longer period than Australian immigration. Even after more diverse immigration was becoming the norm in Australia, between 1976 and 1980 (at the beginning of bicentennial planning), 53 percent of Australian immigrants came from Britain (compared to only 5 percent of American immigrants in the comparable pre-bicentennial period, between 1966 and 1970). But compared to *prior experience*, immigration in Australia was more diverse and more significant in the period before bicentennial planning than it was in the United States by comparison with earlier American experience. For instance, after immigrants from Britain, the next largest category of Australian immigration between 1976 and 1980 was immigration from (the puzzling and perhaps symptomatic category of) "Asia and Egypt," 35 percent of Australian immigration in the period and an important increase since the ending of the White Australia Policy. (In the United States, on the other hand, 16 percent of American immigrants between 1966 and 1970 came from Asia.) And in 1970 only 4.7 percent of the American population was foreign-born, compared with 21 percent of the Australian population in 1981. (Comparisons developed from

R. V. Jackson, *The Population History of Australia* [Melbourne: McPhee Gribble/Penguin, 1988], 30, 38; US Department of Commerce, *Historical Statistics of the United States: Colonial Times to 1970* [Washington, DC: Government Printing Office, 1975], 105, 107, 8, 14.) So although the Australian population was much less diverse in absolute terms than the American, diversity was highly salient to Australian bicentennial planners – and indeed, has become a key theme in talk of Australian national identity, at least among dominant cultural producers. As a result, "diversity" characterizations were used about as frequently during the Australian as during the American bicentenary.

Immigration has been a significant theme in Australian as in American historiography: for a useful overview, including important developments in that historiography since the 1970s, see James Jupp, *Immigration* (Melbourne: Sydney University Press with Oxford University Press, 1991); see especially 95–107 on "multicultural" changes since 1947. See also his review article, "Immigration: Some Recent Perspectives," *Australian Historical Studies* 24 (91) April 1990, 285–91; Ann-Mari Jordens, *Redefining Australians: Immigration, Citizenship, and National Identity* (Sydney: Hale and Iremonger, 1995). Charles Price, "Immigration," in J. D. B. Miller, *Australians and British*, 13–44, tells the story with an emphasis on the Britishness of Australians. For relevant comparisons, see Gary P. Freeman and James Jupp, eds., *Nations of Immigrants: Australia, the United States, and International Migration* (Melbourne: Oxford University Press, 1992); Glenn Withers, ed., *Commonality and Difference: Australia and the United States*, vol. I, *Australian Fulbright Papers* (Sydney: Allen and Unwin in association with the Australian–American Educational Foundation, 1991); John M. Liu, "A Comparative Historical Perspective of Post-World War II Asian Immigration to North America and Australia" (paper presented at the Annual Meeting of the American Sociological Association, Washington, DC, August 1990). Also useful, though now somewhat dated, on Australian ethnic politics is Andrew Parkin, "Ethnic Politics: A Comparative Study of Two Immigrant Societies, Australia and the United States," *Journal of Commonwealth and Comparative Politics* 15 (1) March 1977, 22–38. See also n. 73 below.

65 ARBA, *BT* 337, 417. Fourteen percent of themes in sampled ARBA newsletter stories involved diversity; 9 percent of themes in sampled community listings were diversity themes. Diversity was more often a major theme, and not only a casual reference, in the ARBA newsletter than in the community listings. See also Bodnar, *Remaking America*, 240–41.

66 ABA, *B '88* 8 (4): 21; 8 (2): 19. On ethnic festivals, see Penny Van Esterik, "Celebrating Ethnicity: Ethnic Flavour in an Urban Festival," *Ethnic Groups* 4 (1982), 207–27.

67 ARBA, *BT* 417; ARBA, *Final Report*, vol. I, 194–95; ARBA, *BT* 334. See also Bodnar, *Remaking America*, 241. Barthes says of inoculation: "one immunizes the contents of the collective imagination by means of a small inoculation of acknowledged evil; one thus protects it against the risk of a generalized

subversion." See Roland Barthes, *Mythologies*, selected and trans. by Annette Lavers (New York: Hill and Wang, 1972 [1957]), 150. Early ARBC newsletters gave prominent attention to a Washington, DC-based Afro-American Bicentennial Corporation, but this organization does not seem to have been active by 1976 (see also *Congressional Record*, 92nd Cong., 1st sess., 1971, 117, pt. 36: 47590; 93rd Cong., 1st sess., 1973, 119, pt. 11: 13352–54). Despite ARBA's pluralist claims, specifically black participation seems to have been limited to activities at an elite level, and overall, African Americans are notably absent from the official publications of the bicentennial. This absence is particularly notable because, according to Kammen (*Mystic Chords*, 682–84), from the 1960s, there were increasing attempts at racial inclusion in formulations of collective memory. For a useful review of some black opinion on the bicentennial, see *Congressional Record*, 94th Cong., 1st sess., 1975, 121, pt. 27: 35545–49, and *Congressional Record*, 94th Cong., 2nd sess., 1976, 122, pt. 18: 22971.

68 ARBA, *BT* 335. See also n. 21 above.

69 ABA, *Ninth Annual Report*, vol. I, 45; ABA, *B '88* 8 (4): 29; ABA, *Eighth Annual Report*, 23. See also Hutchinson, "State Festivals, Foundation Myths, and Cultural Politics," 20–22. On the changing place of Aborigines in Australian national identity, see Bain Attwood and John Arnold, eds., *Power, Knowledge, and Aborigines*, special edn. of *Journal of Australian Studies* (Melbourne: La Trobe University Press with the National Centre for Australian Studies, Monash University, 1992); Annette Hamilton, "Fear and Desire: Aborigines, Asians, and the National Imaginary," *Australian Cultural History* 9 (1990), 14–35; Chilla Bulbeck, "Aborigines, Memorials, and the History of the Frontier," *Australian Historical Studies* 24 (96) April 1991, 168–78.

70 ABA, *B '88* 8 (3): 27; ARBA, *BT* 376.

71 Compared to the centennial, bicentennial rhetoric rarely worked to integrate different national regions. However, occasional attempts at geographic inclusion could be seen in the full range of organizers' attempts to address national differences; for example, American organizers described how a "Bicentennial Bridge Across the Nation Links West Coast to Original Colonies" (ARBA, *BT* 307). Geographic inclusion was more frequently a minor theme in Australian rhetoric than it was in the language of American organizers. See also n. 23 above.

72 On Americanization as assimilation, see, for example, Roy Rosenzweig, *Eight Hours for What We Will: Workers and Leisure in an Industrial City, 1870–1920* (Cambridge and New York: Cambridge University Press, 1983); Jean H. Baker, *Affairs of Party: The Political Culture of Northern Democrats in the Mid-Nineteenth Century* (Ithaca, NY: Cornell University Press, 1983), 71–107; Stephen F. Brumberg, *Going to America, Going to School: The Jewish Immigrant Public School Encounter in Turn-of-the-Century New York City* (New York: Praeger, 1986); Michael Rogin, "Political Repression in the United States," in *"Ronald Reagan," the Movie, and Other Episodes in Political Demonology* (Berkeley and Los Angeles: University of California Press, 1987); W. Lloyd

Warner, "The Past Made Present and Perfect," in his *The Living and the Dead: A Study of the Symbolic Life of Americans* (Greenwich, CT: Greenwood Press, 1975 [1959]), 156–225. On "melting pot" ideas, see, for example, Fred Matthews, "Cultural Pluralism in Context: External History, Philosophic Premise, and Theories of Ethnicity in Modern America," *Journal of Ethnic Studies* 12 (2) 1984, 63–79; April Schultz, "'The Pride of Race Had Been Touched': Norse–American Immigration Centennial and Ethnic Identity," *Journal of American History* 77 (4) 1991, 1265–95. On "diversity," see, for instance, Susan Hegeman, "Shopping for Identities: 'A Nation of Nations' and the Weak Ethnicity of Objects," *Public Culture* 3 (2) 1991, 71–92; Marjorie R. Esman, "Festivals, Change, and Unity: The Celebration of Ethnic Identity Among Louisiana Cajuns," *Anthropological Quarterly* 55 (4) 1982, 199–210; Van Esterik, "Celebrating Ethnicity."

73 Jordens, *Redefining Australians*, 156. On "tactical pluralism," see Cochrane and Goodman, "Great Australian Journey," 32–35. Multiculturalism and its limits have been discussed extensively in recent Australian social analysis and commentary. In addition to Jordens, *Redefining Australians*, examples of useful overviews include Lois Foster and David Stockley, *Australian Multiculturalism: A Documentary History and Critique* (Clevedon, UK, and Philadelphia: Multilingual Matters, 1988); K. S. Inglis, "Multiculturalism and National Identity," in Charles A. Price, ed., *Australian National Identity* (Canberra: Academy of the Social Sciences in Australia, 1991), 13–31, and other essays in that volume; Murray Goot, "Multiculturalists, Monoculturalists, and the Many in Between: Attitudes to Cultural Diversity and Their Correlates," *Australian and New Zealand Journal of Sociology* 29 (2) August 1993, 226–53; Stephen Castles, Mary Kalantzis, Bill Cope, and Michael Morrissey, *Mistaken Identity: Multiculturalism and the Demise of Nationalism in Australia* (Sydney: Pluto Press, 1988); Castles, "The Bicentenary and the Failure of Australian Nationalism," *Race and Class* 29 (3) 1988, 53–68; and Castles, "Australian Multiculturalism: Social Policy and Identity in a Changing Society," in Freeman and Jupp, *Nations of Immigrants*, 184–201. For an assessment of Australian multiculturalism stressing the depth of ethnocentrism dominating Australian culture before the 1960s, see Horne, *Ideas for a Nation*, 185–200; Bruce Kapferer, *Legends of People*, 215, is one among many students of Australian national identity to suggest that it is deeply structured on the denial of difference. For an intriguing case study of ethnic politics and the bicentenary, see Toby Miller, "Unmarking of Soccer." See also n. 64 above.

74 Emile Durkheim, *The Elementary Forms of Religious Life*, trans. and intro. by Karen Fields (New York: Free Press, 1995 [1912]); Kammen, *Mystic Chords*, ch. 19; Michael Rogin, "'Make My Day!': Spectacle as Amnesia in Imperial Politics," *Representations* 29 (1990), 99–123. This form of expressing imagined community, and more generally the use of strategies of ideological ambiguity to encourage participation, suggest intriguing comparisons to be drawn with the case described in Mabel Berezin, "Cultural Form and Political Meaning:

State-Subsidized Theater, Ideology, and the Language of Style in Fascist Italy," *American Journal of Sociology* 99 (March 1994), 1237–86.

75 ABA, *B '88* 8 (1): 9; ARBA, *BT* 301.

76 ARBA, *BT* 322, 301; ABA, *B '88* 8 (3): 12; ARBA, *BT* 423, 346.

77 ARBA, *BT* 288; ABA, *B '88* 8 (2): 22; ARBA, *Final Report*, vol. III, 467, 491, 355, 118 and vol. IV, 456. For an intriguing instance of increasing emphasis on spectacle in local celebration in the twentieth century, see Debra Gold Hansen and Mary P. Ryan, "Public Ceremony in a Private Culture: Orange County Celebrates the Fourth of July," in Rob Kling, Spencer Olin, and Mark Poster, eds., *Postsuburban California: The Transformation of Orange County Since World War II* (Berkeley and Los Angeles: University of California Press, 1991), 165–89.

78 There may have been more appeal to the abstract, emotional symbolizing of the nation in spectacle in the United States than Australia, but the evidence on this difference is ambiguous. Comparing random samples from each country's bicentennial newsletters, substantially more American stories than Australian ones used this sort of appeal as a ground for national identity – 13 compared to 7 percent of themes in the sample – but the difference was not statistically significant. The slightly different format of the newsletter stories – more like newspaper stories in the United States, and like news-magazine articles in Australia – may have had an impact on any measured differences. Another contributing factor may have been the comparatively small emphasis on the Australian flag in Australian bicentennial rhetoric; the Australian flag is a more contested symbol (with vocal republican and Aboriginal critics) than the American flag. Australian critics did stress and challenge what they saw as presentation of a sort of "contentless consensus," somewhat similar to the emphasis on spectacle, in the Australian Bicentennial Exhibition, a major project of the Australian organizers. Desmond Kennard, director of the exhibition, had aimed to "reach *all* people – the 'football crowd'" and saw "entertainment as the principal purpose to get people there," arguing that "museums cater for the middle and upper-middle classes – they're designed to do that – I wanted to go beyond the educated elite, to people who didn't know much about Australian history and would come for entertainment" (Desmond Kennard, interview with author, January 17, 1989). For example, one contro-versial aspect of the exhibition initially designed with this end in view was the minimization of exhibition labeling. Intriguingly, the postmodern effect of apparently random mixes of uninterpreted Australian artifacts and symbols in exhibition displays may have turned out to be more comprehensible to educated elites than to others (author's notes, Australian Bicentennial Exhibition, December 18, 1988, Blacktown, Sydney; Cochrane and Goodman, "Great Australian Journey"). See also n. 15 above.

References

Primary sources

A rich store of documents produced for the American centennial of 1876 is held at the Library of Congress in Washington, DC. Holdings of documents produced for the Australian centennial were examined at the Mitchell and Dixson Libraries in Sydney and the National Library of Australia in Canberra. Primary documents pertaining to the American bicentennial of 1976 are held in many collections of government documents: most of those cited here are available at the University of California at Berkeley. Primary sources on the Australian bicentenary of 1988 are comprised mostly of documents collected and held by the author: with the exception of ephemera and interview records, main sources are typically available in state and national libraries in Australia.

Only those primary documents cited in notes are listed here.

American centennial

[American Association of School Administrators]. *Education at the Centennial. Extracts from the Proceedings of the Department of Superintendance of the National Education Association, Washington, January 27 & 28, 1875.* Washington, DC: Government Printing Office, 1875.

Bailey, David. *"Eastward Ho!" or Leaves from the Diary of a Centennial Pilgrim: Being a Truthful Account of a Trip to the Centennial City . . .* Highland County, OH: published by the author, 1877.

Brotherhead, William. *The Centennial Book of the Signers of the Declaration of Independence.* Philadelphia: J. M. Stoddart, ?1872.

Bruce, Edward C. *The Century: Its Fruits and Its Festival. Being a History and Description of the Centennial Exhibition, with a Preliminary Outline of Modern Progress. With Numerous Illustrations.* Philadelphia: J. B. Lippincott, 1877.

Bullitt, John C. "Address . . . delivered at the banquet given by the citizens of Philadelphia, to the President, Supreme Court, and Senate and House of

Representatives of the United States, at Horticultural Hall, upon their Visit to the Centennial International Exhibition Grounds, Saturday, Dec. 18, 1875." Philadelphia: King and Baird, Printers, 1875.

Centennial Board of Finance (CBF). *Celebration of the Ninety-Ninth Anniversary of American Independence in Fairmount Park, Philadelphia, July 5th, 1875.* Philadelphia: King and Baird, Printers, 1875.

The Centennial Eagle. In Twelve Numbers, July–September. An Illustrated Descriptive History of the Centennial Exhibition. Philadelphia: Centennial Eagle Company, 1876.

"A Centennial Fourth of July Democratic Celebration: The Massacre of Six Colored Citizens of the United States at Hamburgh, SC, on July 4, 1876." In *Pamphlets on US History and Politics.* N.p., n.d. Held in Doe Library, University of California at Berkeley.

Clarke, William J., S. J. "Centennial Discourse, Delivered July 4, 1876, in St. Joseph's Church, Philadelphia." Philadelphia: P. F. Cunningham and Son, 1876.

Coates, Isaac T. "1776 Centennial 1876, Fourth of July Oration Delivered at Chester, Penna. . . . " Philadelphia: J. B. Lippincott, 1876.

Committee on the National Centennial Commemoration. *Proceedings on the One Hundredth Anniversary of the Introduction and Adoption of the "Resolutions Respecting Independency," Held in Philadelphia . . .* Philadelphia: Printed for the Committee, 1876.

Davis, L. H. "The Centennial Celebration at Pottstown, PA, July 4, 1876, and Historical Sketch Written . . . at the Request of the Centennial Committee." Pottstown, PA: n.p., 1876.

Des Moines Public Schools, Third Ward, No. 10. *1876, a Centennial Offering.* Ames, IA: Iowa State University Press, 1977.

Evarts, William M. "Oration, July 4th 1876, Philadelphia." Reprinted in *His Royal Highness Prince Oscar at the National Celebration of the Centennial Anniversary of American Independence Held in Philadelphia, USA, July 4, 1876.* Boston: Printed at the Riverside Press for Private Distribution, 1876.

[Executive Committee of the Women's Branch of the Centennial Association for Connecticut]. *Spirit of 'Seventy-Six.* June 1875–March 1877.

Farrand, Max, ed. *The Records of the Federal Convention of 1787.* Rev. edn. 4 vols. New Haven and London: Yale University Press, 1966.

Forney, John W. *A Centennial Commissioner in Europe, 1874–1876.* Philadelphia: J. B. Lippincott, 1876.

Guide to the Centennial Exposition and Fairmount Park. Philadelphia: J. H. Smythe, c1876.

Harrington, Kate [Rebecca Smith Pollard]. *Centennial and Other Poems.* Philadelphia: J. B. Lippincott, 1876.

Howells, William D. "A Sennight at the Centennial." *Atlantic Monthly* 38 (July 1876), 93–107.

Ingram, J. S. *The Centennial Exposition, Described and Illustrated, Being a Concise and Graphic Description of This Grand Enterprise, Commemorative of the First Centenary of American Independence . . .* Philadelphia: Hubbard Bros., 1876.

International Order of Oddfellows, Sovereign General Lodge. *Centennial Celebration in Honor of the Anniversary of American Independence . . . September, 1876.* Philadelphia: Burk & Caldwell, Printers, 1876.

Johnson, George J. *The Roll Call and Other Poems.* Philadelphia: J. B. Lippincott, 1876.

Kelley, William D. "National Centennial Celebration and Exposition." Speech delivered in the House of Representatives, January 10, 1871. Washington, DC: F. J. Rives and Geo. A. Bailey, Reporters and Printers of the Debates of Congress, 1871.

"Key to the Star Monument." Held in Broadside Collection, Rare Books and Special Collections, Library of Congress, Washington, DC.

Kidder, Charles H., ed. *Burley's United States Centennial Gazetteer and Guide, 1876.* Philadelphia: S. W. Burley, Proprietor and Publisher, 1876.

Ladies' Centennial Committee of Rhode Island. *Herald of the Centennial.* February 1875–January 1876.

Lilley, Celinda A. B. *Centenary Tract. The Coming Centennial, A.D. 1876.* East Calais, VT: published by the author, 1873.

Livermore, A. A. *The Centennial International Exhibition of 1876: A Lecture Delivered in the Court House, Meadville, PA, Before the City Library Association, December 8, 1874.* Meadville, PA: n.p., 1875.

Lossing, Benson J. *The American Centenary: A History of the Progress of the Republic of the United States During the First One Hundred Years of Its Existence.* Philadelphia: Porter & Coates, 1876.

Love, D. L. *Love's Southerner's Illustrated Guide to the Centennial Exposition. "Multum in Parvo." All About the Centennial, How to Go: Where to Stop, What to See, How to See It &c &c.* New York: Wheat and Cornell, Printers, 1876.

McCabe, James D. *The Illustrated History of the Centennial Exhibition, Held in Commemoration of the One Hundredth Anniversary of American Independence . . .* Philadelphia: National Publishing Co., 1876.

Memorial Certificate. Held in Broadside Collection, Rare Books and Special Collections, Library of Congress, Washington, DC.

Moore, Jacob Bailey, comp. *New Hampshire at the Centennial. The Address of Governor Cheney, The Oration of Professor E. D. Sanborn, of Dartmouth College . . .* Manchester, NH: Published by John B. Clarke, 1876.

Morse Brothers, Druggists and Pharmacists. *Ye Centennial Almanac.* Rutland, VT: Tuttle and Co., Printers, 1876.

National Liberal League. *Equal Rights in Religion: Report of the Centennial Congress of Liberals and Organization of the National Liberal League, at Philadelphia, on the Fourth of July, 1876.* Boston: National Liberal League, 1876.

[New Jersey State Centennial Board]. *Report of the New Jersey Commissioners on the Centennial Exhibition*. Trenton, NJ: Naar, Day, and Naar, Printers, 1877. Held in Doe Library, University of California at Berkeley.

[*New York Tribune*]. *New York Tribune Extra No. 35: Letters About the Exhibition*.

"Noah Webster, 'The Schoolmaster of the Republic.' . . . United States Centennial." Poster. Springfield, MA: Clark W. Bryan and Company, Printers, 1876. Held in Broadside Collection, Rare Books and Special Collections Division, Library of Congress, Washington, DC.

Norwood, Thomas M. "Centennial Exposition: Speech in the Senate of the United States, February 10, 1876." Washington, DC: Government Printing Office, 1876.

"Order of Musical Exercises on the Occasion of the Ushering in of the Centennial Anniversary of American Independence . . . " Held in Broadside Collection, Rare Books and Special Collections, Library of Congress, Washington, DC.

Pepper, William, medical director, Bureau of Medical Service. Report submitted to Alfred Goshorn, director-general of the USCC, 1877. Advance proofsheets held in Toner Collection, Rare Books and Special Collections Division, Library of Congress, Washington, DC.

Report of the Board on Behalf of the United States Executive Departments at the International Exhibition, Held at Philadelphia, PA, 1876, Under Acts of Congress of March 3, 1875, and May 1, 1876. 2 vols. Washington, DC: Government Printing Office, 1884.

Saunders, Frederick, ed. *Our National Centennial Jubilee: Orations, Addresses, and Poems Delivered on the Fourth of July, 1876, in the Several States of the Union*. St. Clair Shores, MI: Scholarly Press, 1976 (1877).

Sayen, W. Henry, ed. *The Grand International Centennial Chess Congress, held in Philadelphia in August, 1876, During the Celebration of the American Centennial*. Annotated by Jacob Elson, B. M. Neil, and W. H. Sayen. Philadelphia: Claxton, Remsen, and Haffelfinger, 1876.

Shortcut, Daisy [pseud.], and 'Arry O'Pagus [David Solis Cohen]. *Our Show; a Humorous Account of the International Exposition in Honor of the Centennial Anniversary of American Independence, . . . etc.*. Illustrated by A. B. Frost. Philadelphia: Claxton, Remson, and Haffelfinger, 1876. Held in Rare Books and Special Collections Division, Library of Congress, Washington, DC.

Spaulding, Elbridge G. "Address at the Bank Officers and Bankers Building, Centennial Grounds, Fairmount Park, Philadelphia, on the Occasion of the Formal Opening, May 30, 1876." Philadelphia: Richard Magee and Son, Printers, 1876.

Taylor, Bayard. "Aspects of the Fair." In [*New York Tribune*], *New York Tribune Extra No. 35: Letters About the Exhibition*.

Trout, S. Edgar. *The Story of the Centennial of 1876: Golden Anniversary*. Lancaster, PA: n.p., 1929.

United States Centennial Commission (USCC). Complimentary Pass. Held in Broadside Collection, Rare Books and Special Collections Division, Library of Congress, Washington, DC.

International Exhibition 1876. Appendix to the Reports of the USCC and Centennial Board of Finance. Philadelphia: J. B. Lippincott, 1879. Held in Bancroft Library, University of California at Berkeley.

Journal of the Proceedings of the United States Centennial Commission, at Philadelphia, 1872. Philadelphia: E. C. Markley and Son, Printers, 1872.

Meeting of the Executive Committee, Philadelphia, August 1872. Philadelphia: n.p., 1872.

The National Celebration of the Centennial Anniversary of the Independence of the United States by an International Universal Exhibition, to be held in Philadelphia in the Year 1876. Accompanied by a Classified Compilation of the Journal of the Proceedings of the Commission and other Papers. Compiled and arranged by H. D. Pratt. Washington, DC: Government Printing Office, 1873.

The National Centennial: The International Exhibition of 1876. Message of the President of the United States to Congress Transmitting the Third Report of the USCC on the Progress of the Work . . . Embracing the Report on the Vienna Exhibition of 1873. Washington, DC: Government Printing Office, 1874.

[United States Centennial Commission]. *1776–1876. The United States International Exhibition . . . Origin, Rise & Progress of the Work, Description of the Buildings, etc. . . . .* Philadelphia: n.p., 1873.

. . . The United States International Exhibition . . . The Organization, The Work Proposed, The Work Already Done. Philadelphia: n.p., 1875.

[?United States Centennial Commission]. *Additional Notes on the International Exhibition and the Centennial.* N.p.: n.p., ?1874.

Virginius [Dr. Geo. M. Brown]. "Centennial Dirge: A Song of Wrong." ?Continsville, VA: n.p., 1877.

Walker, Francis A. *The World's Fair. Philadelphia 1876. A Critical Account.* New York: A. S. Barnes & Co., 1877.

Wilmshurst, Zavarr. *Liberty's Centennial, A Poem of 1876.* New York: Stephen English, 1876.

Women's Centennial Executive Committee. *First Annual Report (February 16, 1874).* Philadelphia: J. B. Lippincott, 1874.

Second Annual Report. Philadelphia: Thomas S. Dando, Steam-Power Printer, 1875.

"Women's Department. International Exhibition, Fairmount Park, Philadelphia." *Third Annual Report, March 31, 1876.* Philadelphia: Press of Henry B. Ashmead, 1876.

Australian centenary

Agricultural Society. Invitation. Luncheon, January 25, 1888. Held in Ephemera 1888, Petherick Collection, National Library of Australia, Canberra.

Allen, W. "Centennial Cantata." Music by H. J. King, Jr. In [CIE Commission], *Official Record.*

[?Appleton, Savory]. *The Exhibition Historical and Descriptive Geography of the*

Australian Colonies, by Mrs Savory Appleton. Melbourne: n.p., 1888. Held in Dixson Library, Sydney.

[*Argus*]. *The Centennial International Exhibition, Melbourne, 1888, Inaugural Ceremony*. Souvenir Extract and Reprint from *Argus*, August 2, 1888.

Brisbane Courier, 1888.

Buddivent, P. Lucien. *The "CENTENNIAL," or Simple Rhymes of an "Idle Rhymster"*. Sydney: Wm MacLardy, Printer, 1888. Held in Petherick Collection, National Library of Australia, Canberra.

Bulletin, 1888.

Celebration in Commemoration of the Centennial of Australia and the Jubilee Year of the Foundation of the Order of the Sisters of Charity in Australia, St. Vincent's Convent, 23rd January 1888. Sydney: J. G. O'Connor, Nation Office, 1888. Held in National Library of Australia, Canberra.

Centennial Almanac '88: Facts About Ourselves and the Land We Live In: Guide to Sorrento. In Pamphlet Collection, vol. 270, National Library of Australia, Canberra.

[Centennial International Exhibition (CIE) Commission]. *Official Daily Programme*. Held in Mitchell Library, Sydney.

The Official Catalogue of the Exhibits, with Introductory Notices of the Countries Exhibiting. 2 vols. Melbourne: published by M. L. Hutchinson, printed by Mason, Firth, and McCutcheon, 1888. Bound with Centennial International Exhibition Melbourne 1888, *Commission. List of Commissioners, Rules, and Regulations*, and *Official Guide to the Picture Galleries and Catalogue of Fine Arts*, compiled and edited for the commissioners by J. Lake, superintendent of Fine Arts. 4th edn., 1889. Held in Mitchell Library, Sydney.

Official Record . . . Melbourne, 1888–1889, Containing a Sketch of the Industrial and Economic Progress of the Australasian Colonies During the First Century of Their Existence: and of the Exhibition Held in Melbourne, Victoria, to Commemorate the Close of That Period . . . Published by the authority of the Executive Commissioners. Melbourne: Sands and McDougall Limited, Printers, 1890.

Comettant, Oscar. *In the Land of Kangaroos and Gold Mines*. Trans. by Judith Armstrong. Adelaide: Rigby, 1980 (1899).

Ferguson, David G. "The Future of the Australian Colonies." In *Centennial Magazine* 1 (1888–89), 763–69.

Harper, Samuel. *Australia and Mnason: A Centennial Poem, Being a Poetical History of the Colony of New South Wales*. Sydney: F. Cunningham & Co, Steam Machine Printers, 1885.

Herbert, Robert. *Australian Centennial Ode, 1888*. Sydney: n.p., 1892. Held in Mitchell Library, Sydney.

Hutchinson's Australian Almanac 1889. Melbourne: M. L. Hutchinson, 1889. Held in Mitchell Library, Sydney.

Jefferis, James, "Australia's Mission and Opportunity." *Centennial Magazine* 1 (1888–89), 101–04.

Jones, E. Handel. *The Centennial of Australasia: An Address Delivered . . . at a United Thanksgiving Service Held in St. George's Presbyterian Church, East St. Kilda, January 26, 1888, Commemorative of British Settlement in Australasia.* Melbourne: Crabb and Yelland, Printers, ?1888.

Moore, J. Sheridan. *Memorials of the Celebration of the Australasian Centenary in New South Wales, 1888.* Sydney: Charles Potter, Government Printer, 1888.

Morrison, W. Frederick. *Aldine Centennial History of New South Wales.* 2 vols. Sydney: n.p., 1888.

Notes on Exhibits and Exhibitors, Centennial International Exhibition, Melbourne 1888. ?Melbourne: McLean Brothers and Prigg Limited, Publishers, 1888.

Official Programme, New South Wales Centennial Regatta. Held in Miscellaneous Publications File, Centennial Celebrations Box 2, Mitchell Library, Sydney.

Official Reports of the National Australian Convention Debates. Adelaide: C. E. Bristow, Government Printer, 1897.

Plummer, John. "Choral Parts of the Centennial Ode." Music by Hugo Alpen. Sydney: John Sands, General Printer, 1887.

Sydney Morning Herald. 1888–89.

Tribune and News of the Week. 1888.

West Australian, 1888.

American bicentennial

American Revolution Bicentennial Administration (ARBA). *First Report to the Congress.* 2 vols. Washington, DC: Government Printing Office, 1974–75.

Second Report to the Congress. 3 vols. Washington, DC: Government Printing Office, 1975–76.

Final Report to the People. 5 vols. Washington, DC: Government Printing Office, 1977.

Bicentennial Times: Commemorative Reprints (cited as *BT*). Washington, DC: Government Printing Office, 1977.

Call for Achievement. Washington, DC: Government Printing Office, c1976.

"Minutes, 1975." Bound with ARBA, *Second Report to the Congress.*

National Bicentennial Ethnic and Racial Council Conference Report, Washington, DC, January 20–22, 1975 (cited as *BERC*). Washington, DC: Government Printing Office, 1975.

American Revolution Bicentennial Commission (ARBC). *Annual Report, 1972.* In Hawkens and Associates, *Sourcebook*, A–25–59.

Bicentennial Era.

California American Revolution Bicentennial Commission (California ARBC). *The California Plan, Submitted to the National ARBC, April 1970.* Held in Doe Library, University of California at Berkeley.

Minutes, 1968–1970. Held in Doe Library, University of California at Berkeley.

Congressional Record. 1970–76. Washington, DC.

Hartje, Robert G. *Bicentennial USA: Pathways to Celebration.* Nashville, TN: American Association for State and Local History, 1973.

Hawkens and Associates. *Bicentennial Sourcebook.* Washington, DC: n.p., c1973.

Heritage Foundation. *The Great Bicentennial Debate: History as Political Weapon.* Record of a debate between Jeremy Rifkin, director, People's Bicentennial Commission, and Jeffrey St. John, author and historian, held at St. Olaf's College, Minnesota, 1976. Held in Doe Library, University of California at Berkeley.

People's Bicentennial Commission (PBC). *America's Birthday: A Planning and Activity Guide for Citizens' Participation During the Bicentennial Years.* New York: Simon and Schuster, 1974.

Rifkin, Jeremy. *Commonsense II: The Case Against Corporate Tyranny.* Boston: People's Bicentennial Commission, 1975.

United States. General Accounting Office. *Planning for America's Bicentennial Celebration – A Progress Report, June 6, 1975.* Washington, DC: Government Printing Office, 1975.

United States. Senate Judiciary Committee. Subcommittee to Investigate the Administration of the Internal Security Act and Other Internal Security Laws. *The Attempt to Steal the Bicentennial.* 1976.

Australian bicentenary

Australia. Department of Prime Minister and Cabinet. *Annual Report, 1984–1985.* Canberra: Government Printing Office, 1985.

Australia, 1788–1988: Historical Newsletter. Held in Mitchell Library, Sydney.

Australian Bicentennial Authority (ABA). *First Annual Report on Activities to 30 June 1981.* Sydney: Australian Bicentennial Authority, 1981.

Second Annual Report on Activities to 30 June 1982. Sydney: Australian Bicentennial Authority, 1982.

Third Annual Report on Activities to 30 June 1983. Sydney: Australian Bicentennial Authority, 1983.

Fourth Annual Report on Activities to 30 June 1984. Sydney: Australian Bicentennial Authority, 1984.

Fifth Annual Report on Activities to 30 June 1985. Edited by Robert Campbell. Sydney: Australian Bicentennial Authority, 1985.

Sixth Annual Report on Activities to 30 June 1986. Edited by Kate Richardson. Sydney: Australian Bicentennial Authority, 1986.

Seventh Annual Report on Activities to 30 June 1987. Edited by Kate Richardson. Sydney: Australian Bicentennial Authority, 1987.

Eighth Annual Report 1988: On Activities to 30 June 1988. Edited by Kate Richardson. Sydney: Australian Bicentennial Authority, 1988.

Ninth Annual Report 1989: On Activities to 30 June 1989. 2 vols. Edited by Bruce Pollock. Sydney: Australian Bicentennial Authority, 1989.

Australia Live! The Celebration of a Nation. Produced by Peter Faiman for the ABA. 1988. Video cassette. Author's notes from videocassette lent by ABA.

Bicentenary '88 (cited as *B '88*).

Australian Bicentennial Exhibition. December 18, 1988, Blacktown, Sydney. Author's notes.

Australian Broadcasting Commission. *Australia's Day*. Produced by ABC Bicentennial Unit, 1988. 92 min. Video cassette.

Canberra College of Advanced Education. "The 29th International Mathematical Olympiad July 9–21, 1988, Canberra, Australia." 1985. Brochure held by author.

Capoletto, Dorothy. Interview with author. Sydney, January 17, 1989.

"Captain Arthur Phillip R. N. 250th Anniversary Programme, 1988." Miscellaneous Publications File: Commonwealth Celebrations 2, in Mitchell Library, Sydney.

Kennard, Desmond. Interview with author. Sydney, January 17, 1989.

"Linking the Nation: Bicentennial Birthday Beacons, 18 June 1988." Pamphlet held in Mitchell Library, Sydney.

McCarthy, Wendy. Interview with author. Sydney, January 6, 1989.

O'Brien, Denis. Interview with author. Sydney, January 6, 1989.

Treaty '88 Campaign. "Aboriginal Sovereignty – Never Ceded." In Janson and MacIntyre, *Making the Bicentenary*, 1–2.

Tapperell, Kathleen. Interview with author. Canberra, January 13, 1989.

Secondary sources

Abbott, G. J. "The Botany Bay Decision." *Journal of Australian Studies* 16 (May 1985), 21–40.

Abbott, G. J., and N. B. Nairn, eds. *Economic Growth of Australia, 1788–1821*. Melbourne: Melbourne University Press, 1969.

Abercrombie, Nicholas, and Bryan Turner. "The Dominant Ideology Thesis." *British Journal of Sociology* 29 (2) June 1978, 151–63.

Abercrombie, Nicholas, Stephen Hill, and Bryan Turner. *The Dominant Ideology Thesis*. London: George Allen and Unwin, 1980.

Aitken, Don. "Australian Political Culture," *Australian Cultural History* 5 (1986), 5–11.

Aitken, Hugh G. J., ed. *The State and Economic Growth*. Papers of a Conference held on October 11–13, 1956, under the Auspices of the Committee on Economic Growth. New York: Social Science Research Council, 1959.

Alexander, Fred. *Moving Frontiers: An American Theme and Its Application to Australian History*. Port Washington, NY: Kennikat Press, 1969 (1946).

Alexander, Jeffrey C. "Culture and Political Crisis: 'Watergate' and Durkheimian Sociology." In Jeffrey C. Alexander, ed., *Durkheimian Sociology: Cultural Studies*, 187–224. Cambridge and New York: Cambridge University Press, 1988.

Alexander, Jeffrey C., and Philip Smith. "The Discourse of American Civil Society: A New Proposal for Cultural Studies." *Theory and Society* 22 (2) April 1993, 151–207.

Alexander, Malcolm. "Australia: A Settler Society in a Changing World." In Walter, *Australian Studies*, 51–60.

Allen, Judith. "From Women's History to a History of the Sexes." In Walter, *Australian Studies*, 220–41.

"'Mundane' Men: Historians, Masculinity, and Masculinism." *Historical Studies* 22 (89) October 1987, 717–28.

Allin, C. D. *The Early Federation Movement of Australia*. Kingston, Ontario: Press of the British Whig Publishing Co., 1907.

A History of the Tariff Relations of the Australian Colonies. University of Minnesota Studies in the Social Sciences, VII. Minneapolis, MN: Bulletin of the University of Minnesota, February 1918.

Alomes, Stephen. *A Nation at Last? The Changing Character of Australian Nationalism, 1880–1988*. North Ryde and London: Angus and Robertson, 1988.

Altman, Dennis. "The Creation of Sexual Politics in Australia." *Journal of Australian Studies* 20 (May 1987), 76–82.

Anderson, Benedict. *Imagined Communities: Reflections on the Origin and Spread of Nationalism*. Rev. edn. London and New York: Verso, 1991.

Anderson, H., ed. *Tocsin: Radical Comments Against Federation, 1897–1900*. Melbourne: Melbourne University Press, 1977.

Andres, William D. "Women and the Fairs of 1876 and 1893." *Hayes Historical Journal* 1 (1976–77), 173–83.

Appelbaum, Diana Karter. *The Glorious Fourth: An American Holiday, An American History*. New York and Oxford: Facts on File, 1989.

Arieli, Yehoshua. *Individualism and Nationalism in American Ideology*. Cambridge, MA: Harvard University Press, 1964.

Ashton, Paul, and Kate Blackmore. *Centennial Park: A History*. Kensington, New South Wales: New South Wales University Press, 1988.

Astbury, Leigh. "Cash Buyers Welcome: Australian Artists and Bohemianism in the 1890s." *Journal of Australian Studies* 20 (May 1987), 23–37.

Atkinson, Alan. "The First Plans for Governing New South Wales, 1786–1787." *Australian Historical Studies* 24 (94) April 1990, 22–40.

Attwood, Bain. *The Making of the Aborigines*. Sydney: Allen and Unwin, 1989.

Attwood, Bain, and John Arnold, eds. *Power, Knowledge, and Aborigines*. Special edn. of *Journal of Australian Studies*. Melbourne: La Trobe University Press with the National Centre for Australian Studies, Monash University, 1992.

Bailyn, Bernard. *The Ideological Origins of the American Revolution*. Cambridge, MA, and London: Belknap Press of Harvard University Press, 1967.

The Origins of American Politics. New York: Alfred A. Knopf, 1970.

Baker, Jean H. *Affairs of Party: The Political Culture of Northern Democrats in the Mid-Nineteenth Century*. Ithaca, NY: Cornell University Press, 1983.

Barham, Susan Baggett. "Conceptualizations of Women Within Australian Egalitarian Thought." *Comparative Studies in Society and History* 30 (3) July 1980, 483–510.

Barrett, John. "Melbourne and the Bush: Russel Ward's Thesis and a La Trobe Survey." *Meanjin* 31 (1972), 462–70.

Barthes, Roland. *Mythologies*. Selected and trans. by Annette Lavers. New York: Hill and Wang, 1972 (1957).

Bean, Clive. "Orthodox Political Participation in Australia." *Australian and New Zealand Journal of Sociology* 25 (3) November 1989, 451–79.

Becker, Carl. *The Declaration of Independence: A Study in the History of Political Ideas*. New York: Alfred A. Knopf, 1960 (1922).

Beever, Margot, and F. B. Smith, eds. *Historical Studies: Selected Articles*. 2nd edn. Melbourne: Melbourne University Press, 1967.

Bellah, Robert. "Civil Religion in America." In W. G. McLoughlin and R. Bellah, eds., *Religion in America*, 3–23. Boston: Beacon Press, 1968.

Bendix, Reinhard. *Kings or People: Power and the Mandate to Rule*. Berkeley and Los Angeles: University of California Press, 1978.

Benedict, Burton. "The Anthropology of World's Fairs." In Benedict, ed., with Marjorie M. Dobkin, Gray Brechin, Elizabeth N. Armstrong, and George Starr, *The Anthropology of World's Fairs: San Francisco's Panama Pacific International Exposition of 1915*, 1–65. London and Berkeley: Lowie Museum of Anthropology in association with Scolar Press, 1983.

Bennett, Scott. *Aborigines and Political Power*. Sydney: Allen and Unwin, 1989.

Bennett, Tony. "The Shaping of Things to Come: Expo '88." *Cultural Studies* 5 (January 1991), 30–51; reprinted in Bennett *et al.*, *Celebrating the Nation*, 123–41.

Bennett, Tony, Pat Buckridge, David Carter, and Colin Mercer, eds. *Celebrating the Nation: A Critical Study of Australia's Bicentenary*. Sydney: Allen and Unwin, 1992.

Bercovitch, Sacvan. *The American Jeremiad*. Madison, WI: University of Wisconsin Press, 1978.

Berezin, Mabel. "Cultural Form and Political Meaning: State-Subsidized Theater, Ideology, and the Language of Style in Fascist Italy." *American Journal of Sociology* 99 (March 1994), 1237–86.

Billig, Michael. *Banal Nationalism*. London and Thousand Oaks, CA: Sage, 1995.

Blackton, Charles. "Australian Nationality and Nationalism: The Imperial Federationist Interlude, 1885–1901." *Historical Studies* 7 (1955), 1–16.

  "The Dawn of Australian National Feeling, 1850–1856." *Pacific Historical Review* 24 (2) May 1955, 121–38.

Blight, David W. "'For Something Beyond the Battlefield': Frederick Douglass and the Struggle for the Memory of the Civil War." In David Thelen, ed., *Memory and American History*, 27–39. Bloomington and Indianapolis, IN: Indiana University Press, 1990.

Bloom, William. *Personal Identity, National Identity, and International Relations*. Cambridge and New York: Cambridge University Press, 1990.

Bock, Kenneth. "Theories of Progress, Development, Evolution." In Tom Bottomore and Robert Nisbet, eds., *A History of Sociological Analysis*, 39–79. New York: Basic Books, 1978.

Bodnar, John. *Remaking America: Public Memory, Commemoration, and Patriotism in the Twentieth Century*. Princeton, NJ: Princeton University Press, 1992.

Bolton, G. C. "Louis Hartz," *Australian Economic History Review* 13 (2) September 1973, 168–76.

Bourdieu, Pierre. "Thinking About Limits." *Theory, Culture, and Society* 9 (1) February 1992, 37–49.

Breckinridge, Carol A. "The Aesthetics and Politics of Colonial Collecting: India at World Fairs." *Comparative Studies in Society and History* 31 (2) April 1984, 195–216.

Breuilly, John. *Nationalism and the State*. New York: St. Martin's Press, 1982.

Brody, M. Kenneth. "Sociological Theories of Symbolic Activity: A Case Study Application to the Bicentennial Observance." Ph.D. dissertation, University of Iowa, 1977.

Broude, Henry W. "The Role of the State in American Economic Development, 1820–1890." In Hugh Aitken, *State and Economic Growth*, 4–25.

Brown, Dee. *The Year of the Century: 1876*. New York: Charles Scribner's Sons, 1966.

Brumberg, Stephen F. *Going to America, Going to School: The Jewish Immigrant Public School Encounter in Turn-of-the-Century New York City*. New York: Praeger, 1986.

Buckley, Ken, and Ted Wheelwright. *No Paradise for Workers: Capitalism and the Common People in Australia, 1788–1914*. Melbourne: Oxford University Press, 1988.

Bulbeck, Chilla. "Aborigines, Memorials, and the History of the Frontier." *Australian Historical Studies* 24 (96) April 1991, 168–78.

"Australian History Set in Concrete? The Influence of the New Histories on Australian Memorial Construction." *Journal of Australian Studies* 28 (March 1991), 3–16.

Burgmann, Verity. "Racism, Socialism, and the Labour Movement, 1887–1917." *Labour History* 47 (November 1984), 39–54.

Burns, Gene. *The Frontiers of Catholicism: The Politics of Ideology in a Liberal World*. Berkeley and Los Angeles: University of California Press, 1992.

"The Sociology of Ideology: Social Structure, Autonomy, and Ambiguity." Paper presented at the annual meeting of the American Sociological Association, San Francisco, August 1989.

Butlin, N. G. "Colonial Socialism in Australia, 1860–1890." In Hugh Aitken, *State and Economic Growth*, 26–78.

Investment in Australian Economic Development, 1861–1900. Cambridge: Cambridge University Press, 1964.

Cain, P. J., and A. G. Hopkins. *British Imperialism: Innovation and Expansion, 1688–1914*. New York: Longman, 1993.

Calhoun, Craig. "Nationalism and Civil Society: Democracy, Diversity, and Self-Determination." In Craig Calhoun, ed., *Social Theory and the Politics of Identity*, 304–35. Oxford and Cambridge, MA: Blackwell, 1994.

Campbell, James W. *America in Her Centennial Year, 1876*. Washington, DC: University Press of America, 1980.

Carroll, John, ed. *Intruders in the Bush: The Australian Quest for Identity*. Melbourne: Oxford University Press, 1982.

Carter, David, with Gillian Whitlock. "Institutions of Australian Literature." In Walter, *Australian Studies: A Survey*, 112–29.

Castles, Stephen. "Australian Multiculturalism: Social Policy and Identity in a Changing Society." In Freeman and Jupp, *Nations of Immigrants*, 184–201.

——— "The Bicentenary and the Failure of Australian Nationalism." *Race and Class* 29 (3) 1988, 53–68.

Castles, Stephen, Mary Kalantzis, Bill Cope, and Michael Morrissey. *Mistaken Identity: Multiculturalism and the Demise of Nationalism in Australia*. Sydney: Pluto Press, 1988.

Cawelti, John. "America on Display, 1876, 1893, 1933." In Frederic C. Jaher, ed., *America in the Age of Industrialism*, 317–63. New York: Free Press, 1968.

Cerulo, Karen A. *Identity Designs: The Sights and Sounds of a Nation*. ASA Rose Book Series. New Brunswick, NJ: Rutgers University Press, 1995.

Cochrane, Peter. *Industrialization and Dependence: Australia's Road to Economic Development, 1870–1939*. St. Lucia, Queensland: University of Queensland Press, 1980.

Cochrane, Peter, and David Goodman. "The Great Australian Journey: Cultural Logic and Nationalism in the Postmodern Era." In Janson and MacIntyre, *Making the Bicentenary*, 21–44.

Cole, Douglas. "The Crimson Thread of Kinship: Ethnic Ideas in Australia, 1870–1914." *Historical Studies* 14 (April 1971), 511–25.

Collins, Hugh. "Political Ideology in Australia: The Distinctiveness of a Benthamite Society." *Daedalus* 114 (Winter 1985), 147–69.

Connors, Jane. "The 1954 Royal Tour of Australia." *Australian Historical Studies* 25 (100) April 1993, 371–82.

Craik, Jennifer. "Expo '88: Fashions of Sight and Politics of Site," in Bennett *et al.*, *Celebrating the Nation*, 142–59.

Crisp, L. F. *The Later Australian Federation Movement, 1883–1901: Outline and Bibliography*. Canberra: Australian National University Research School of Social Sciences, 1979.

Cronin, Kathryn. "The Yellow Agony." In Raymond Evans, Kay Saunders, and Kathryn Cronin, *Exclusion, Exploitation, and Extermination: Race Relations in Colonial Queensland*, 235–340. Sydney: ANZ Book Co., 1975.

Curti, Merle. *Probing Our Past*. Gloucester, MA: Peter Smith, 1962.

The Roots of American Loyalty. New York: Russell and Russell, 1967.

Darian-Smith, Kate, and Paula Hamilton, eds. *Memory and History in Twentieth-Century Australia*. Melbourne: Oxford University Press, 1994.

Davidson, Alastair. *The Invisible State: The Formation of the Australian State, 1788–1901*. Cambridge: Cambridge University Press, 1991.

Davies, Glenn A. "A Brief History of Australian Republicanism." In George Winterton, ed., *We, the People: Australian Republican Government*, 49–62. Sydney: Allen and Unwin, 1994.

Davies, Susanne. "Diggers and Sportsmen." *Arena* 97 (1991), 30–36.

Davies, Wallace E. *Patriotism on Parade: The Story of Veterans' and Hereditary Organizations in America, 1783–1900*. Cambridge, MA: Harvard University Press, 1955.

Davis, Susan G. *Parades and Power: Street Theatre in Nineteenth-Century Philadelphia*. Philadelphia: Temple University Press, 1986.

Davison, Graeme. "Festivals of Nationhood: The International Exhibitions." In Goldberg and Smith, *Australian Cultural History*, 158–77.

"Sydney and the Bush: An Urban Context for the Australian Legend." *Historical Studies* 18 (71) October 1978, 191–209.

[Davison, Graeme]. "Centennial Celebrations." In Graeme Davison, J. W. McCarty, and Ailsa McLeary, eds., *Australians 1888*, 1–29. Sydney: Fairfax, Syme, and Weldon, 1988.

Day, David. "Aliens in a Hostile Land: A Re-appraisal of Australian History." *Journal of Australian Studies* 23 (November 1988), 3–15.

Dayan, Daniel, and Elihu Katz. *Media Events: The Live Broadcasting of History*. Cambridge, MA, and London: Harvard University Press, 1992.

"Television Ceremonial Events." In Arthur Asa Berger, ed., *Television in Society*, 41–55. New Brunswick, NJ: Transaction Books, 1987.

de Certeau, Michel. *The Practice of Everyday Life*. Berkeley and Los Angeles: University of California Press, 1988.

de Garis, B. K. "The Colonial Office and the Commonwealth Constitution Bill." In A. W. Martin, *Essays in Australian Federation*, 94–121.

de Lepervanche, Marie. "Nineteenth-Century Experiments with Cheap Coloured Labour." In *Indians in a White Australia: An Account of Race, Class, and Indian Immigration to Eastern Australia*, 36–55. Sydney: George Allen and Unwin, 1984.

Deacon, Desley. "Political Arithmetic: The Nineteenth-Century Australian Census and the Construction of the Dependent Woman." *Signs* 11 (1985), 27–47.

Dennis, Matthew. "America (Re)Invents Itself: Centenary Celebrations of Columbus's Voyage of 'Discovery,' 1792–1992." Paper presented at the 107th annual meeting of the American Historical Association, Washington, DC, 1992.

Detweiler, Philip F. "The Changing Reputation of the Declaration of Independence: The First Fifty Years." *William and Mary Quarterly* 19 (October 1962), 557–74.

Dibble, Vernon K. "Four Types of Inference from Documents to Events." *History and Theory* 2 (1963), 203–21.

Dillon, Sam. "He's the Explorer/Exploiter You Just Have to Love/Hate." *New York Times*, October 12, 1992, B5.

"Schools Growing Harsher in Scrutiny of Columbus." *New York Times*, October 12, 1992, A1, B5.

Dixson, Miriam. "Gender, Class, and the Women's Movements in Australia, 1890, 1980." In Grieve and Burns, *Australian Women*, 14–26.

Dobbin, Frank. *Forging Industrial Policy: The United States, Britain, and France in the Railway Age.* Cambridge: Cambridge University Press, 1994.

Dogan, Mattei, and Dominique Pelassy. *How to Compare Nations: Strategies in Comparative Politics.* Chatham, NJ: Chatham House Publishers, 1984.

Dunn, Michael. *Australia and the Empire: From 1788 to the Present.* Sydney: Fontana/Collins, 1984.

Durkheim, Emile. *The Elementary Forms of Religious Life.* Trans. and intro. by Karen Fields. New York: Free Press, 1995 (1912).

Eddy, John. "Nationalism and Nation-making from Federation to Gallipoli." In John Eddy and Deryck Schreuder, eds., *The Rise of Colonial Nationalism*, 132–37. Sydney: Allen and Unwin, 1988.

"What Are the Origins of Australia's National Identity?" In F. G. Castles, ed., *Australia Compared: People, Policies and Politics*, 17–37. Sydney: Allen and Unwin, 1991.

Eisenstein, Hester. *Gender Shock: Practising Feminism on Two Continents.* Sydney: Allen and Unwin, 1991.

Ely, Richard. "Secularisation and the Sacred in Australian History." *Historical Studies* 19 (77) October 1981, 553–66.

Erika, Sabine. "Nationalism and Women." *Politics* 21 (1) May 1986, 82–88.

Esman, Marjorie R. "Festivals, Change, and Unity: The Celebration of Ethnic Identity Among Louisiana Cajuns." *Anthropological Quarterly* 55 (4) 1982, 199–210.

Evans, Raymond. "'The Nigger Shall Disappear...': Aborigines and Europeans in Colonial Queensland." In Raymond Evans, Kay Saunders, and Kathryn Cronin, *Exclusion, Exploitation, and Extermination: Race Relations in Colonial Queensland*, 25–146. Sydney: ANZ Book Co., 1975.

Faeges, Russell. "Why a Soviet Union?" Department of Political Science, University of California at Berkeley. Photocopy.

Farber, David, ed. *The Sixties: From Memory to History.* Chapel Hill and London: University of North Carolina Press, 1994.

Fischer, David Hackett. *Historians' Fallacies: Toward a Logic of Historical Thought.* New York: Harper and Row, 1970.

Flaherty, Chris, and Michael Roberts. "The Reproduction of Anzac Symbolism," *Journal of Australian Studies* 24 (May 1989), 52–69.

Fletcher, Brian H. "The 1888 Celebrations." In *Australian History in New South*

Wales, 1888–1938, 1–19. Kensington, New South Wales: New South Wales University Press, 1993.

Foner, Philip S. "Black Participation in the Centennial of 1876." *Negro History Bulletin* 39 (February 1976), 532–38.

Foss, Paul, ed. *Island in the Stream: Myths of Place in Australian Culture*. Sydney: Pluto Press, 1988.

Foster, Lois, and David Stockley. *Australian Multiculturalism: A Documentary History and Critique*. Clevedon, UK, and Philadelphia: Multilingual Matters, 1988.

Freeman, Gary P., and James Jupp, eds. *Nations of Immigrants: Australia, the United States, and International Migration*. Melbourne: Oxford University Press, 1992.

Frost, Alan. "The Conditions of Early Settlement: New South Wales, 1788–1840." In Carroll, *Intruders in the Bush*, 69–81.

"Historians, Handling Documents, Transgressions, and Transportable Offences." *Australian Historical Studies* 25 (99) October 1993, 192–219.

Galligan, Brian. "The State in Australian Political Thought." *Politics* 19 (2) November 1984, 82–92.

Gellner, Ernest. *Nations and Nationalism*. Oxford and New York: Basil Blackwell, 1983.

Giddens, Anthony. *The Nation State and Violence*. Berkeley: University of California Press, 1985.

Gillis, John R., ed. *Commemorations: The Politics of National Identity*. Princeton, NJ: Princeton University Press, 1994.

Glassberg, David. *American Historical Pageantry: The Uses of Tradition in the Early Twentieth Century*. Chapel Hill and London: University of North Carolina Press, 1990.

Glynn, Sean. "Urbanisation in Australian History." In Whitlock and Carter, *Images of Australia*, 229–39.

Goldberg, S. L., and F. B. Smith, eds. *Australian Cultural History*. Cambridge: Cambridge University Press, 1988.

Gollan, R. A. "Nationalism, the Labour Movement, and the Commonwealth, 1880–1900." In Gordon Greenwood, ed., *Australia: A Social and Political History*, 145–95. North Ryde and London: Angus and Robertson, 1955.

Goot, Murray. "Multiculturalists, Monoculturalists, and the Many in Between: Attitudes to Cultural Diversity and Their Correlates." *Australian and New Zealand Journal of Sociology* 29 (2) August 1993, 226–53.

Gordon, Richard, ed. *The Australian New Left: Critical Essays and Strategy*. Melbourne: William Heinemann, 1970.

Gordon, Richard, and Warren Osmond. "An Overview of the Australian New Left." In Gordon, *Australian New Left*, 3–39.

Gourevitch, Peter. *Politics in Hard Times: Comparative Responses to International Economic Crises*. Ithaca, NY, and London: Cornell University Press, 1986.

Greene, Jack P. "A Fortuitous Convergence: Culture, Circumstance, and Contingency in the Emergence of the American Nation." In *Religion, Ideology, and Nationalism in Europe and America: Essays Presented in Honor of Yehoshua Arieli*, 243–61. Jerusalem: Historical Society for Israel and the Zalman Shazar Center for Jewish History, 1986.

The Intellectual Construction of America: Exceptionalism and Identity from 1492 to 1800. Chapel Hill and London: University of North Carolina Press, 1993.

Peripheries and Center: Constitutional Development in the Extended Polities of the British Empire and the United States, 1607–1788. Athens, GA, and London: University of Georgia Press, 1986.

"Search for Identity: An Interpretation of the Meaning of Selected Patterns of Social Response in Eighteenth-Century America." *Journal of Social History* 3 (1969–70), 189–220.

Greenfeld, Liah. *Nationalism: Five Roads to Modernity*. Cambridge, MA, and London: Harvard University Press, 1992.

Greenhalgh, Paul. *Ephemeral Vistas: The Expositions Universelles, Great Exhibitions, and World's Fairs, 1851–1939*. Manchester: Manchester University Press, 1988.

Grieve, Norma, and Ailsa Burns, eds. *Australian Women: New Feminist Perspectives*. Melbourne: Oxford University Press, 1986.

Griffiths, Tom. "Past Silences: Aborigines and Convicts in Our History-Making." *Australian Cultural History* 6 (1987), 18–32.

Grimshaw, Charles. "Australian Nationalism and the Imperial Connection, 1900–1914." *Australian Journal of Politics and History* 3 (2) May 1958, 161–82.

Grimshaw, Patricia. "'Man's Own Country': Women in Colonial Australian History." In Grieve and Burns, *Australian Women*, 182–209.

Habermas, Jürgen. "Legitimation Problems in the Modern State." *Communication and the Evolution of Society*, ch. 5. Trans. by Thomas McCarthy. Boston: Beacon Press, 1976.

Hackett, David G. "The Social Origins of Nationalism: Albany, New York, 1754–1835." *Journal of Social History* 21 (1987–88), 659–81.

Haines, Robin, and Ralph Shlomowitz. "Immigration from the United Kingdom to Colonial Australia: A Statistical Analysis." *Journal of Australian Studies* 34 (September 1992), 43–52.

Hall, Peter D. *The Organization of American Culture, 1780–1900: Private Institutions, Elites, and the Origins of American Nationality*. New York: New York University Press, 1982.

Hamilton, Annette. "Fear and Desire: Aborigines, Asians, and the National Imaginary." *Australian Cultural History* 9 (1990), 14–35.

Hansen, Debra Gold, and Mary P. Ryan. "Public Ceremony in a Private Culture: Orange County Celebrates the Fourth of July." In Rob Kling, Spencer Olin, and Mark Poster, eds., *Postsuburban California: The Transformation of Orange County Since World War II*, 165–89. Berkeley and Los Angeles: University of California Press, 1991.

Harris, Neil. "All the World a Melting Pot? Japan at American Fairs, 1876–1904." In Akira Iriye, ed., *Mutual Images: Essays in American–Japanese Relations*, 24–54. Cambridge, MA: Harvard University Press, 1975.

Hartz, Louis. "Comments." *Comparative Studies in Society and History* 5 (3) April 1963, 279–84.

The Founding of New Societies. New York: Harcourt, Brace, and World, 1964.

Hay, Robert Pettis. "Freedom's Jubilee: One Hundred Years of the Fourth of July, 1776–1876." Ph.D. dissertation, University of Kentucky, 1967.

Head, Brian. "Political Dependency and the Institutional Framework." In Walter, *Australian Studies*, 275–80.

"Political Ideologies and Political Parties." In Walter, *Australian Studies*, 284–94.

"The Role of State Intervention." In Walter, *Australian Studies*, 295–303.

Head, Brian, ed. *State and Economy in Australia.* Melbourne: Oxford University Press, 1983.

Headon, David. "Preparing for the Grandest Experiment – Daniel Deniehy's New-World Vocabulary." *Journal of Australian Studies* 17 (November 1985), 59–68.

Headon, David, James Warden, and Bill Gammage, eds. *Crown or Country: The Traditions of Australian Republicanism.* Sydney: Allen and Unwin, 1994.

Hegeman, Susan. "Shopping for Identities: 'A Nation of Nations' and the Weak Ethnicity of Objects." *Public Culture* 3 (2) 1991, 71–92.

Hicks, John. "The United States Centennial Exhibition of 1876." Ph.D. dissertation, University of Georgia, 1972.

Hills, E. R. "The Imaginary Life: Landscape and Culture in Australia." *Journal of Australian Studies* 29 (June 1991), 12–27.

Hirst, J. B. "Keeping Colonial History Colonial: The Hartz Thesis Revisited." *Historical Studies* 21 (82) April 1984, 85–104.

"The Pioneer Legend." *Historical Studies* 18 (October 1978), 316–37.

The Strange Birth of Colonial Democracy: New South Wales, 1848–1884. Sydney: Allen and Unwin, 1988.

Hobsbawm, E. J. *Nations and Nationalism Since 1780.* Cambridge and New York: Cambridge University Press, 1990.

Hobsbawm, E., and T. Ranger, eds. *The Invention of Tradition.* Cambridge and New York: Cambridge University Press, 1984.

Hoffenberg, Peter. "Colonial Innocents Abroad? Late Nineteenth-Century Australian Visitors to America and the Invention of New Nations." Paper presented at the 107th annual meeting of the American Historical Association, Washington, DC, 1992.

Hoffenberg, Peter, and Marc Rothenberg. "Australia at the 1876 Exhibition in Philadelphia." *Historical Records of Australian Science* 8 (1990), 55–60.

Holt, Elizabeth Gilmore, ed. *Universal Expositions and State-Sponsored Fine Arts Exhibitions.* Vol. I, *The Expanding World of Art, 1874–1902.* New Haven and London: Yale University Press, 1988.

Horne, Donald. *Ideas for a Nation.* Sydney: Pan Books, 1989.

Howe, Renate, ed. *Women and the State.* Special edn. of *Journal of Australian Studies.* Bundoora, Victoria: La Trobe University Press, 1993.

Hudson, W. J., and M. P. Sharpe. *Australian Independence: Colony to Reluctant Kingdom.* Melbourne: Melbourne University Press, 1988.

Hunt, Lynn. *Politics, Culture, and Class in the French Revolution.* Berkeley: University of California Press, 1984.

Hutchinson, John. "State Festivals, Foundation Myths, and Cultural Politics in Immigrant Nations." In Tony Bennett, *et al., Celebrating the Nation,* 3–25.

Inglis, K. S. "The Anzac Tradition," *Meanjin* 24 (1) 1965, 25–44.

"Australia Day." *Historical Studies* 13 (49) October 1967, 20–41.

"The Imperial Connection: Telegraphic Communication Between England and Australia, 1872–1902." In Madden and Morris-Jones, *Australia and Britain,* 21–38.

"Multiculturalism and National Identity." In Charles A. Price, ed., *Australian National Identity,* 13–31. Canberra: Academy of the Social Sciences in Australia, 1991.

Inkeles, Alex. "National Character Revisited." In Jesse R. Pitts and Roland Simon, eds., *Tocqueville Review* 12 (1990–91), 83–117.

Jackson, R. V. *Australian Economic Development in the Nineteenth Century.* Canberra: Australian National University Press, 1977.

The Population History of Australia. Melbourne: McPhee Gribble/Penguin, 1988.

Jacques, T. D., and G. R. Pavia. *Sport in Australia: Selected Readings in Physical Activity.* Sydney: McGraw Hill, 1976.

Jaffa, Harry V. "Conflicts Within the Idea of the Liberal Tradition." *Comparative Studies in Society and History* 5 (3) April 1963, 274–78.

Janson, Susan, and Stuart MacIntyre, eds. *Making the Bicentenary.* Special edn. of *Australian Historical Studies* 23 (91) 1988. Melbourne: Australian Historical Studies, 1988.

Jenkins, J. Craig. "Interpreting the Stormy 1960s: Three Theories in Search of a Political Age," *Research in Political Sociology* 3 (1987), 269–303.

Jordens, Ann-Mari. *Redefining Australians: Immigration, Citizenship, and National Identity.* Sydney: Hale and Iremonger, 1995.

Jupp, James. *Immigration.* Melbourne: Sydney University Press with Oxford University Press, 1991.

"Immigration: Some Recent Perspectives." *Australian Historical Studies* 24 (91) April 1990, 285–91.

Kammen, Michael. *A Machine That Would Go of Itself: The Constitution in American Culture.* New York: Vintage Books, 1987.

Mystic Chords of Memory: The Transformation of Tradition in American Culture. New York: Knopf, 1991.

A Season of Youth: The American Revolution and the Historical Imagination. New York: Oxford University Press, 1978.

Spheres of Liberty: Changing Perceptions of Liberty in American Culture. Madison, WI: University of Wisconsin Press, 1986.

Kapferer, Bruce. *Legends of People, Myths of State: Violence, Intolerance, and Political Culture in Sri Lanka and Australia.* Washington, DC, and London: Smithsonian Institution Press, 1988.

Kapferer, Judith L. "Rural Myths and Urban Ideologies." *Australian and New Zealand Journal of Sociology* 26 (1) March 1990, 87–106.

Keller, Morton. *Affairs of State: Public Life in Late Nineteenth-Century America.* Cambridge, MA, and London: Belknap Press of Harvard University Press, 1977.

Kennedy, Brian. "Regionalism and Nationalism: Broken Hill in the 1880s." *Australian Economic History Review* 20 (1) March 1980, 64–76.

Kertzer, David. *Ritual, Politics, and Power.* New Haven: Yale University Press, 1989.

Ketchum, Alton. *Uncle Sam: The Man and the Legend.* New York: Hill and Wang, 1959.

Kingston, Beverley. *1860–1900: Glad, Confident Morning.* Vol. III, *The Oxford History of Australia.* Melbourne: Oxford University Press, 1988.

"The Lady and the Australian Girl: Some Thoughts on Nationalism and Class." In Grieve and Burns, *Australian Women,* 27–41.

Kirkby, Diane. "Frontier Violence: Ethnohistory and Aboriginal Resistance in California and New South Wales, 1770–1840." *Journal of Australian Studies* 6 (June 1980), 36–48.

Kohn, Hans. *American Nationalism: An Interpretive Essay.* New York: MacMillan, 1957.

Nationalism: Its Meaning and History. Princeton, NJ: D. Van Nostrand Co., 1955.

Prelude to Nation States. Princeton, NJ: D. Van Nostrand Co., 1967.

Kohn, Melvin L. "Cross-National Research as an Analytic Strategy." *American Sociological Review* 52 (December 1987), 713–31.

Krieger, Leonard. "A View from the Farther Shore." *Comparative Studies in Society and History* 5 (3) April 1963, 269–73.

La Nauze, J. A. *The Making of the Australian Constitution.* Melbourne: Melbourne University Press, 1972.

Lake, Marilyn. "The Politics of Respectability: Identifying the Masculinist Context." *Historical Studies* 22 (86) April 1986, 116–31.

Lamont, Michele. *Money, Morals, and Manners: The Culture of the French and American Upper-Middle Class.* Chicago and London: University of Chicago Press, 1992.

Lane, Christel. *The Rites of Rulers: Ritual in Industrial Society – The Soviet Case.* Cambridge: Cambridge University Press, 1981.

Lawson, Alan. "Acknowledging Colonialism: Revisions of Australian Tradition." In Madden and Morris-Jones, *Australia and Britain,* 135–44.

Lipset, Seymour M. *Continental Divide: The Values and Institutions of the United States and Canada.* New York: Routledge, 1990.

The First New Nation: The United States in Comparative and Historical Perspective. New York: W. W. Norton and Co., 1979 (1973).

"The Social Requisites of Democracy Revisited." *American Sociological Review* 59 (1) February 1994, 1–22.

LiPuma, Edward, and Sarah Keene Meltzoff. "Ceremonies of Independence and Public Culture in the Solomon Islands." *Public Culture* 3 (1990), 77–92.

Litwak, Leon E. "Trouble in Mind: The Bicentennial and the Afro-American Experience." *Journal of American History* 74 (2) September 1989, 315–37.

Liu, John M. "A Comparative Historical Perspective of Post-World War II Asian Immigration to North America and Australia." Paper presented at the annual meeting of the American Sociological Association, Washington, DC, August 1990.

Livingston, K. T. "Anticipating Federation: The Federalising of Telecommunications in Australia." *Australian Historical Studies* 26 (102) April 1994, 97–118.

Lukes, Steven. "Political Ritual and Social Integration." *Sociology* 9 (2) May 1975, 289–308.

McAllister, Ian. "Patriotism Beats in Aussie Hearts." *Australian Society* 4 (10) October 1985, 25–26.

McCarty, J. W. "Australia as a Region of Recent Settlement in the Nineteenth Century." *Australian Economic History Review* 13 (2) September 1973, 148–67.

McConville, Chris. "Rough Women, Respectable Men, and Social Reform: A Response to Lake's 'Masculinism.'" *Historical Studies* 22 (88) April 1987, 432–41.

McDonald, Forrest. *Novus Ordo Seclorum: The Intellectual Origins of the Constitution.* Lawrence, KS: University Press of Kansas, 1985.

McGerr, Michael. *The Decline of Popular Politics: The American North, 1865–1928.* New York: Oxford University Press, 1986.

McGrath, Ann. "Travels to a Distant Past: The Mythology of the Outback." *Australian Cultural Studies* 10 (1991), 113–24.

McMichael, Philip. "Incorporating Comparison Within a World-Historical Perspective: An Alternative Comparative Method." *American Sociological Review* 55 (June 1990), 385–97.

Settlers and the Agrarian Question: Foundations of Capitalism in Colonial Australia. Cambridge: Cambridge University Press, 1984.

"State Formation and the Construction of the World Market." In Maurice Zeitlin, ed., *Political Power and Social Theory: A Research Annual* 6 (1987), 187–237.

McMinn, W. G. *A Constitutional History of Australia.* Melbourne: Oxford University Press, 1979.

Nationalism and Federalism in Australia. Melbourne: Oxford University Press, 1994.

McNaughton, I. D. "Colonial Liberalism, 1851–1892." In Gordon Greenwood, ed., *Australia: A Social and Political History*, 98–114. North Ryde and London: Angus and Robertson, 1955.

McQueen, Humphrey. *A New Britannia: An Argument Concerning the Social Origins of Australian Radicalism and Nationalism.* Rev. edn. Ringwood, Victoria: Penguin, 1986 (1970).

Madden, A. F., and W. H. Morris-Jones, eds. *Australia and Britain: Studies in a Changing Relationship.* Sydney: Sydney University Press in association with the Institute of Commonwealth Studies, University of London, 1980.

Magarey, Susan, Sue Rowley, and Susan Sheridan, eds. *Debutante Nation: Feminism Contests the 1890s.* Sydney: Allen and Unwin, 1993.

Main, J. M. "Making Constitutions in New South Wales and Victoria, 1853–1854." In Beever and Smith, *Historical Studies,* 51–74.

Mandle, W. F. "Cricket and Australian Nationalism in the Nineteenth Century." *Journal of the Royal Australian Historical Society* 57 (4) December 1973, 225–46.

"Pommy Bastards and Damn' Yankees: Sport and Australian Nationalism." In *Going It Alone: Australia's National Identity in the Twentieth Century,* 24–46. Ringwood, Victoria: Allen Lane, 1978.

"Sport." In J. D. B. Miller, *Australians and British,* 140–57.

Mann, Michael. "The Social Cohesion of Liberal Democracy." *American Sociological Review* 35 (3) June 1970, 423–39.

Markey, Ray. "Populism and the Formation of a Labor Party in New South Wales, 1890–1900." *Journal of Australian Studies* 20 (May 1987), 38–48.

Martin, A. W. "Australia and the Hartz 'Fragment' Thesis." *Australian Economic History Review* 13 (2) September 1973, 131–47.

"Australian Federation and Nationalism: Historical Notes." In R. L. Mathews, ed., *Public Policies in Two Federal Countries: Canada and Australia,* 27–46. Canberra: Centre for Research on Federal Financial Relations, Australian National University, 1982.

Martin, A. W., ed. *Essays in Australian Federation.* Melbourne: Melbourne University Press, 1969.

Martin, Ged, ed. *The Founding of Australia: The Argument About Australia's Origins.* Sydney: Hale and Iremonger, 1978.

Matthews, Fred. "Cultural Pluralism in Context: External History, Philosophic Premise, and Theories of Ethnicity in Modern America." *Journal of Ethnic Studies* 12 (2) 1984, 63–79.

Matthews, Jill Julius. "'A Female of All Things': Women and the Bicentenary." In Janson and MacIntyre, *Making the Bicentenary,* 90–102.

Matthews, T. V. "Business Associations and the State, 1850–1976." In Head, *State and Economy in Australia,* 115–49.

Menadue, J. E. *A Centenary History of the Australian Natives' Association.* Melbourne: Horticultural Press, n.d.

Merrett, Richard L. *Symbols of American Community, 1735–1775.* New Haven and London: Yale University Press, 1966.

Meyer, John W., David Tyack, Joane Nagel, and Audri Gordon. "Public Education as Nation-Building in America: Enrollments and Bureaucratization in the American States, 1870–1930." *American Journal of Sociology* 85 (3) November 1979, 591–613.

Middleton, David and Derek Edwards, eds. *Collective Remembering*. London and Newbury Park, CA: Sage, 1990.

Millar, T. B. *Australia in Peace and War: External Relations, 1788–1977*. New York: St. Martin's Press, 1978.

Miller, J. D. B. "An Empire That Don't Care What You Do . . ." In Madden and Morris-Jones, *Australia and Britain*, 90–100.

Miller, J. D. B., ed. *Australians and British: Social and Political Connections*. Sydney: Methuen, 1987.

Miller, Lillian B. "Engines, Marbles, and Canvases: The Centennial Exposition of 1876." In Lillian B. Miller, Nugent, and Morgan, *Centennial Year*, 3–29.

Miller, Lillian B., Walter T. K. Nugent, and H. Wayne Morgan. *1876: The Centennial Year. Indiana Historical Society Lectures, 1972–1973*. Indianapolis: Indiana Historical Society, 1973.

Miller, Toby. "The Unmarking of Soccer: Making a Brand New Subject." In Tony Bennett, *et al.*, *Celebrating the Nation*, 104–20.

Miner, H. Craig. "The United States Government Building at the Centennial Exhibition, 1874–1877." *Prologue* 4 (1972), 203–18.

Minogue, Kenneth R. *Nationalism*. New York: Basic Books, 1967.

Mitchell, Timothy. "The World as Exhibition." *Comparative Studies in Society and History* 31 (2) April 1984, 217–36.

Mosse, George L. "Caesarism, Circuses, and Monuments." *Journal of Contemporary History* 6 (2) 1971, 167–82.

"Mass Politics and the Political Liturgy of Nationalism." In Eugene Kamenka, ed., *Nationalism: The Nature and Evolution of an Idea*, 39–54. New York: St. Martin's Press, 1973.

Murphy, John. "Conscripting the Past: The Bicentenary and Everyday Life." In Janson and MacIntyre, *Making the Bicentenary*, 45–54.

Murphy, William P. *The Triumph of Nationalism: Sovereignty, the Founding Fathers, and the Making of the Constitution*. Chicago: Quadrangle Books, 1967.

Murrin, John M. "A Roof Without Walls: The Dilemma of American National Identity." In Richard Beeman, Stephen Botein, and Edward C. Carter II, eds., *Beyond Confederation: Origins of the Constitution and American National Identity*, 333–48. Chapel Hill and London: University of North Carolina Press, published for the Institute of Early American History and Culture, Williamsburg, VA, 1987.

Myers, Marvin. "Louis Hartz, *The Liberal Tradition in America*: An Appraisal." *Comparative Studies in Society and History* 5 (3) April 1963, 261–68.

Nagel, Paul C. *One Nation Indivisible*. New York: Oxford University Press, 1964.

Nugent, Walter T. K. *Crossings: The Great Transatlantic Migrations, 1870–1914*. Bloomington, IN: Indiana University Press, 1992.

"Seed Time of Modern Conflict: American Society at the Centennial." In Lillian B. Miller, Nugent, and Morgan, *Centennial Year*, 30–45.

O'Brien, Peter. "Some Overseas Comparisons." In Gordon, *Australian New Left*, 219–34.

Oldfield, Audrey. *Woman Suffrage in Australia: A Gift or a Struggle?* Cambridge: Cambridge University Press, 1992.

Olick, Jeffrey K., and Daniel Levy. "Mechanisms of Cultural Constraint: Holocaust Myth and Rationality in German Politics." Department of Sociology, Columbia University. Photocopy.

Onuf, Peter S. *The Origins of the Federal Republic.* Philadelphia: University of Pennsylvania Press, 1983.

Pacheco, Josephine F. "Introduction." In Josephine Pacheco, ed., *Antifederalism: The Legacy of George Mason*, 1–23. Fairfax, VA: George Mason University Press, 1992.

Parkin, Andrew. "Ethnic Politics: A Comparative Study of Two Immigrant Societies, Australia and the United States." *Journal of Commonwealth and Comparative Politics* 15 (1) March 1977, 22–38.

Patterson, G. D. "The Murray River Border Customs Dispute, 1853–1880." *Business Archives and History* 2 (1962), 122–50.

Peterson, Richard. "Cultural Studies Through the Production Perspective: Progress and Prospects." In Diana Crane, ed., *The Sociology of Culture: Emerging Theoretical Perspectives*, 163–89. Oxford and Cambridge, MA: Blackwell, 1994.

"Revitalizing the Culture Concept." *Annual Review of Sociology* 5 (1979), 137–66.

Pettman, Jan. "The Australian Natives' Association and Federation in South Australia." In A. W. Martin, *Essays in Australian Federation*, 122–36.

"Learning About Power and Powerlessness: Aborigines and White Australia's Bicentenary." *Race and Class* 29 (3) 1988, 69–85.

Price, Charles. "Immigration." In J. D. B. Miller, *Australians and British*, 13–44.

Priessnitz, Horst. "Dreams in Austerica: A Preliminary Comparison of the Australian and the American Dream." *Westerly* 3 (Spring 1994), 45–64.

Pye, Lucien W. "The Politicians' Search for Identity." In *Politics, Personality, and Nation Building: Burma's Search for Identity*, 244–66. New Haven: Yale University Press, 1962.

Quartly, Marian. "Mothers and Fathers and Brothers and Sisters: The AWA and the ANA and Gendered Citizenship." In Howe, *Women and the State*, 22–30.

"Racist Group Challenges Government." *West Australian*, January 2, 1990, 13.

Raichle, Donald. "The Image of the Constitution in American History: A Study in Historical Writing from David Ramsay to John Fiske (1789–1888)." Ph.D. dissertation, Columbia University, 1956.

Ramcharan, B. G., ed. *Human Rights: Thirty Years After the Universal Declaration.* The Hague, Boston, and London: Martinus Nijhoff, 1979.

Ramirez, Francisco O. "Institutional Analysis." In George M. Thomas, *et al.*, *Institutional Structure*, 316–28.

Randel, William Pierce. *Centennial: American Life in 1876*. Philadelphia and New York: Chilton Book Co., 1969.

Ranum, Orest, ed. *National Consciousness, History, and Political Culture in Early Modern Europe*. Baltimore and London: Johns Hopkins University Press, 1975.

Reekie, Gail. "Contesting Australia: Feminism and Histories of the Nation." In Whitlock and Carter, *Images of Australia*, 145–55.

"Nineteenth-Century Urbanization." In Walter, *Australian Studies*, 84–96.

Reynolds, Henry. *Frontier: Aborigines, Settlers, and Land*. Sydney: George Allen and Unwin, 1987.

The Other Side of the Frontier: An Interpretation of the Aboriginal Response to the Invasion and Settlement of Australia. Ringwood, Victoria: Penguin, 1982.

"Racial Thought in Early Colonial Australia." *Australian Journal of Politics and History* 20 (1) April 1974, 45–55.

Rinhart, Floyd, and Marion Rinhart. *America's Centennial Celebration: Philadelphia – 1876*. Winter Haven, FL: Manta Books, 1976.

Roe, Jill. "Chivalry and Social Policy in the Antipodes." *Historical Studies* 22 (88) April 1987, 395–410.

Roe, Michael. "Vandiemenism Debated: The Filming of 'His Natural Life,' 1926–1927." *Journal of Australian Studies* 24 (May 1989), 35–51.

Rogin, Michael. "Liberal Society and the Indian Question." In *"Ronald Reagan," The Movie and Other Episodes in Political Demonology*, 134–68. Berkeley and Los Angeles: University of California Press, 1987.

"'Make My Day!': Spectacle as Amnesia in Imperial Politics." *Representations* 29 (1990), 99–123.

"Political Repression in the United States." In *"Ronald Reagan," the Movie, and Other Episodes in Political Demonology*. Berkeley and Los Angeles: University of California Press, 1987.

Rose, Richard. "National Pride in Cross-National Perspective." *International Social Science Journal* 37 (1) 1985, 85–96.

Rosenzweig, Roy. *Eight Hours for What We Will: Workers and Leisure in an Industrial City, 1870–1920*. Cambridge and New York: Cambridge University Press, 1983.

Rowse, Tim. *Australian Liberalism and National Character*. Melbourne: Kibble Books, 1978.

Royal Institute for International Affairs. "The Rise of National Feeling in Western Europe." In *Nationalism*, 8–24. London: Oxford University Press, 1939.

Rubinstein, W. D. "Men of Wealth." In Goldberg and Smith, *Australian Cultural History*, 109–22.

Ryan, J. A., Geoffrey Bartlett, B. K. de Garis, and C. T. Stannage. "Colonial Politics in Australia: A Symposium," *Australian Economic History Review* 8 (1) March 1968, 37–61.

Rydell, Robert. *All the World's a Fair: Visions of Empire at American International Expositions, 1876–1916*. Chicago and London: University of Chicago Press, 1984.

　World of Fairs: The Century of Progress Exhibitions. Chicago and London: University of Chicago Press, 1993.

"St. Francis Won't Support Kiwis in Court." *San Francisco Chronicle*, January 31, 1990, D9.

Santayana, George. *Soliloquies in England and Later Soliloquies*. London, Bombay, and Sydney: Constable and Company, 1922.

Saunders, Kay. "The Black Scourge." In Raymond Evans, Kay Saunders, and Kathryn Cronin, *Exclusion, Exploitation, and Extermination: Race Relations in Colonial Queensland*, 147–234. Sydney: ANZ Book Co., 1975.

　"'The Middle Passage?' Conditions on Labour Vessels from Queensland to Melanesia, 1863–1907." *Journal of Australian Studies* 5 (November 1979), 38–49.

Savelle, Max. "Nationalism and Other Loyalties in the American Revolution." *American Historical Review* 67 (July 1962), 901–23.

Sawer, Marian. "Reclaiming Social Liberalism: The Women's Movement and the State." In Howe, *Women and the State*, 1–21.

Schaffer, Kay. *Women and the Bush: Forces of Desire in the Australian Cultural Tradition*. Cambridge and Melbourne: Cambridge University Press, 1988.

Schlereth, Thomas J. "The 1876 Centennial: A Model for Comparative American Studies." In *Artifacts and the American Past*, 130–42. Nashville, TN: American Association for State and Local History, 1980.

Schudson, Michael. "Culture and the Integration of National Societies." In Diana Crane, ed., *The Sociology of Culture: Emerging Theoretical Perspectives*, 21–43. Oxford and Cambridge, MA: Blackwell, 1994.

　"The Present in the Past Versus the Past in the Present." *Communication* 11 (1989), 105–13.

　Watergate in American Memory: How We Remember, Forget, and Reconstruct the Past. New York: Basic, 1992.

Schultz, April. "'The Pride of Race Had Been Touched': Norse–American Immigration Centennial and Ethnic Identity." *Journal of American History* 77 (4) 1991, 1265–95.

Schwartz, Barry. *George Washington: The Making of an American Symbol*. Ithaca, NY, and London: Cornell University Press, 1987.

　"The Reconstruction of Abraham Lincoln." In David Middleton and Derek Edwards, *Collective Remembering*, 81–107. London and Newbury Park, CA: Sage, 1990.

　"Social Change and Collective Memory: The Democratization of George Washington." *American Sociological Review* 56 (2) April 1991, 221–36.

　"The Social Context of Commemoration: A Study in Collective Memory." *Social Forces* 61 (December 1982), 372–402.

Serle, Geoffrey. "The Digger Tradition and Australian Nationalism," *Meanjin* 24 (2) 1965, 148–58.

"Victoria's Campaign for Federation." In A. W. Martin, *Essays in Australian Federation*, 1–56.

Shaw, A. G. L. "London and the Governors: Relations in Eastern Australia, 1825–1845." In Madden and Morris-Jones, *Australia and Britain*, 1–20.

Sheridan, S. "Louisa Lawson, Miles Franklin, and Feminist Writing, 1888–1901." *Australian Feminist Studies* 7–8 (Summer 1988), 29–48.

Shils, Edward. "Center and Periphery: An Idea and Its Career, 1935–1987." In Liah Greenfeld and Michel Martin, eds., *Center: Ideas and Institutions*, 250–82. Chicago and London: University of Chicago Press, 1988.

Center and Periphery: Essays in Macrosociology. Chicago and London: University of Chicago Press, 1975.

Shortus, Stephen P. "'Colonial Nationalism': New South Welsh Identity in the Mid–1880s." *Journal of the Royal Australian Historical Society* 59 (March 1973), 31–51.

Shy, John. "The American Revolution: The Military Conflict Considered as a Revolutionary War." In Stephen G. Kurtz and James H. Hutson, eds., *Essays on the American Revolution*, 121–56. Chapel Hill: University of North Carolina Press, 1973.

Siskind, Janet. "The Invention of Thanksgiving: A Ritual of American Nationality." *Critique of Anthropology* 12 (2) 1992, 167–91.

Skocpol, Theda, ed. *Vision and Method in Historical Sociology*. Cambridge and New York: Cambridge University Press, 1984.

Skowrenek, Stephen. *Building a New American State: The Expansion of National Administrative Capacities, 1877–1920*. Cambridge: Cambridge University Press, 1982.

Slotkin, Richard. *The Fatal Environment: The Myth of the Frontier in the Age of Industrialization, 1800–1890*. New York: Atheneum, 1985.

Smelser, Neil. *Comparative Methods in the Social Sciences*. Englewood Cliffs, NJ: Prentice-Hall, 1976.

"The Methodology of Comparative Analysis of Economic Activity." In Smelser, *Essays in Social Explanation*, 62–75. Englewood Cliffs, NJ: Prentice-Hall, 1968.

Smith, Anthony D. *The Ethnic Origins of Nations*. Oxford and New York: Basil Blackwell, 1986.

Theories of Nationalism. 2nd edn. New York: Holmes and Meier, 1983.

Spate, Oskar. "Geography and National Identity in Australia." In David Hoosen, ed., *Geography and National Identity*, 277–82. Oxford and Cambridge, MA: Blackwell, 1994.

Spearritt, Peter. "Celebration of a Nation: The Triumph of Spectacle." In Janson and MacIntyre, *Making the Bicentenary*, 3–20.

"Royal Progress: The Queen and Her Australian Subjects." In Goldberg and Smith, *Australian Cultural History*, 138–57.

Spillman, Lyn. "Culture, Social Structure, and Discursive Fields." *Current Perspectives in Social Theory* 15 (1995), 129–54.

"'Neither the Same Nation Nor Different Nations': Constitutional Conventions in the United States and Australia." *Comparative Studies in Society and History* 38 (1) January 1996, 149–81.

Stampp, Kenneth M. "The Concept of Perpetual Union." *Journal of American History* 65 (June 1978), 5–33.

Stoddart, Brian. "Sport, Cultural Imperialism, and Colonial Response in the British Empire." *Comparative Studies in Society and History* 30 (1988), 649–73.

Stromberg, Peter. "Consensus and Variation in the Interpretation of Religious Symbolism: A Swedish Example." *American Ethnologist* 8 (3) August 1981, 544–59.

Swidler, Ann. "Culture in Action: Symbols and Strategies." *American Sociological Review* 51 (2) April 1986, 273–86.

Tarver, Heidi. "The Creation of American National Identity, 1774–1796." *Berkeley Journal of Sociology* 37 (1992), 55–99.

Thomas, George M., John W. Meyer, Francisco O. Ramirez, and John Boli. *Institutional Structure: Constituting State, Society, and the Individual.* Newbury Park, CA: Sage, 1987.

Thomas, Julian. "1938: Past and Present in an Elaborate Anniversary." In Janson and MacIntyre, *Making the Bicentenary*, 77–89.

Thompson, Ailsa. "The *Bulletin* and Australian Nationalism." MA thesis, Canberra University College, 1953.

Tilly, Charles, ed. *The Formation of National States in Western Europe.* Princeton, NJ: Princeton University Press, 1975.

Tocqueville, Alexis de. *Democracy in America.* Edited by J. P. Mayer and trans. by George Lawrence. Garden City, NY: Doubleday, 1969.

Trachtenberg, Alan. *The Incorporation of America: Culture and Society in the Gilded Age.* New York: Hill and Wang, 1982.

Trennert, Robert A. "A Grand Failure: The Centennial Indian Exhibition of 1876." *Prologue* 6 (Summer 1974), 118–29.

Trotter, Robin. "Pioneering the Past: A Study of the Stockman's Hall of Fame." In Tony Bennett, *et al.*, *Celebrating the Nation*, 160–74.

Trouillot, Michel-Rolph. "Good Day Columbus: Silences, Power, and Public History (1492–1892)." *Public Culture* 3 (1) Fall 1990, 1–24.

United States. Department of Commerce. *Historical Statistics of the United States, Colonial Times to 1970.* Washington, DC: Government Printing Office, 1975.

Vamplew, Wray, and Brian Stoddart, eds. *Sport in Australia: A Social History.* Cambridge: Cambridge University Press, 1994.

Van Esterik, Penny. "Celebrating Ethnicity: Ethnic Flavour in an Urban Festival." *Ethnic Groups* 4 (1982), 207–27.

Voss, Kim. *The Making of American Exceptionalism: The Knights of Labor and Class Formation in the Nineteenth Century.* Ithaca, NY, and London: Cornell University Press, 1993.

Walshe, R. D. *Australia's Fight for Independence and Parliamentary Democracy.* Sydney: Current Books, 1956.

Walter, James, ed. *Australian Studies: A Survey.* Melbourne: Oxford University Press, 1989.

Ward, Russel. *The Australian Legend.* 2nd edn. Melbourne: Oxford University Press, 1966 (1958).

"The Australian Legend Re-visited." *Historical Studies* 18 (71) October 1978, 171–90.

Warhurst, John. "The Politics and Management of Australia's Bicentenary Year." *Politics* 22 (1) May 1987, 8–18.

Warner, W. Lloyd. "The Past Made Present and Perfect." In Warner, *The Living and the Dead: A Study of the Symbolic Life of Americans,* 156–225. Greenwich, CT: Greenwood Press, 1975 (1959).

Warren, Charles. "Fourth of July Myths." *William and Mary Quarterly* 2 (1945), 237–72.

Watts, Rob. "'Bringing Them Home': Vietnam and the Sixties Revisited." *Journal of Australian Studies* 34 (September 1992), 82–86.

Weber, Max. "Structures of Power: The Nation." In H. H. Gerth and C. Wright Mills, eds., *From Max Weber: Essays in Sociology,* 171–76. New York: Oxford University Press, 1946.

Weiler, Patrick, and Dean Jaensch, eds. *Responsible Government in Australia.* Special edn. of *Politics* 15 (2) November 1980. Richmond, Victoria: Drummond Publishing for the Australian Political Studies Association, 1980.

White, Richard. *Inventing Australia: Images and Identity, 1688–1980.* Sydney: George Allen and Unwin, 1981.

Whitlock, Gillian, and David Carter, eds. *Images of Australia.* St. Lucia, Queensland: University of Queensland Press, 1992.

Wilkins, Mira. *The History of Foreign Investment in the United States to 1914.* Cambridge, MA, and London: Harvard University Press, 1989.

Wilson, John. *Playing by the Rules: Sport, Society, and the State.* Detroit: Wayne State University Press, 1994.

Wilson, Mary. "The Making of Melbourne's Anzac Day," *Australian Journal of Politics and History* 20 (2) August 1974, 197–209.

Withers, Glenn, ed. *Commonality and Difference: Australia and the United States.* Vol. I, *Australian Fulbright Papers.* Sydney: Allen and Unwin in association with the Australian–American Educational Foundation, 1991.

Wolfe, Patrick. "On Being Woken Up: The Dreamtime in Anthropology and in Australian Settler Culture." *Comparative Studies in Society and History* 33 (2) April 1991, 197–224.

Wuthnow, Robert. *Communities of Discourse: Ideology and Social Structure in the Reformation, the Enlightenment, and European Socialism.* Cambridge, MA: Harvard University Press, 1989.

Yarwood, A. T., and M. J. Knowling. *Race Relations in Australia: A History.* Sydney: Methuen, 1982.

York, Barry. "Sugar Labour: Queensland's Maltese Experiment, 1881–1884." *Journal of Australian Studies* 25 (November 1989), 43–56.

Zagorski, Krzysztof. "Australian 'Left' and 'Right': (Social Composition and Ideological Integrity)." *Politics* 23 (1) May 1988, 90–100.

Zainu'ddin, Ailsa G. "The Early History of the Bulletin." In Beever and Smith, *Historical Studies*, 199–216.

Zelinsky, Wilbur. *Nation into State: The Shifting Symbolic Foundations of American Nationalism.* Chapel Hill and London: University of North Carolina Press, 1988.

Zuckerman, Michael. "Identity in British America: Unease in Eden." In Nicholas Canny and Anthony Pagden, eds., *Colonial Identity in the Atlantic World, 1500–1800*, 115–57. Princeton, NJ: Princeton University Press, 1987.

Index